MAKING A

MONSTROUS

HALLOWEEN

ALSO BY CHRIS KULLSTROEM

Monster Parties and Games:
Fifteen Film-Based Activities
(McFarland, 2009)

MAKING A MONSTROUS HALLOWEEN

THEMED PARTIES, ACTIVITIES AND EVENTS

CHRIS KULLSTROEM

McFarland & Company, Inc., Publishers
Jefferson, North Carolina, and London

Illustrations by Karli Hendrickson.
Information from The Shadowlands website used with permission.

LIBRARY OF CONGRESS CATALOGUING-IN-PUBLICATION DATA

Kullstroem, Chris, 1979–
Making a monstrous Halloween : themed parties,
activities and events / Chris Kullstroem.
p.   cm.
Includes bibliographical references and index.

ISBN 978-0-7864-4438-0
softcover : 50# alkaline paper ∞

1. Halloween.   2. Halloween decorations.
3. Parties — Planning.   I. Title.
GT4965.K85 2009   394.2646 — dc22   2009016889

British Library cataloguing data are available

Manufactured in the United States of America

*McFarland & Company, Inc., Publishers
Box 611, Jefferson, North Carolina 28640
www.mcfarlandpub.com*

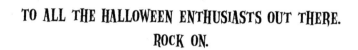

TO ALL THE HALLOWEEN ENTHUSIASTS OUT THERE.
ROCK ON.

Acknowledgments

A big thanks to some very special monsters out there:

Mollie Clarke
The Connecticut Gravestone Network
Jonathan M. and Michael J. Covault
Dean Davis of Monster Guts
Matt and Joan Greene
Bill and Elaine Keegan
Anders Kullstroem
New Haven Paranormal Society
Michael Nolan
Harold Rodriguez
Jaimie Sixsmith
Don Staub
Jim and Kathy Walsh
Jim Wieloch

Table of Contents

Introduction of Insanity

Welcome to Halloween, the greatest time of year. A time when the world turns upside-down and around every corner could lurk a band of zombies fresh from the grave, the Grim Reaper hosting a party from the other side or a hearse and rotting chauffer escorting mortals to the House of Horrors. It's the time of year long anticipated for its parties and haunts, shows and scares, so that when it arrives we think, Why can't it last all year? Let's face it, celebrating Halloween for one night just doesn't cut it.

This book serves to give ideas and inspiration for bringing all your passions of Halloween to life at home, at work and for play. After all, Halloween isn't just a night — it's a season. You'll discover an ensemble of events and activities including yard displays, events at the office, travel ideas, party themes and much more for Halloween enthusiasts of all levels.

The first section, "Starting the Season," helps get you ready for all the events that will be coming to your area so that you don't miss a thing. The second section, "Making the Season," focuses on a series of displays, celebrations and adventures that you can put together yourself to embrace Halloween throughout September and October. The third section, "Keeping the Season," goes into a variety of ways to keep the spirit of Halloween alive in the off-season, from November through the summertime. Topics range from cemetery outings, conventions, parties, howling at the moon and explorations into the furthest haunted realms of the earth.

This book focuses primarily on the spirit of Halloween in the adult realm, rather than going into many activities for children. Although the celebrations can be carried out by all ages, this collection calls to the adult monsters out there to take their passion for the spook and run wild with it, as crazy for fun-size candy bars as you still may be. However, some of the activities discussed are intended for those with school groups, as seen in Chapter 6, "Halloween in the Classroom," and for entertaining trick-or-treaters on Halloween night, as seen in Chapter 9, "Setting up for the Big Night."

Most of the horrifying endeavors in this book have been experimented and long-celebrated by monsters throughout the most insane laboratories. Others are yet to be brought to life and are just waiting to be explored. Indulge in all those that call out to you, and let them inspire you to take your love for the holiday and create your own adventures of insanity.

Please note that this book does not speak of Halloween as a religious holiday in any way but focuses on celebration for the sake of fun and entertainment. By adding this guide to your Halloween library, you now have something to pick up year after year for creating countless adventures.

And now, let us take our beloved Halloween and make a monstrous season of celebration.

STARTING

THE

SEASON

The world changes at Halloween. Of course, the world changes every day, but with the retreating rays of summer and the return of brisk autumn winds, a certain feeling returns with them. It's the feeling that reaches the monsters, werewolves, lunatics and other hiding creatures in each of us. It arises like the determined drive of a mad scientist to create a world we may have always wanted to live in: filled with fantasy, fun, anticipation and terror.

Holidays, like life, are what we make of them. Halloween, therefore, is a different form of madness to different people. As kids, it was probably a night for getting as much candy as possible before curfew, running around the streets as vampires, super heroes, scarecrows, and butterflies. We grew up with this tradition of role-playing and make-believe, and some of us—the fortunate ones—held onto that custom. Now, as adults, Halloween may mean something more. As full-fledged lovers of Halloween it is a passion, and perhaps even a lifestyle, and those autumn changes come to reflect a clearer picture of our truer, inner monster. Some may take their passion and create huge yard displays, run wild along the streets of endless haunted attractions or hit every Halloween celebration within a 100-mile radius.

We'll begin our adventure before the season even starts, researching fun and frightening events that may be going on in the outside world for the Halloween season and making a special Halloween calendar of all our devious plans.

1

RESEARCHING HALLOWEEN HAPPENINGS

One of the best aspects of the Halloween season that sets it apart from any other time of year is all of the fun, demented events that creep up. Whether your interests lie in scares and haunts, mystifying shows, dazzling displays or pleasant strolls through the pumpkin patch, there's something for everyone to enjoy in their own way.

The list of what's out there in that never-ending monster party changes every year. But to make sure you don't miss a thing, start researching all the Halloween happenings that will be crawling up from the grave in your area as early as mid-summer. Look for events such as:

Haunted Houses. No Halloween season is complete without a trip to a haunted house to be attacked by a monster or two. Haunted houses can turn up anywhere from a single-family home to a converted tire factory. You'll also find haunts with all different themes, such as a haunted funeral parlor or a circus of killer clowns.

Where to look: Haunted houses are usually advertised online. Check out sites that list all the haunts in each state, such as Hauntedhouses.com and Horrorfind.com/haunted_houses.

Amusement Parks and Zoos. Look for theme parks and zoos that change into horrifying worlds of Halloween when the sun goes down with haunted houses, walk-through displays, stage performances and live monsters on the prowl. Theme parks and zoos provide an entire night of fun because there's so much to do and all in one location.

Where to look: Check out the websites of the amusement parks and zoos in your area to see which ones turn over to the dark side during September and October. Bigger parks and zoos usually post their event information months in advance.

Horror Theme Parks. Unlike regular theme parks, horror theme parks are only open for the Halloween season and have a complete theme of ghosts and ghouls. The entire grounds can be lined with haunted houses, shows, haunted hayrides, merchandise and more for the ultimate night of terror.

Where to look: The internet is the best resource for horror theme parks, as well as listening for commercials on the radio and TV. Also, keep an eye out for coupons at local businesses with haunted attraction advertisements in their windows and on the horror park's website.

Magic Shows and Hypnotist Shows. Magic and hypnotist shows appear out of thin air this time of year. Whether you want to volunteer to be up on stage or sit back and watch from the safety of the audience, these are shows that will amaze you on a fun night out.

Where to look: Magic and hypnotist shows can appear anywhere from theme parks to small museums. Your best bet is to search under "magic show" and "hypnotist show" in your area on a search engine online.

Halloween Parades. Who doesn't love a parade? Especially one with monsters, action heroes, political figures and long-dead movie stars. Get into character yourself and stretch out those arms for flying candy and bead necklaces!

Where to look: For smaller Halloween parades, keep an eye on your local newspapers. For more elaborate Halloween parades, look online for parades being held in bigger cities, such as the Greenwich Village Halloween parade in New York.

Dark Art Exhibits. Art galleries big and small can get into the season with special exhibits geared towards the spirit of Halloween. They may also include dark artwork that's for sale by local artists, so you can walk out with a new piece of the macabre for your Halloween indoor décor.

Where to look: Museums and galleries try to get their advertising out a few months before their openings. Check out tourism guides in your area and look at the websites of your favorite galleries to see if they're holding any special showings in September and October.

Monster Stage Performances. Check out the stage theatres and playhouses in your area for special fall productions. You'll probably find a few dark plays and musicals such as *The Phantom of the Opera, Sweeney Todd, Frankenstein, Dracula* and other smaller shows on their world premier.

Where to look: Look at the websites of your favorite theatres or type in the keywords "theatre, October," the current year and your state to see what good shows pop up.

Movie Theater Special Showings. Check to see if your local movie theater is holding a special movie marathon of thriller, horror or science fiction films. Dress up as your favorite character and rest up for a night of blissful suspense and nightmares.

Where to look: In addition to your regular movie theater websites, look at small, independent theaters and larger IMAX theaters.

Pumpkins and Jack-o'-Lantern Displays. Pumpkin and jack-o'-lantern shows are dazzling displays for the Halloween season that can be held anywhere from town greens to amusement parks. Experience hundreds to thousands of glowing jack-o'-lanterns in a world of orange light.

Where to look: Since pumpkin displays can appear almost anywhere, keep your eye on the newspaper and your ears tuned to the radio for advertisements.

Ghost Tours and Graveyard Tours. Although these can be found year round, Halloween is the time when ghost tours and graveyard tours flourish. From the smallest, overlooked alleyways to the biggest, most infamous cities, you'll be amazed as you learn their haunted histories on a nightly stroll through seemingly ordinary streets, historic homes and foreboding graveyards.

Where to look: Ghost and graveyard tours are best unearthed online. Do a search for tours going on in your state and surrounding states. Some tours may only run for one night, so get your tickets fast!

Halloween Parties. Good grief, don't forget the parties! Huge, elaborate parties of the damned are a must for going all out on your Halloween adventures. Attend a costume ball at a haunted hotel or a rustic tavern ... or both!

Where to look: Check out the hotels and inns in towns that have a lot of other haunted happenings going on, such as big Halloween parades and horror theme parks.

Halloween Concerts. Many goth, rock, horror instrumental and other groups from the underworld put on special shows for the Halloween season. Howl at the moon or right along with the lyrics in a deadly concert you'll never forget.

Where to look: Check out the websites of arenas, concert halls and stadiums in your area to see what shows will be coming in the fall.

Hay Rides. Hay rides are great fun, especially when you find the haunted ones. Zombies stagger after you, vampires fly above you and madmen with chainsaws are just a few steps behind. It's the perfect evening! Even if you choose a "safer" non-haunted hayride, it makes a great atmosphere for enjoying the season.

Where to look: Hay rides are popular attractions at large farms. Go to the websites of your local apples orchards, berry farms and pumpkin growers to see if they're holding hayrides, as well as checking in the Sunday paper.

Autumn Festivals. All kinds of autumn festivals take place around Halloween with a variety of Halloween displays, raffles and contests, foods to sample and crafts for sale. Festivals make great day trips and make you feel as if you've entered an entire town of Halloween.

Where to look: Festivals are usually held in town greens and advertised in daily and weekly newspapers. You're also likely to find advertisements posted in libraries and community centers.

Museums. Museums of all kinds set up special displays and events for the Halloween season. You may find a living history museum bringing classic campfire tales to life or a marine life museum introducing some of Halloween's most famous critters to their collection. These events can take place either during regular admission hours or as special events after dark.

Where to look: Tourism guides are a good resource for listing all the museums and their exhibits in your state, as well as your state tourism website.

Murder Mystery Dinner Shows. Become a central character in a tale of murder by attending a murder mystery dinner and show. In these interactive productions, you can sit back and relax while putting together a series of clues to help solve the mystery yourself ... unless of course, you're the killer!

Where to look: Murder mysteries are generally held in restaurants and playhouses. Do an online search for "murder mystery dinners" in your state for a full listing.

Halloween Warehouses. In addition to the local stores that serve all your Halloween needs, Halloween warehouses pop up for the season with just about everything you could ever want for putting together parties, yard displays, Halloween business events and other adventures for the season.

Where to look: Halloween warehouses creep up fast, and they mainly rely on TV and radio commercials. Keep your eyes and ears perked and let friends know that you're on the lookout.

Has your head exploded yet? There's so much out there, and these are just some of the exciting adventures you can take part in for the Halloween season to make it last for weeks on end. In addition to researching haunted happenings in mid- to late summer, stay on the lookout straight through October as new nightmares emerge one by one. You'll find that bigger attractions and events post their schedules and sell tickets months in advance, while smaller events are scheduled much later. By researching what's out there before the Halloween season begins, you'll have the opportunity to buy the best seats for Halloween shows and concerts, get into the biggest parties before they sell out and take advantage of discounted tickets for early buyers.

To look for all the awesome Halloween activities listed above as well as others rising with the October moon, use the following resources to go where the monsters go:

Online: Do a grand-scale search of everything Halloween-oriented in your area (or any other area where you would like to celebrate the season), by typing "Halloween," the specific state and the current year into a search engine. Some haunted happenings will only be found online because it's cheap advertisement and a popular source for Halloween listings.

In Print: Not all Halloween events are listed online, so it's always good to check out your local magazines, newspapers and tourism guides, as well. Start in mid- to late summer and pick up a couple Sunday papers for the *Living* or *Local* section. Some Halloween events mainly advertise in print because they're not affiliated with a website. This is often the case with smaller events such as ghost walks, pumpkin sales, festivals and hay rides.

Radio Stations: Other Halloween events are solely advertised over the radio to reach a broader audience than a newspaper would. Keep your ears perked during those commercial breaks, especially since radio stations are known for giving away prizes during the season, such as VIP (or RIP) tickets to Halloween haunts and parties.

Word of Mouth: Let friends, family and co-workers know that you're looking for Halloween activities so they'll keep you in mind and pass on any info they come across. Odds are they probably know of some annual Halloween happenings that go on in their home town.

2

THE HALLOWEEN CALENDAR

Now that you've looked down every dark alley and behind every tombstone for all the Halloween events that will be going on in your area, create a special calendar to keep all your skulls in a row. A Halloween calendar is a fun project that will give you a nice, haunted image to look at throughout the season and — most importantly — will provide a good visual of the best times to embark on each adventure.

Choosing Your Top Haunts

Did you find about fifty Halloween events coming up over the next two months, but now you can only remember three of them? Rats! To make things a bit easier, put together a list of all the attractions, shows and other events you want to hit before you start working on the calendar. Include the location, dates and times for each event.

Theme Parks:
Six Flags Fright Fest
   Agawam, Massachusetts, September 25–October 31, 6–11 PM
The Haunted Graveyard at Lake Compounce
   Bristol, Connecticut, September 25–October 31, 6–11 PM
Spookyworld
   Salem, New Hampshire, October 2–31, 5–10 PM

Haunted Houses:
Trails to Terror
   Wakefield, Rhode Island, October 3–31, 7–10 PM
Barrett's Haunted Mansion
   Abington, Massachusetts, September 25–October 31, 7–10:30 PM
Headless Horseman Hayride and Haunted Houses
   Ulster Park, New York, September 12–October 31, 6:30 PM–midnight

Halloween Parties:
Salem Halloween Party at Hawthorne Hotel
   Salem, Massachusetts, October 31, 8:00 PM

Tours:
Nautical Nightmares Tour
   Mystic Seaport, Connecticut, October 16–31, 6:30–9 PM
Haunted Graveyard Tour
   Newport, Rhode Island, October 10–11, 17–18, 6:30–10 PM

Art Exhibits:
Creep Show Art Show
   New London, Connecticut, October 10–31, 10 AM–7PM

Movies in the Theaters:
Haunted Castle
   IMAX, Providence, Rhode Island, October 10–November 14, 7:15, 9:30 PM

Local Events:

Haunted Car Wash

Norwich, Connecticut, October weekends, 7–11 PM

Once you've got your creepy dream destinations down, choose your top priorities that you definitely don't want to miss. With each event, notice the specific days it will be open. Some may only be open on a particular weekend, or only on Saturdays or Sundays. If you want to go to a particular event on Halloween night, make sure that the event will be going on that night, especially if Halloween falls on a weeknight, and if purchasing advance tickets is recommended.

Top Haunt Choices:

1. Fright Fest
2. The Haunted Graveyard
3. Nautical Nightmares
4. Haunted Castle movie
5. Salem Halloween Party

Making the Calendar

To make your Halloween calendar reflect your true dementia, go with a haunting theme. Choose one of your favorite icons of the season, such as a graveyard, pumpkins, ghosts or vampires, and pick out different colors and styles of craft paper and stickers that go with the theme.

For making a calendar that's big enough to mark down all your haunting events, use the following supplies for a 12 × 24" vertical calendar:

- 2 sheets of 12 × 12" scrapbooking paper
- 2 sheets of 9 × 12" light-colored cardstock
- 1–2 sheets of 9 × 12" dark-colored cardstock
- 1 piece of 22 × 28" poster board
- 2 sheets of alphabet stickers
- Rubber cement or a glue stick
- Pens and/or markers
- Halloween cut outs, stickers or other images

1. To make the calendar, paste 2 sheets of scrapbooking paper onto the poster board using rubber cement or a glue stick. Cut off the remaining poster board.

2. On a piece of light-colored cardstock, spell out "October" with your alphabet stickers and cut it out. Cut out the same size piece of the darker-colored cardstock and fit it behind the first to create a shadow effect. Use the same technique for each day of the week, spelling out only "Mon," "Tue," etc. to save letters and space. Glue onto the calendar with the "October" piece so that it hangs vertically.

3. To make the individual days of the week, use the light-colored cardstock to cut out squares at least 2 × 2". Cut out some of the days in shapes that reflect your haunting theme,

such as tombstones, pumpkins, witch hats, etc. Make shadows for some of the days with the dark-colored cardstock fitted behind.

4. Arrange the days of the week on the calendar in any fashion you like, such as straight or crooked, overlapping or separated before gluing them onto the calendar.

5. Paste a couple Halloween ad-ons or stickers throughout the calendar. You can also place them onto random days of the week — particularly on days when you're not planning any Halloween events.

6. Number each of the date boxes and mark all your activities for the season.

Hang your Halloween calendar in a place where you'll see it often to brighten your days and frighten your nights. To make sure you have all the specifics ready when it's time to head out on the adventures, make a list of all the haunting details that includes dates, times and directions for each excursion.

Halloween Events List

1. *Fright Fest*
Six Flags New England
Friday, October 2, 6–11 PM
Rt. 159, Agawam, Massachusetts
1 hour, 15 minutes from home
91N to exit 47W
190W to 159N

2. *The Haunted Graveyard*
Lake Compounce
Friday, October 9, 6–11 PM
822 Lake Ave, Bristol, Connecticut
45 minutes from home
I-84 to exit 31, right onto 229N

3. *Nautical Nightmares*
Mystic Seaport
Saturday, October 24, 7 PM
Rt. 27, Mystic, Connecticut
25 minutes from home
I-95 N, exit 90
Turn right onto Rt. 27

4. *The Haunted Castle movie*
Feinstein IMAX theaters
Sunday, October 25, 7:15 PM
9 Providence Place Road, Providence,
  Rhode Island
1 hour, 10 minutes from home
I-95 N to exit 22C

5. *Salem Halloween Party*
Hawthorne Hotel
Saturday, October 31, 8:30 PM
18 Washington Sq. West, Salem,
  Massachusetts
2½ hours from home
I-95 North to exit 45, Rt. 128
Exit 26, straight onto Peabody Street

The What-Ifs. You may find while looking through your list of Halloween activities that some of them take place outside, such as haunted attractions, Halloween parades and tours. Keep the risk of a storm of the century in the back of your head since a downpour would definitely put a damper on that 45-minute walk through the haunted corn field or spooky forest.

To alleviate this setback and keep you from cursing the weather gods, make a separate list of alternate Halloween activities to embark on in the event of rain, storms, the earth catching fire and the like so you won't find yourself dressed up with no where to go. This list may include activities that weren't your top choices so they never made it to the Halloween calendar, but are fun alternatives if your original plans get stomped on. (This is also why it's good to have the dates of each event on your complete attraction listing. If an outdoor event gets rained away, you'll be able to reschedule it easier by seeing the remaining dates that it's open.)

You can also include in your Storm of the Century list some Halloween events and activities to throw right at home.

Storm of the Century (alternative) Halloween Fun List

1. Creep Show Art Show
Hygienic Art, Inc.
79 Bank St., New London, Connecticut
20 minutes from home
Open October 14–31

2. Halloween Warehouse
Worchester, Massachusetts
395N to 290E, exit 19
1 hour from home
Open throughout October

3. Horror Movie Night at Home
Movies: *Child's Play* and *Poltergeist*
Dinner: Pizza from Hell and The Experiment Gone Wrong
Dessert: The Dessert of the Dead

4. Pumpkin-Carving Night at Home

September Mayhem. If you choose to make a Halloween calendar for September, as well, you may find it lacking in haunted house outings and midnight horror shows since many of these don't open until October. But fear not: there are some wonderfully horrific events to embark on during this first month of the season as well, such as:

Start-of-the-Season Halloween Party at Home
Halloween Day Trips (see Chapter 7)
Halloween Story Telling and Poetry Reading (see Chapter 7)
Halloween Movie Marathon Night at Home
Pumpkin Carving Night
Prop-Building Night (see Chapter 3)

In both of your Halloween calendars, remember to leave room for any activities that pop up last-minute, such as smaller haunts, tours, special events and all the Halloween adventures you'll be taking part in around the house. These may include setting up your outdoor and indoor décor, creating dishes from the Halloween menu, working on costumes, making invitations and more.

MAKING
THE
SEASON

Okay, you've scouted out every haunted house, mad house, clown house, costume house, magic house and mystery house that's open for the season. Sounds like it's going to be a couple months just filled with adventure, doesn't it?

But wait! Everything you've researched is only what the outside world is putting together, and there's still one very important Halloween world to explore: yours. And there are countless ways to create your own haunts and displays, nightmarish events and eerie endeavors where you create the stories, characters, rules and chaos.

In this section, we'll discover ways to dive into Halloween and make the season your very own at home, at work, and in between those top haunts and storm of the century outings. And with the leaves starting to fall, the scarecrows popping up in the corn fields and skeletons waving in the shop windows, the season has officially begun. So hang up that Halloween calendar and open the gates of your Insane Asylum, because away we go!

3

OUTDOOR DÉCOR

Let us begin the season with our own humble abode: the Insane Asylum we call home. For those of us who love the art of outdoor demonic design, the Halloween season is the ultimate excuse for building some demented scenery in our very own back yard, front yard, and any other stretch of property we can get our hands on. That peaceful rolling hill of purple flowers suddenly becomes a foreboding, fog-filled graveyard; the stretch of land beside the garden now a battlefield of plotting scarecrows; and the pathway along the roadside is the perfect field of nightmarish jack-o'-lanterns.

Outdoor displays share the spirit of the season with the whole neighborhood by creating a piece of Halloween that becomes a gateway into another realm. Outdoor displays can also create themes and even adventures for throwing Halloween parties and other home haunted events like never before.

In this chapter, we'll explore ways to create different outdoor Halloween displays as well as a walk-through display and home haunted attraction. We'll go into detail with themes, plots, characters and props to build true horror stories of your very own.

The Halloween Graveyard

If you're a graveyard fan (and who isn't?), then turn your yard into the ultimate resting place. But not just any resting place ... one that tells its own demented tale of a horrid past, a terrible demise or even of gruesome creatures that roam its grounds.

There are all kinds of ways to build a haunted graveyard using your own particular style of madness. Here, we'll explore ways of making a scene of the dead that's in-depth and original by developing a theme or storyline that the imagery will bring to life.

Themes from the Beyond. Anyone can put up a few painted gravestones by the front porch and call it a haunted graveyard, but where's the lunacy in that? To put together something above and beyond, create a theme for your graveyard. Is it cursed or haunted? Is it the home of ungodly creatures, hovering figures or madmen on an evil pursuit? Did something happen to the people of the town that the graveyard dwells in, their tale now told through the writings on the stones?

Write a short description of your graveyard's theme, such as:

They Lurk...!

The graveyard has long been a hunting ground for mad scientists who steal body parts for their horrendous experiments. Anyone who should happen by late at night is sure to find these madmen lurking behind stones next to freshly dug graves. In early mornings, coffins can be found removed from the earth, scattered about with random, discarded body parts left behind.

Another way to set up a background for the graveyard is to write a complete storyline for it. Tell a tale that involves something strange, scary or silly that happened either at the graveyard or to its inhabitants. For example:

Murder in Decrepit Town

Over 100 years ago, there was a series of murders in Decrepit Town. Over 60 men, women and children were killed, torn to pieces in a way that seemed to suggest animal attacks. The killings went on for almost 10 years until it was discovered that the beast responsible was actually a werewolf! The creature was shot and killed with silver bullets, and as the body returned back to human form it was revealed that the town dairy farmer was the tortured soul behind it all. His body was buried in an unmarked grave in Decrepit Town cemetery. The many gravestones tell the story of the killings through their images, epitaphs and offerings.

Writing up a storyline is also a great way to build a theme for a Halloween party that revolves around the display. For example, you may invite your guests to come dressed as man scientists and grave robbers to accompany your *They Lurk..!* display, or to dress as either werewolves or werewolf victims to match *Murder in Decrepit Town*. If you're putting together a tour for trick-or-treaters on Halloween night (discussed in Chapter 9), a haunted graveyard is also a good starting point for building the rest of your tour.

The Graveyard Look. Once you have an idea for a theme or storyline for your graveyard, think about how you want to bring it to life with the display. What images and atmosphere do you want for the stones and surroundings? Are those buried there the innocent victims of a terrible fate so that their stones are surrounded with bright flowers and positive images? Were some of them vicious killers, even monsters or demons, so that their stones have been vandalized or bear dark symbols to show their evil nature?

Setting up props and imagery in such a way will tell the tale of your haunted graveyard in greater detail. Some graveyard props can be found right at home while others can be dug up at your local Halloween shop or Halloween websites. Consider the following sceneries and additions to work with your specific theme or storyline:

Tombstones
- Older-looking stones with weathering damage, decay, cracks, lichen and faded engravings for those buried ages ago
- Newer-looking stones with fresh dirt before them for the innocents just laid to rest
- Vandalized stones that have curses spray-painted onto them, have been broken or have evil objects placed around them for those despised by who outlived them
- Sinister stones with blood sprayed on them and broken ground before them for those who died a bloody death or have come back to life
- Sunken stones, crooked and half-concealed in the grass for those almost completely forgotten in time

Stone Symbols and Engravings
- Positive symbols such as crosses, cherubs, willow trees and flowers for the innocents
- Negative symbols such as grinning skulls, crossbones, knives, axes, dripping blood or triple sixes for evil-doers
- Descriptions of how the people died or their last words
- Epitaphs that consist of the eerie, strange, sinister or just plain pathetic way they lived

Creatures in the Graveyard
- Night creatures such as skeletons crawling out of the graves, zombies staggering out

into the night, vampires, werewolves or demons either hidden among the stones or prominently out before them
- Night animals such as black cats, bats, rats and owls that may guard the graveyard by night or be the familiars of those who inhabit it
- Madmen such as mad scientists digging up body parts, gravediggers working the night shift and groundskeepers with their nightly animal friends

Other Graveyard Props
- Lights for a night scene such as candles, lanterns and jack-o'-lanterns to light the sections you want visible and for shadow effect
- A fog machine to create a dismal atmosphere with rolling fog in which anything could be lurking unseen
- Scattered remains such as coffins lying hap-hazardously about and random body parts littering the grounds, or offerings such as urns with flowers (either alive or long dead), framed pictures, teddy bears, skulls or thick, leather-bound books of the dead

Now that you've got all your tombstones and evil creatures laid out perfectly in your head, pick out an area of the yard where your graveyard will look its deadliest. Notice if there are any areas containing trees, shrubs, outcropping rocks, etc. that would go well with the grounds.

You may find it helpful to draw a sketch of how you want the graveyard to look before you start building or buying props. Don't worry, you can be scribbly with crayons or defined with ink and quill and both will work great. Draw the layout of the stones and creatures and how much space you want in between them. You may discover that you have a lot more room to work with than you had originally thought ... to add an extra monster or two!

Finding the Stonecutter in You. To get just the right style of tombstones to match your story, consider making them yourself rather than buying them. By making the stones you can be as creative as you want with size, shape, texture, color, imagery and epitaphs, all while becoming the stonecutter you always wanted to be.

A simple way to make tombstones is to use Styrofoam. Use the following steps to make 2' high, 1½' wide tombstones while adding your own touch of madness to the process.

Supplies:

One 8 × 2' sheet of plastic foam	Sandpaper
Electric saw or deep cut saw	Ruler
Pen or marker	Dremel tool
Acrylic paints (gray, white, black, etc.)	Various paints for additional touches
3" bristle paintbrush	

1. Cut the plastic foam into 1½ × 2' sections with an electric saw or deep cut saw for the individual stones.

2. Take one of the plastic foam pieces and draw the outline of the tombstone with a pen or marker. Different tombstone shapes may include a curved top, a curved top with square corners, a cross, etc. Cut out the shape and smooth out the edges with a piece of sandpaper.

3. Draw the inscription outlines of the stone, such as the person's name, RIP, birth

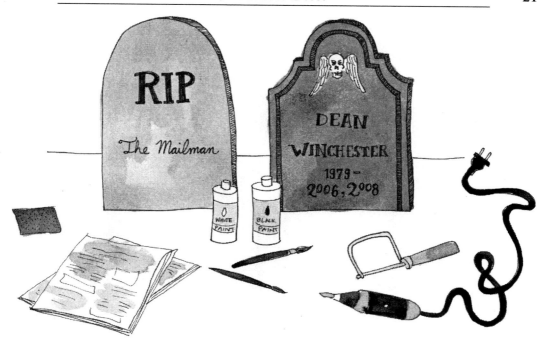

and death date, etc., using a ruler to keep the lettering straight. Include any symbols and images that go with your theme. Carve out all the inscriptions with your Dremel tool.

4. Once the inscriptions are made, paint the tombstone with acrylic paints and let it dry.

5. Once the paint is completely dry, dry-brush on additional layers of light and dark colors to create lichen, wind damage, fading marks or shadowing. Dry brushing is done by dipping the brush in paint and then brushing most of it off onto newspaper so that only a little remains and can be lightly applied to the stones. Other effects to produce through dry brushing include cracks, claw marks, blood splatter or painted warnings.

Setting It All Up. To put the stones into the ground, insert thin metal rods half-way into each tombstone on either side of its base. Push the remaining rod into the ground to keep it firm and steady. Working with your theme, set up some of the stones at odd angles to make them lean forward, backward, or to be partially sunken into the ground.

If you've set up your graveyard in a small section of yard rather than a large area, you may want to make a small stonewall around it. You can do this simply by using rocks of all sizes found right within your yard. Or would you prefer a wooden fence but all you have is half-rotted, uneven stubs of boards? Perfect! Post them up around the parameter for the ultimate look of depreciation.

GRAVEYARD INHABITANTS

Putting gravediggers, zombies and other life-sized characters in your graveyard? Check out "Those Halloween Dummies" in Chapter 4 for simple ways to build them.

The Legacy of the Grounds. Now that your haunted graveyard has truly come to life with a theme and look all its own, create its legacy. Write out the complete story of the display to send along with invitations to your Halloween party:

Murder in Decrepit Town

Back in 1851, a small farming area known as Decrepit Town fell victim to a series of massive killings. For over 2 years, the cattle had been attacked one by one by what seemed like a large animal. It was suspected that a wolf or a bear was the beast responsible, but over time the cattle were all but gone, and the townsfolk became the ones targeted.

One October night, Robert and Martha Kiley were discovered completely torn apart outside their home in the same way the cattle had been. At first, everyone thought it nothing more than a terrible isolated incident, until the killings started occurring at least once per month, and always around the time of the full moon.

For almost 10 years, the men of the town kept watch by night. They hunted out bears and wolves in all the surrounding forests, wiping them out almost completely in an effort to keep their families safe. And still, the killings continued. No one ever saw the beast responsible — except for those who never lived to tell the tale.

Then, one October night during a full moon, a little girl named Eleanor Bishop was heard screaming from her bedroom. When her father, Thomas Bishop, rushed in with his rifle, it was already too late: the girl was dead, and the animal had vanished out the window. A drawing was later discovered that Eleanor had done that night: a picture of an animal with the features of a wolf, but as large as a man.

Thomas Bishop showed the drawing to the people of the town. The minister, the Reverend Townsend, recognized the beast as a werewolf, which he concluded was the reason for the monthly pattern of deaths around the full moon.

The Reverend Townsend told the men to melt down all of their silver to make into bullets, as it would be the only thing that could kill the beast, and to hang wolfsbane around all their windows and doors.

The following month when the moon was full, the men kept watch: their weapons loaded with silver bullets. Late into the night, a loud rustling was heard in the woods behind a farmer's field. Suddenly an enormous werewolf jumped out and attacked Seamus Butler, a young man of 21 who had been standing guard.

Others came quickly and several shots were fired. When the beast fell lifeless to the ground, it slowly changed into the form of a man, the local dairy farmer named Gregory Bane, whose cattle had been the first to be killed off long ago.

The townsfolk buried Bane alongside all of his victims throughout those 10 years. To this day, wolfsbane is laid around his grave in every season, which some believe is what has kept the town at peace for the past 150 years.

PARTYING GRAVEDIGGERS!

Want to turn your haunted graveyard into the ultimate Halloween party adventure? Bury bones, skulls and body parts in each of the graves and make a game so that the guests have to dig up a precise number of body parts for their science experiment!

The Scarecrow Show

Who better to bring out for the season than our old pals, the scarecrows? They're spooky, they're goofy, and best of all, they'll probably end up scaring the neighbors after dark. Scarecrows are perfect for creating an outdoor display because they're life-sized and, all too often, life-*like*, standing frozen in time to tell a tale that can range from warm and friendly to conniving and evil.

There are actually two types of scarecrows that work well together in a scarecrow show: the traditional scarecrow that stands upright on a pole and the seated and stuffed Halloween dummy.

Scarecrow Stories. Before you start picking out the old plaid shirts, brainstorm a theme or storyline to build your scarecrow show around like you did with the haunted grave-yard. After all, if you're going to bring some of these monstrous creations to life, they'll need a good story, won't they?

A basic theme can involve one particular scenario or style that all the scarecrows can fit into, setting them apart from your basic stiff. Are they possessed or pondering the mysteries of life? Are they making a fashion statement or a statement of mass murder? For example:

The Possessed

These scarecrows come to life when no one's watching to steal the goodies — and souls — of trick-or-treaters. Some stand posed in their original scarecrow attire: plaid shirts, overalls and straw hats. But others are mysteriously dressed in children's Halloween costumes, torn hap-haz-ardously over them with treat bags and plastic pails in their grip and (depending on the severity of your theme) blood sprayed on their clothes. These deadly scarecrows have glowing eyes, evil grins and loose dirt beneath their poles from when they jumped down onto their victims.

To make an entire storyline for your scarecrow show, consider working with a par-ticular plot that's filled with fun, turmoil or nightmares to tell through the scarecrows' expressions, postures, costumes and layout. Think about how a beginning, middle and end could be developed for a happy Halloween story or an utter tale of horrors. For example:

Scarecrows Awaken!

Several scarecrows were made on a small farm and have since gone crazy with fear of the crows they were built to scare away.

Throughout the field newly-posted scarecrows look terrified towards the sky, while others silently scream with crows perched calmly on top of them. Eventually the scarecrows turn evil and band together to take revenge on the farmer who made them, climbing off their poles to attack him with shovels, pitch-forks and hoes. They then hide themselves within the farmer's barn, grinning maliciously after sticking him on a pole for the crows to torment.

Creating a particular theme or story for your scarecrow show will also help you pick out clothing, make their facial expressions and give you a better idea on how to construct a layout of the scene.

Sketches. Once you have a playful or demonic theme or storyline thought out, draw some sketches of how you want the layout of the display to look. Consider which areas of the yard will work for visibility and atmosphere, and if you want to work around areas such as trees, swings and the porch.

Include in your sketch any additional props that you plan on setting in the background or giving to the scarecrows to hold, guard or attack with. For example, some objects that can be used to create a farm atmosphere include:

- Pumpkins
- Gourds
- Rakes
- Hoes
- Pitch forks
- Shovels
- Indian corn
- Corn stalks
- Strands of autumn leaves
- Bales of hay
- Empty barrels
- Wheelbarrows

Drawing a sketch will also give you a good visual of how much room you have in your yard to work with, how big you want the scarecrows and dummies to be and how far apart you want them. Depending on your theme or story, pose them in areas such as:

Standing scarecrows:
- Throughout the lawn
- Along the walkway
- In the garden
- Along the fence
- Peeking out behind trees

Sitting dummies:
- On the front porch
- On a swing
- On the front stairs
- On a low, sturdy branch
- In a wheelbarrow
- On or in the car

Getting the Goods. To make your creations, load up on some old, raggy clothes. Dress some scarecrows in old shirts, jeans and overalls while others wear large rags and scrap cloth draped over them like a Reaper's robe. The best places to get all your scarecrow clothes are thrift shops and tag sales so you can load up on materials for the whole show for only a few dollars per heap.

To make a show with 10 scarecrows and 5 dummies, use the following supplies:

- 10 old plaid shirts
- 10 thick branches or poles at least 5' long
- 10 thick branches or poles about 2' long
- 5 old pillowcases
- 5 large pieces of cloth
- 3 pumpkins
- 3 potato sacks
- Big bags of leaves, straw or grass
- Old newspapers
- Hammer and nails

- 5 pairs of worn, faded pants
- 4 craft pumpkins
- 3 pairs of overalls

- Thin rope and scissors
- Paints and paint brushes
- Carving tools

Building 'Em Up. Set yourself up for a day of creativity or invite friends and family over for a Crazy Project party (see Chapter 8) so that everyone can help bring the show to life. Use the steps below for building the scarecrows and dummies, adding your own mad touches along the way:

Standing Scarecrows:

1. Run a 2' branch or pole through the sleeves of a scarecrow shirt.
2. Place a 5' branch or pole behind it and nail or tie the two together, depending on their thickness and durability.
3. If using pants, run one pant leg up the longer branch. Run a thin rope through the belt loops of the pants and tie tightly. Use safety pins to attach the pants to the shirt.
4. To make scarecrows with a large scrap cloth rather than a shirt and pants, cut a small hole in the cloth and drape over the nailed branches to create a "cape look" that will blow in the breeze.
5. For the scarecrow heads, use anything from pumpkins, craft pumpkins, stuffed potato sacks or old, stuffed pillowcases. Carve the pumpkins and paint the sacks with varied expressions, such as scary, silly, surprised, menacing, frightened or crazy.
6. When using pumpkins, make very small holes in the base for fitting snugly onto the pole. (If the hole is cut too big, the head will hang and sway in the breeze, which would be a whole other look entirely.) For potato sack and pillowcases, stuff and tie the base firmly to the pole.

Sitting Dummies:

1. Stuff a shirt and pair of pants with hay, grass or bunched-up newspapers and tuck the shirt into the pants. If the dummy slumps too much, run a thin rod from the seat of its pants up through the shirt.
2. Tie up the sleeves and pant legs with thin rope so the stuffing doesn't fall out.
3. For the heads, place a pumpkin on top of the shirt, making sure that there is support behind it (such as the back of a chair) so it can sit firmly. When using stuffed pillow cases or potato sacks for heads, tie at the base and use safety pins to attach to the shirt.

Setting Up the Stiffs. For setting up the standing scarecrows, dig small, deep holes in the ground. Bury the poles about one third of their height so that they won't be blown over. When shoveling the loose dirt back into the holes, include as many small rocks as you can. This will help prevent the poles from tilting in the breeze.

When setting up the dummies in chairs, swings, low branches, etc., make sure they can sit sturdy without falling over with their heads rolling down the street. If the dummies feel too light, weigh them down by putting rocks in the seat of their pants or something heavy in their lap, such as a pumpkin or murder victim.

To keep the scarecrow show going at night, place lanterns and jack-o'-lanterns next to each scene in the show. You can also use candles in glass jars or strings of orange lights on the porch and windows, complimented by strands of autumn leaves or corn stalks. Just remember not to put anything with a live flame too close to hay or anything else that's flammable. Use glow sticks to light carved jack-o'-lanterns or craft pumpkin heads.

The Written Word. Finally, write up the story of your scarecrow show to include with the invitations to your scarecrow Halloween party, game night or other event that includes a special showing of your display.

Scarecrows Awaken!

Something terrible has happened at Butcher Farm. After making scarecrows for over 20 years to protect his crops from the insatiable crows, Farmer Fritz has started to notice that his creations are starting to come alive!

The scarecrows started showing signs of life by moving their heads from side to side, changing facial expressions and even signaling to each other. They have also developed a horrible fear of crows that torment them day and night. They tremble in fear at the loud, harassing creatures, and some of them have even been seen silently screaming at the obnoxious birds.

Farmer Fritz, not at all a sympathetic man, has actually taken this torture of his creations as a new pastime. He delights in building new scarecrows and posting them in his open fields for the crows to prey upon.

But the scarecrows have begun to learn through their art of communication, and are planning their revenge on the evil farmer. With each new scarecrow he makes, Farmer Fritz comes closer to bringing on his own demise as their plans begin to unfold...

Come witness *Scarecrows Awaken!* on Saturday, October 10th from 7 to 11 PM for a fun night of dark games, kitchen experiments and this frightening Halloween display.

The Jack-o'-Lantern Light Show

Looking for a display that will really light up the night? Then turn to the number one natural Halloween icon: the pumpkin! If carving jack-o'-lanterns and getting pumpkin slop up to your elbow is one of your favorite parts of the season, why stop at two when

you can go for twenty? Create an entire light show of pumpkins for the ultimate outdoor display.

A jack-o'-lantern light show isn't your typical line of pumpkins on the doorstop, but an entire world of lights that can encompass part, if not *all*, of your yard. It's a pumpkin patch gone nuts, brought to life in a show that can be cheerful, funny, foreboding, mysterious or maniacal and, like your other outdoor displays, can have a theme all its own.

Light Show Themes. If you've been to other jack-o'-lantern light shows, you've probably noticed that not all of them work with a specific theme. But you may find that creating one will make your own display that much more original and unique while also helping you come up with ideas for all the different carvings. Basing your light show around a theme can also help to provide a basis for your own trick-or-treaters' Halloween tour, haunted attraction or party theme later on.

Just like you brainstormed with the other outdoor displays, do the same with your jack-o'-lantern light show. Consider themes that would work especially well with small, glowing images only visible after dark. What types of faces, monsters, creatures or symbols would work well together for a show of eerie, flickering lights? For example:

Monsters!

Carve faces of all different types of monsters from classic horror or sci-fi films, modern films and your own unique creations. Create zombies, werewolves, mummies, vampires, ghosts, aliens and others that haunt and hover over the grounds.

The Watching Eyes

Rather than carving entire faces into the pumpkins, carve only various sets of eyes so that after dark you can't tell just what type of evil creatures are lurking out there. Make each set of eyes unique in their size, shape, emotion and intention.

Ghosts

Glowing images of ghosts throughout the yard and creeping their way towards the house work well to create an eerie haunted atmosphere. Carve ghosts of all shapes and sizes and place them on tree stumps, crates and other raised surfaces to better give an impression of floating specters.

Designs. Once you decide on a particular theme for your jack-o'-lantern light show, consider the many different images that can expand on it. What sorts of expressions can you create for your monsters, eyes and other creatures? Also think about inscriptions, names and icons that would work well with the theme and provide good glowing backgrounds. For example:

Expressions and Eyes
- Happy, innocent and care-free
- Confused, contorted or tortured
- Nervous, scared or terrified
- Evil, menacing or insane

Inscriptions
- Famous or horrific locations where your monsters came from, such as King Tut's Tomb, Area 51, Dracula's Castle or Sleepy Hollow
- The birth and death dates of your infamous characters and their last words
- Warnings, threats or pleas for help

Icons
- Coffins, stakes, dripping blood and crosses to go along with vampire carvings
- Sarcophagi, pyramids and hieroglyphics to go with mummy carvings
- Space ships, stars and planets to go with alien carvings

As you come up with different faces and images to include in the light show, draw a rough sketch of each one so that you get the exact look you want before you begin carving.

Carve 'Em Till You Drop! Now that you've got a good stack of design ideas, head out to do some pumpkin shopping. Farm stands and local growers who sell pumpkins by the side of the road generally sell pumpkins for less than what you would pay in the store, so why not buy twice as many? Choose a wide variety of pumpkins so that each image will be vastly different, using pumpkins from tiny to jumbo, oddly shaped pumpkins and those with unusual coloring.

With pumpkins spilling out of your car, you're now reading for a day of carving. But don't do it alone: make the project a group effort and save your hands and arms from aching until you tear them off. Get a bunch of friends and family together and have a pumpkin carving party. Send out invitations that tell the theme of your coming display (even if it's just the basic idea) so that everyone gets excited about it and wants to help out.

Since jack-o'-lanterns won't last forever, arrange to have your carving day the same day you want to set up the show. Depending on weather conditions, your show should last from 5–7 days before the pumpkins start to rot. You can also make the show and story evolve as the season goes on by adding a few more pumpkins every few days.

Setting Up the Joint. When picking out different areas of the yard to set up the show, consider using any and all locations that will provide a flat surface, such as the fence, walkway, trees, porch swing and window ledges. Place others randomly throughout the yard where there is level ground or on flat objects such as crates and hay bales so that they will keep steady. To make the light show appear bigger, space some groups of pumpkins a good distance apart with others scattered in between, as well as hanging mini pumpkins from trees and fence posts.

Additional props in the display can include hanging lanterns in trees, standing lanterns throughout the yard and strings of orange lights on the fence and porch railings.

Use tea-light candles to light the jack-o'-lanterns and other candles each night at sundown. You can buy big bags of these candles in most craft stores for only a few dollars so it won't cost you a bundle to keep the show going for a week or more. Keep all the candles in a big basket or cauldron by your front door along with a grill lighter that can easily fit into the narrower pumpkins. Keeping these supplies where you will readily see them will help you remember to light the show each night.

The Pumpkin That Would Not Die. Don't like the idea of all your pumpkins going bad after the season is over? Well, not *all* pumpkins die. Pick up a couple foam craft pumpkins and include them in the show. You can also carve your favorite patterns and designs into these immortal pumpkins so that you'll be able to reuse them each year. Keep in mind, though, that craft pumpkins are flammable and not to be used with candles. Instead, you'll need glow sticks or a string of lights and an extension cord to light them.

When it comes to outdoor décor, the sky's the limit. Use the display ideas we've covered so far to inspire you to develop new themes based on your favorite aspects of the season. Other Outdoor Décor displays may include:

Alien Crash Landing	Torture Chamber
Jack the Ripper	Conjurer's Circle
Invading Zombies	Crop Circles
Vampire's Lair	Night of the Undead Trick-or-Treaters
Skeleton Parade	Night of the Houseguests

The Walk-Through Display

Now that you've got some different ideas for making a Halloween spectacular out of your yard, consider making the display into one where you and a group of unsuspecting mortals can actually *enter* the world you've created. By turning your outdoor décor into a walk-through display, all of your friends, party guests and random aliens visiting our planet will be able to step right into the story rather than seeing it from afar.

Creating a walk-through display is slightly different than setting up a regular Halloween

display in that you set up the scenes on a designated path. This way, the victims you bring in will get to see the story unfold while surrounded by its images and, if you choose, its sounds. This is most efficiently done by using borders to create a pathway throughout the scenes.

Big Bad Borders. Borders are simply props that work to separate your Halloween displays from a walking path. This way, spectators won't have to worry about accidentally stepping on anything and you won't have to worry about killing anyone because they did.

Many borders can be made out of items already being used in the outdoor display, while others can be found right at home or be easily made. Work with the theme of your display to figure out which type of border would look best. For example:

The Haunted Graveyard: If you're turning your haunted graveyard into a walk-through, line several tall tombstones on either side of the path to mark it, or you can even make a small fence or short stone wall to show the way. Standing lanterns and jack-o'-lanterns also work well, especially for night shows. Just make sure the jack-o'-lanterns are visible enough that no one steps on them.

The Scarecrow Show: For the scarecrow show, the scarecrows themselves will actually be big enough to be the borders. However, if you want them to be further back so that people aren't walking right up to them (or *into* them), use hay stacks, wheelbarrows, shovels or other farming tools stuck into the ground.

Jack-o'-Lantern Light Show: Haystacks, wheelbarrows and farming tools can also be used for your jack-o'-lantern light show. Other items include tiki torches and tall standing lanterns. Prop some of the pumpkins up on bales of hay, crates and sturdy boxes so they can be viewed easily throughout the trail.

Display Layouts. Set up your walk-through display so that the story is told as the spectators move along the path. One way to begin the trail is to post a sign bearing the name of your display. As the trail goes on, set up the scenes so that they unravel more and more of the story. For example, using the story:

The Island of Hell's Bounty

Over 200 years ago, infamous Captain Robert the Lion stole a secret treasure that was so powerful and so deadly, it cursed him for life. Whoever laid eyes upon it was stricken blind. Whoever touched it fell victim to the disease of rotting flesh and bone. And any who even learned of the treasure became completely obsessed with it.

Capt. Robert the Lion, so known for his incredible strength and strong will, knew of the curse of the treasure, and spent his life never setting eyes upon it. He alone knew of its awesome power and lived with the stolen goods on an island far off in the West Indies, which was forever after known as the Island of Hell's Bounty.

Thousands came and died trying to steal the treasure for themselves. But they never went very far, as one by one they fell victim to either the curse or each other. The captain made examples out of every one of them, displaying the dead bodies in plain view to warn off any who would dare step foot onto his island.

Though no one ever discovered just what the treasure was — coins, jewels, gold or silver — it is believed that it could only be something so terrible that it came from the dark underworlds below.

Capt. Robert the Lion wasted away on his Island of Hell's Bounty, where he remains to this day with the thousands of souls who followed him.

For the walk-through set-up, write a summary of the different displays that will tell the tale. This will help you figure out the types of props you need and how much space will be used throughout the trail. For example:

The Island of Hell's Bounty
Layout Summary

Location: Side yard and backyard
Theme: Island of dead pirates killed in various ways

1. Trail begins with torn and faded pirate flags stuck in the ground next to an old sign reading *The Island of Hell's Bounty.* Warnings of "Keep away!" and "This place is cursed!" are painted over the sign. Small, long burnt-out fires line the walkway with scattered bones in and around them.

2. A few yards down, pirates (skeletons) are hanged from a large tree, some of which hang upside-down. Others lay on the ground, their hands tied behind their backs and some with swords in their ribs. One sits tied to the tree. Background music plays from speakers hidden behind the tree.

3. Further along the trail, scattered bones of a long dead pirate line the ground. Rope is tied to his detached hands and feet, extending to nearby trees or poles to show how the pirate was stretched until finally withering away and falling apart. Gold coins lay scattered on the ground.

4. Further along, pirates are trapped in large cages that were once used to store animals in cargo. Their outstretched arms lay on the ground, reaching out of the cage. More background music plays from hidden stereo speakers underneath the pirate rags.

5. Further along, 3–4 skulls are placed on wooden stakes with tiki torches in between them. Small circles of bones surround the stakes and bandanas are tied to each.

6. The last display is a huge treasure chest. Next to it sits Capt. Robert the Lion, blindfolded and bearing a sword, on his thrown of sticks and bones. Inside the treasure chest — for those who dare to open it — are bags of goodies for party guests.

Setting It All Up. To set up the walk-through, mark where you want the borders to be placed so that you'll know how much room is available for each display. For a pirate walk-through such as this one, borders can be made out of tiki torches, bamboo sticks stuck into the ground, wood (representing broken pieces of ships or life boats), piles of bones and small extinguished fires made from circles of rocks. If you have room, make the path wide enough so that more than one person can walk-through it. Additional props and effects throughout the trail can include rags and bandanas of long lost pirates, blood stains and claw marks in the grass of those dragged off by animals.

For playing music throughout the walk-through, set up speakers behind the borders or hidden among the props. You can also play eerie music from the windows of your house if you don't want to lay speakers throughout the yard. Use a Halloween CD with sound effects or horror instrumental music that works with your theme. Once the borders and speakers are in place, set up your props and ensure that all of them are sturdy enough so that they won't blow away.

Shiver Me Timbers! Making the Perfect Pirate.

To make your buccaneers out of skeletons, there are a few options. You can either purchase life-sized skeletons made out of foam or plastic, or you can buy big bags of skeleton bones from the same materials. Each prop will make a good dead pirate, depending on how visible they will be and how they died in your story.

Full skeletons work well for pirates that are completely visible and haven't been dismembered, such as those who have been hanged, impaled, rotted in cages, tied up on the ground and the like. For pirates that have been torn to pieces in one way or another or are only partially exposed, a bag of bones comes in very handy. Use this method to construct pirates that have been eaten by wild animals, burned, hacked to pieces, had only their head impaled, stretched on a stretcher wheel, and so on. You can also use a bag of bones to scatter loose bones around the display and make decorative objects such as thrones of bones, finger and toe necklaces and more.

To dress your pirates (or at least their remains), pick up a barrel full of rags and raggy clothes at your local thrift shop or wipe out the next yard sale you come across. Load up on:

- Bandanas
- Button-down puffy shirts
- Old pants, ripping and tearing the pant legs
- Cut-off shorts
- Old t-shirts to tear into sleeveless shirts
- Faded vests
- Old sandals, shoes and boots
- Worn leather straps and bags

Roll the clothes around in dirt to get that nice decayed-pirate look and smell. Dress the pirates differently so that each one has it own style, keeping in mind that the costumes will shape the characters and tell more of the story. Also use accessories such as:

- Gold teeth
- Eye patches
- Chains around their necks
- Rags tied around their arms and heads
- Old rings
- Ropes and bags of gun powder draped across their chests
- Leather straps around their wrists and ankles

STORY SHACK

Want to tell the story of your walk-through display before your guests embark on the journey? Check out Chapter 9 for setting up a ghost story shack for the perfect location!

The Haunted Attraction

Okay, so you've thought about putting up an outdoor display and walk-through but you want something more intense ... something for your Halloween party that will make your friends run for their lives and possibly traumatize them for life. Great! Because isn't that what friends are for? Bring on the spooks and scares like they'll never forget by creating your own home haunted attraction.

But just what makes a haunted attraction different than a display to really bring on the screams? Walking, talking characters! Admit it: you're just dying to dress yourself up like a rotting zombie to moan, stagger, lunge at and attack people. Even if you already do it at work, do it even better at home and become a part of your killer story.

Here, we'll explore two different types of haunted attractions to build from the ground up: the interactive attraction where your guests have just as much of a role as you do, and the traditional attraction where guests just need to focus on getting out alive.

Some home haunters put thousands of dollars into building a haunted attraction through buying props, building sets and adding special effects. But not all of us are prepared to do that. After all, there are lots of weekend adventures to embark on and Halloween vacations to fly off to that the Halloween fund has to cover, as well. But that's okay, because putting together a home haunted attraction can be simple, inexpensive and an awesome adventure.

The House Is Starting to Seem Mighty Small... The first step of putting together an attraction is thinking about where you want it. It can be held outdoors, indoors, or a combination of both. Each location has its advantages: building a haunt outdoors gives you more space to work with and leaves more room for characters to hide. On the other hand, building your haunt indoors will keep your props (and your live characters) out of possible wind, rain and cold temperatures.

Whichever you choose, you can utilize the space to create any type of nightmare you dream up. Consider building your haunt in an area such as:

- The yard
- A path through the woods
- The basement
- The garage
- The attic
- The first story of your house
- The shed
- The porch

Also think about the type of attraction you want to make when considering where to have it. If it will include a lot of decorative displays, then setting it up in the house may be your best bet. This way your whole Halloween party can take place in the haunted atmosphere, rather than going through all that work to build it in the shed and have everyone marvel in its splendor for a whole ten minutes.

On the other hand, if you want to make your attraction super-gory, think twice before splattering your entire living room with fake blood, or if you would rather save that image for the garage.

Good Ol' Themes. Once you decide on the best area to have the attraction, think about if you want it to be an interactive haunt or a traditional haunt. In an interactive haunt, your party guests or visitors will not only be threatened by horrific monsters in one form or another, but they will become part of the show by taking on a certain challenge and possibly fighting back to save their souls. In a traditional haunt, your characters will scare your guests just the same, whose only challenge will be to keep their sanity through it all.

For an interactive attraction, create characters and a plot that would work well with both the monsters and the visitors in a specific role. For example:

Killer Klowns!

A mass of the ugliest clowns you could ever imagine has invaded and started wiping off everyone in town. Only a small group of survivors know that these evil "klowns" are actually from another planet, and they have figured out how to destroy them once and for all. Each participant is armed with a Nerf-ball gun and must aim for the killer klown's nose as he sneaks up and attacks from almost any corner. The group must reach the other end of the psycho circus

You're Invited to the...

KILLER KLOWN INTERACTIVE HAUNTED ATTRACTION!

PRESENTED BY THE CANNIBAL'S DINER

"You Better Get Here ... Before the Klowns Take Over!"

Something very unusual is happening in Crescent Cove. A comet was seen crashing down somewhere deep in the woods, and the town hasn't been the same since. A band of strange, huge killer klowns has taken to the streets and is blasting away each person they come across!

Only a handful of people remain, and they have discovered that these klowns are actually from outer space and are here to eat humanity for all its worth. The survivors know that every move could be their last as the klowns tail their every move. But through their near-death battles of popcorn guns and banana cream pies, they have discovered the secret to the downfall of these horrible monsters.

The only choice left: to fight!

Your mission: In this interactive haunted attraction, you take on the role of one of these desperate townspeople. Starting at the entrance of the klown's space ship, you must venture through the circus corridors and reach the other end of the ship to take a bag of cotton candy, then make it back before the klown strikes with his deadly supply of silly string.

Each player will be armed with a Nerf ball gun and must try to successfully hit the klown in the nose to destroy him once and for all. Throughout your journey, you must keep on the lookout for the killer klown, as he will be watching your every move and ready to sneak up and attack from any corner.

All participants must work in a team if they hope to survive this alien klown and his demented circus. Some may perish, but others will prevail.

Will you accept this mission?

Killer Klown Interactive Haunted Attraction and Halloween Party

Held at the Cannibal's Diner

Friday, October 23rd

---

to successfully take their share of cotton candy, then make it back alive while avoiding the klown's deadly assault of silly string.

An interactive attraction such as this one gives your guests a mission and makes them each a crucial part of the story. It's also an attraction that will never be the same twice—after you have had the chance to be the alien klown, switch roles with one of the party guests so that they can be the klown and you can be a townsperson.

For a theme or story for your traditional haunt, create a character that you want to portray that doesn't require any assistance from your visitors, but rather intimidates and scares them away. For example:

A Torturer in the Dark Ages

A tormenter loved his work of torturing those in the king's dungeons so much that he brought his work home with him. (Don't we all wish we had jobs like that?)

The torturer's home is full of every kind of torture device used in the Dark Ages, as well as a few pardoned victims who the foul creature just couldn't bear to part with. He is always on the look out for some new souls to torment, especially those who dare enter his private dwelling.

When deciding which type of attraction you want to build, also keep things in mind as to just who you'll be inviting to it. If your party guests tend to be more on the timid (or wimpy) side, then a traditional attraction might be a better fit, as they could become too scared in an interactive haunt and simply run away rather than fight. Also, if you choose to build your attraction indoors, putting your guests in an interactive role could lead to accidentally bumping into furniture, knocking props over and breaking things as they fight back in a panic!

The Attraction Layout: Tasty Food for Thought. Once you know the type of attraction you want to build and where you'll build it, construct a layout of how to bring the nightmare to life. The layout will help you figure out how the story should be acted out with characters, the props you'll need and where everything should be placed. Just like with a walk-through display, set up the scenes so that they tell different pieces of the story.

An example of a traditional haunted attraction layout could be:

The Torture Chamber of Fiendson

Location: Front porch, side porch and back porch
Theme: A simple cottage turned into a torture chamber

1. The attraction begins on the front porch, where skulls line the railings with various candles scattered between them. Tattered netting hangs down from the roof and a fog machine emits fog from underneath the porch. Sinister music emanates out from the cracked windows of the house. A wooden sign reading "Fiendson's house: *Keep Out!*" hangs at the entrance. Guests follow a line of candles to the side porch.

2. Around the corner, the side porch is a huge catacomb. The only light comes from candles beside large piles of skulls and bones along the wall, shelves and a wooden table. An open wooden coffin holds stacks of bodies (stuffed dummies). Large cages contain half-rotted skeletons. Everything is covered in dust and cobwebs. More sinister music plays, reflecting a dungeon atmosphere. A live character suddenly appears underneath rags and crouched in a small cage at the far end of the porch. He is dressed in rags and cackles madly. He instructs the visitors through his jabbering to proceed around the corner, as there is no turning back now...

3. The back porch is a torture chamber. Skeletons and bleeding bodies (more dummies) hang from shackles on the wall and nearby trees. Torture weapons lay on a large, wooden table beside a stretcher wheel. The demented torturer (live actor) comes at the visitors with an axe, shouting at them if they have escaped the King's dungeon, as they look

very familiar. The visitors exit through the back stairs, the way out lit with candles and lanterns.

The Floor Plan: Even Tastier.
You may also find it helpful to draw up a basic sketch or floor plan of the attraction. The floor plan is really useful because you'll have a visual of everything before you build, revealing if you need more or less space in each area than you originally thought, the assortment of props and the location for each live actor.

You can also include visual and audio effects so that your visitors are left not knowing what to expect, especially in the darkness. For example, use dummies for stationary characters as well as your live actors for extra suspense, and play a variety of sound effects throughout the displays. For lighting, set up lights only around the props that you want to be seen to make things dark and frightening as well as keep unwanted surroundings from view. That way the row of garbage cans won't be distracting in your outdoor haunt and your treadmill won't take away from the effect of your indoor haunt. Other effects may include sounding alarms and flashing alarms set on a timer or motion detector.

Characters and Setup.
However many live characters you put into the show, whether you're haunting solo or have an entire army of killer klowns, practice becoming just the right type of monster ahead of time. Even if the haunt isn't completely set up yet, trying out different ways of dressing and acting the part can really improve the quality of your terrifying performance.

Work on styles of:

Costume: Try all different costumes until you find the perfect look. Is your character a high-class serial killer who needs to look his finest, or a rotting zombie that couldn't look shabbier? Play around to see if the costume needs to get dirtier, torn up, painted on, bled on or dolled up with accessories.

Make Up: Try out different ways of applying monster make-up that will suit the type of psycho you're going for. Experiment with shadowed eyes, rotting flesh, scars, scabs and claw marks. Consider if your character will be sneaking up on people after dark and should blend in with his or her surroundings. Take pictures of each new look so that you can remember them all later.

Speech: What would your character do and say, scream or hiss in your story? Does he/she/it talk at all? Does he attack, or try to? If your character does talk, come up with some lines, cackles, gestures or lunges that go with the theme.

Are you coming up with a blank when it comes to some of the props to include in your haunted attraction? You've got a skeleton and a spider ... oh crap, now what?

For a list of props that can be worked into all kinds of attractions and inspire ideas for those unfathomable, check out "Ten Thousand Props" at the end of this chapter. Keep in mind, though, that you don't need a new display every five feet to have a good outdoor attraction, especially since you'll probably be running the show after nightfall. Choose just the right amount of props both big and small and scatter them far and wide, using that surrounding pitch blackness for all its worth ... and it was the easiest part to set up!

Now that you've got the story, layout, props and plan, you're ready to set it all up. Set the stage by putting out the big props up first, such as backdrops, borders, coffins, crates, tombstones, haystacks, and so on. If you'll be using speakers or lighting, set these up next so that you won't have to squeeze them in between a corpse and a pile of clown shoes later. Then add the smaller props and finish with space fillers and added gloom, such as candles, spider webs, netting and blood splattering.

Don't forget the main rule of thumb when it comes to setting up your displays: make it fun! Keep a radio with you at all times to play Halloween party music or your favorite tunes. Invite friends over to "Ooh..!" "Ahh..!" and "...*Yuck!*" as everything comes together.

The Story Unfolds. For a finishing touch, print out the storyline of your attraction as a keepsake and for mailing out to friends as a foreshadowing invitation. You can also create programs for your haunted attraction which include the storyline and brief synopsis of what the guests will be coming to face. Include a picture of one of the displays or of the deadly monster who awaits their arrival.

You may find that creating displays and haunted attractions is down-right addicting. Each year you may concoct bigger and more elaborate props and themes, extending the stories and expanding the chaos. Don't hold back! There are such things as healthy obsessions. Write down those ideas as you get them and draw sketches while they're fresh in your brain to bring more adventures next season and for continuing with the spook all year.

Ten Thousand Outdoor Props

With so many different outdoor display and attraction themes to choose from, you may be wondering what kinds of props would go best with your particular theme, and how much this is all going to cost. Well fear not, because there are endless selections of items out there that can make your nightmare go in any direction you want without emptying the Halloween fund.

The best props are actually items found right around the house, in the wilds of your backyard and by raiding second hand shops for all they're worth. Using everyday items rather than store-bought props also gives the advantage of making your scene look more authentic and original. Why would you go out and buy a plastic shovel for your gravedigger scene when you have a real one in your storage shed? Why buy a plastic chain for the torture chamber when you have almost fifty feet of it in the garage?

Below is just a sample of some of the ten thousand props floating around out there and the different ways to use them in all your outdoor decor, as well as in your ghost story shack and trick-or-treaters' haunted tour (both discussed in Chapter 9). So grab a lantern to scout out the basement and attic, delve into the wonders of your backyard and head to those consignment shops for the following items and more for all your outdoor displays and attractions.

Balloons: Tie balloons into every nook and cranny for a haunted circus display.

Barrels: Scatter barrels and other loose pieces of wood around your shipwreck scene and alien attraction.

Blankets: Toss loose blankets around a slaughter-camp display and possessed child's bedroom display.

Buoys and Life Vests: Hang all types of nautical gear on the walls for your haunted ship ghost story or scatter them throughout the yard for a shipwreck scene.

Camping Gear: Set up a few old and tattered tents, camping chairs and cooking stoves sprayed with blood for your slaughter-camp display.

Cloths: Tear old cloths into tattered flags and fallen sails, shredded clothes and tarps.

Crates: Pile crates, empty boxes, barrels, trunks and chests for your walk-through borders and pirate displays.

Crosses and Crucifixes: Hang crosses and crucifixes on the walls for your demonic possession display or give to guests for an interactive vampire attraction.

Emergency Alarms: Place a few alarms and flashing lights throughout your alien attraction or breeched laboratory scene.

Fake Body Parts: Use old mannequins and dolls as dead bodies or for breaking into individual body parts to lie scattered throughout the scenes.

Furniture: Use old dressers, shelves, tables and chairs for outdoor tour displays that take place in a lab, haunted mansion or torture chamber. Use old recliners for seating your monsters in front porch displays and stools for seating in your ghost story shack.

Garbage Bags: Use large black garbage bags as body bags, storage bags for a mad scientist stealing body parts in the graveyard or to hold toxic waste in a chemical lab.

Gloves: Black gloves work well for the space travelers in your alien attraction and thin, rubber gloves can be used on mad scientists and evil doctors.

Hoses: Scatter odd hoses and cables around the grounds for background in your alien display or laboratory.

Jars: Store alien heads, strange creatures and other evil experiments in large jars.

Jewelry: Fill up those treasure chests in your pirate display with old, cheap jewelry and scatter it among the dead pirates.

Lanterns: Light all your displays with standing lanterns and hanging lanterns and use them to guide your haunted tours.

Mats: Use mats for seating in outdoor tours and your ghost story shack.

Netting: Hang netting from crates and barrels for your alien display, from the walls of your torture chamber or pirate scene.

Pirate Flags: Hang skull and crossbones pirate flags throughout your pirate display as well as other tattered flags of those who dared challenge the scallywags.

Poles: Use poles for supporting scarecrows, impaling skeletons and roasting victims over a fire.

Record Players: Use old record players and track records for playing music of yesteryear throughout your old-fashioned attraction.

Ropes: Hang ropes throughout your shipwreck walk-through and tie up both stationary and live characters in your torture chamber or farmer's display.

Speakers: Place speakers throughout your walk-through or haunted attraction or set them up in the windows for bringing spooky sounds to the grounds.

Spot Lights and Flash Lights: Use spot lights to shine on your displays at night and flashlights for your interactive haunted attraction and tours.

Strings of Lights: Hang up strings of lights and strands of plastic leaves around the porch for your scarecrow show and jack-o'-lantern light show.

Suitcases: Old suitcases can be scattered among the shipwreck scene in your pirate display or around the room of a haunted motel attraction.

Tiki Torches: Line tiki torches along your walk-through to light the way or scatter them throughout your scarecrow show ... just away from all the hay!

Tools: Use farmer's tools such as shovels and pitchforks for your scarecrow show and axes and saws for your torture chamber.

Toy Guns: Get some water guns or Nerf ball guns for your alien or zombie interactive attraction.

Wooden Signs: Make wooden warning signs for your walk-through, haunted attraction or ghost story shack.

Props from the Outside.

And just when you thought your yard wasn't demented. It turns out there are lots of props for your most hideous displays hidden amongst those seemingly innocent rocks and trees that are fooling no one.

Consider using items such as:

Ashes: Use the ashes from your fireplace and grill to create town ruins, crop circles and to sprinkle in long extinguished fires in your pirate display.

Branches: Drape branches throughout your pirate island display and use thick sticks for making scarecrows and old-fashioned grave markers.

Dead Flowers: Fill urns in the haunted graveyard with dead flowers and scatter them around the stones.

Dirt: Pile dirt over recently buried victims in your graveyard and other displays.

Rocks: Use a series of rocks for making extinguished campfires, building a stone wall for the graveyard or paint smaller rocks with glitter gold to serve as treasure in the treasure chests.

Sand: Scatter sand among your treasure chests, rotting pirates and throughout broken ship pieces in your pirate display.

Seaweed: Gather seaweed at the beach for draping over the borders of your alien attraction, *Creature from the Black Lagoon* display or shipwreck scene.

Shells: Scatter different types of shells throughout the path and props of your pirate walk-through.

Wood and Logs: Use wood and logs to create village ruins and extinguished fires, borders for your walk-through or posts in the haunted graveyard. Also use wood for making larger props, such as a guillotine and stocks for your torture chamber.

4

INDOOR DÉCOR

What is Halloween if not getting to turn your comfy, cozy home into your own personal, demented nightmare? An Insane Asylum of your very own filled with maddening displays, haunting images, deranged characters and more to return to each night of the season.

There are numerous ways to bring such horror under your roof. In this chapter, we'll create indoor décor that reflects your favorite aspects of Halloween such as setting up displays that compliment your outdoor décor from within, creating a sinister party atmosphere and inviting a monster or two to stay for the season. These borderline insane projects will allow you to be deliriously creative with props, arts and crafts, photography, set up and design while encouraging you to come up with your own concoctions for a complete indoor metamorphosis.

You've already got the outside world changing for Halloween, so now let us turn to all that which lies within for building the ultimate home of horror.

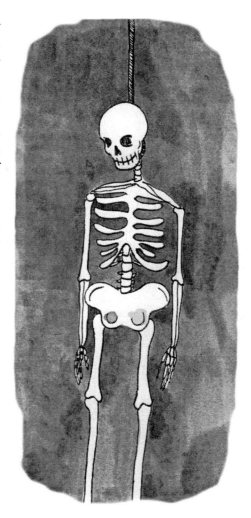

Window Displays

Window displays have a way of looking alive. Unlike outdoor displays which can be set up in a vast area and tell a tale through a series of scenes, window displays consist of limited props in a defined space, a frozen image conveying a still-life quality to a tale. The themes can be scary, silly, serious or maddening, set up in a large picture-window or in several smaller windows throughout the house.

Window displays can be used as part of a story being told throughout the yard or they can be an entirely new story all on their own. They can go along with outdoor displays,

including a walk-through, haunted attraction or tour, or they can create a theme for a Halloween party or other event. But above all, window displays can change the atmosphere of your Insane Asylum by showing a quick glimpse of all that remains hidden inside.

Adding to the Themes. If you're putting together a walk-through or tour that takes place solely outside the house, window displays can serve as nice, deadly visuals of additional nightmares that await your guests beyond the confines of the front door — even if there aren't any! Or if your event or attraction takes place both in and outside the home, window displays work well in extending the story as to what is happening inside after the monsters, killers and other psychos have invaded.

For example:
- **Killer Klowns Outdoor Haunted Attraction:** Show a sneak peak of the demented circus space ship with an evil klown in the window holding a few balloons splattered with blood. Hang red and black streamers and set up a sign that reads "Free Sircus Tonite" in slanted, smeared lettering.
- **Walk-Through Pirate Attraction:** Create a scene that shows the inside of the captain's shack on the island. Hang ropes and flags on the walls, store barrels of food and crates of wine on the floor, set up the captain's journal, quills, candles and coins on an upturned crate for a desk and splatter blood throughout the scene from when a fight broke out.
- **Jack-o'-Lantern Outdoor Display:** Add to your outdoor display with craft pumpkins in the window that require electric lights and a strand of orange lights with jack-o'-lantern garland around the window pane.

If you have bigger props that you want to include in your haunted attraction, outdoor display or tour but you don't want to risk them being damaged outside, putting them in a window display is a good alternative. Keep your coffins and Halloween characters safely inside but still a part of the show, as well as good quality Halloween costumes and accessories used on Halloween dummies.

A World All Their Own. However, window displays don't have to serve as part of the bigger picture of killer klowns or deranged pirates. If you choose to build a window display on its own for creating a Halloween party theme, other Halloween event theme or just to scare the neighbors, you can still work with the concept of what kind of display would look best in a window.

Consider the following:
- **Indoor Décor Theme:** Set up the house to resemble an Insane Asylum with a window display of mental patients trying to escape, pressed up against the glass and crawling through the windows. Use Halloween dummies as mental patients dressed in scrubs, hospital bracelets and bandages around their heads.
- **Halloween Party Theme:** Make a funeral parlor party theme with a window display of a coffin for sale, placed up on a large table or two end tables so that it's completed visible. Make a creepy mortician dressed in an old, dark suit, looking out to all who pass by. Hang a glowing sign that reads "Stiffs 'n' Stuff Funeral Parlor: Walk-Ins Welcome."
- **Horror Movie Night:** Before throwing that horror movie night to watch *Aliens,* build an alien laboratory display with lab tables of large, clear containers filled with glowing water (using glow sticks) and specimens of alien bodies of all sizes. Flash emergency lights and alarms from within, as one of the containers has been broken and the alien vanished!

Set up candles, jack-o'-lanterns or even small lamps around the props and characters to keep the window display visible at night. Use different color light bulbs to create additional effects, such as green lighting for an alien laboratory scene or red lighting for an axe murderer's humble abode.

Finding the Coffin Maker in You. A coffin is a great prop to make for window displays and many other indoor and outdoor displays. You can make a coffin by using simple supplies and tools you may have right at home or can find at your local hardware store. Follow these steps for making a 4' long, 2' wide coffin for your Halloween funeral parlor party and other display themes:

Supplies:
- Four 2 × 4' plywood boards or handypanel wood
- Two 3' wooden posts
- Electric saw (or for the true nineteenth-century coffin-makers: a handsaw)
- Superglue and wood glue
- Electric drill and screws or hammer and nails

1. To make a 4 × 2' coffin, start by drawing the coffin's lid outline on 2 of the plywood boards or handypanel wood. To get the look of a nineteenth-century coffin, shape it

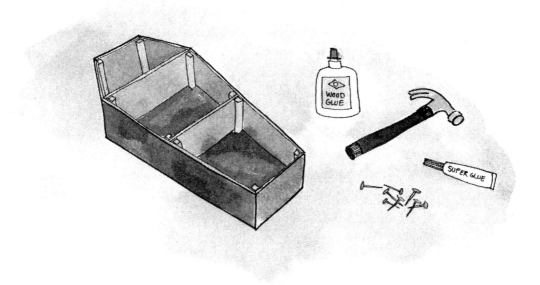

with 6 corners: 1' wide at the top and bottom, 3' in length for either bottom side slanting outwards towards the middle and 1' in length on either top side slanting downwards towards the middle. Cut out both pieces for the lid and base of the coffin.

2. Next, measure the length of your posts for the height you want for your coffin and cut them out. 10" provides a good height, but use any measurement that fits your evil plans. The posts will help keep the coffin firm and steady and provide a good support for nailing or drilling everything together. Use superglue to secure them in place vertically at all 6 corners.

3. While the posts dry, measure and cut the side boards for the coffin. When measuring the height of each side board, remember to add the thickness of the coffin's base to the measurement of your posts. (For example: if the posts are 10" high and the thickness of the base board is ¼", measure the height of the side boards at 10¼".)

4. After all your side boards are cut, your posts should be firmly glued in place. Flip the coffin over and secure them with 2–3 nails or screws in each post for extra support.

5. Flip the coffin back over and nail or drill the side boards in place, attaching each one to its corner support post. If there are any cracks in between the boards, fill them in with wood glue and let dry for 24 hours.

Your coffin is now complete and ready for use! Depending on the look of your display, you can also paint the coffin brown or black, or leave it just as it is to keep that old-fashioned look. Additional features can include engraving a cross, skull or other image into the lid of the coffin or even in the sides with a table saw. If you stand the coffin upright in your display, rest the lid against it at an angle so that it partially exposes who — or *what*— resides inside.

Want to turn your coffin into a bookshelf? Add 2 extra posts about 1½' from the base. Stand the coffin upright and use your extra wood for making shelves that slide right on top of the posts. Apply 2 coats of gloss to protect the wood and paint. You now have the perfect set of shelves for your Halloween collections and library!

Indoor Displays: Bringing the Outside In

Did you come up with some really awesome ideas for outdoor displays, but you're not in a position to turn the yard into a torture chamber or alien invasion scene? If your Insane Asylum lies within an apartment building, condo or if you have other restrictions, fear not. In addition to making window displays, you can create big Halloween displays right in the living room, hallway or any other room you choose for bringing the outside in. Who says a haunted graveyard needs to be in a field? Does a jack-o'-lantern light show *really* need to be under the stars? If the pumpkins don't care, why should we?

Indoor displays are great because they face inwards (rather than window displays which face out and outdoor displays which are *already* out) so they're specifically made for *you* to enjoy throughout the season. They also work well to create themes for events such as Halloween parties and Halloween story telling and poetry readings (discussed in Chapter 7).

There are all kinds of big indoor displays that can be made using outdoor props with an indoor touch. Consider the following examples and create some of your own to bring your favorite Halloween scenes right under your roof.

The Indoor Halloween Graveyard.
Make an indoor haunted graveyard to set the stage for your Grim Reaper party by using the space in your living room, hallway or even stairway. Set up those home-made tombstones by gluing an additional piece of Styrofoam at either side of their base so that they stand upright. Scatter body parts, hang ghosts, stretch webbing, and include a plush black cat or two around the stones.

Scatter various tea light candles throughout the stones or run a string of green or blue electric lights on the floor so that the graveyard glows after dark. Take a few pictures of your indoor graveyard for making cards and invitations to the party.

The Indoor Light Show. Use the same concept of the Halloween graveyard for making an indoor jack-o'-lantern light show. Set up the show by arranging various carved craft pumpkins (real pumpkins would eventually bring in fruit flies) in your living room, kitchen, or whatever space you'll be using for a Halloween party or other event. Set up a few storage boxes draped with dark cloths to resemble a rocky landscape. Scatter orange or green lights throughout the display or give it an outdoor look with fake autumn leaves around the pumpkins.

Tree of the Dead. If you've always wanted to bring a tree into your home, why not make it a tree of the dead? Pick up a 4 to 5 foot black, foreboding tree at your Halloween supply store and surround it with small gravestones, witch's hats, pumpkins and glowing skulls (using glow sticks). Stretch spider webs throughout the branches and hide special party prizes inside. Putting together an interactive haunted attraction in which party guests enter a dark forest? Make a couple different trees of the dead to help set the stage indoors.

The Grim Reaper's Arrival. Everyone gets a visit from the Grim Reaper, so why not have it today? Construct your own Reaper by putting together a hooded Halloween dummy with a skull for a head, holding his scythe on a throne of skulls and bones. Surround him with chained skeletons, glowing skulls, decrepit tombstones and a large-as-life hourglass. If you have a grandfather clock, turn it into a Reaper's clock that's decaying with moss and mold (using Spanish moss) to set behind him.

A Reaper's display can also make a great window display. Put his throne on an end table to turn towards the window, then add a lantern by the Reaper's feet so that a dim light is cast upon his staring eyes.

The Scarecrow Show. Indoor displays also work well for expanding the story of your outdoor displays. Create another chapter in your scarecrow show story of "Scarecrows Awaken!" with an indoor scene that shows scarecrows taking over Farmer Fritz's home. Hang pictures of scarecrows on the walls, write "Death to crows!" on the windows with window paints and make a display of scarecrows carving themselves new jack-o'-lantern heads. This indoor scene will be a special surprise for your party guests as it is not something that the average viewer of the show can see!

Party in the Afterlife! Build a scene of the departed to show mortals the *only* way to spend the afterlife. Lay out your coffin and pose a skeleton lounging inside, wearing sunglasses and hanging his feet over the edge. Surround the coffin with everything he needs for a good afterlife: a portable radio, bags of chips, soda cans and magazines. Finish it off with a few tombstones and shovels.

Halloween Pictures

What we surround ourselves with affects the way we see the world. This is the case not only when we leave our humble Insane Asylum, but when we return there, as well. In addition to elaborate displays, simple images on the wall such as paintings, photographs, artwork, dungeon prisoners and the like work to capture our attention and can put us in peaceful bliss, blinding insanity, deranged hysteria or any other mood we may prefer.

A series of Halloween pictures can also make your Insane Asylum all the nuttier, spookier or just more awesome with many styles to choose from, including those you create yourself. Look through the different types of Halloween pictures below to add to your indoor and outdoor display themes, Halloween party or attraction themes and just for having some great visuals to keep you in the spirit of the season.

Halloween Artwork.

There is a huge variety of Halloween artwork out there from fellow enthusiasts who have put their passion to the paint brush. Why cover up the walls for your mad scientist's laboratory indoor attraction when you can get some paintings of monster creations and other delirious experiments? What better atmosphere for your Halloween monster dance party than a few pictures of werewolves, mummies and vampires boogying the night away?

You can find Halloween artwork in shops specializing in the macabre that are open throughout the year, or check out some Halloween artwork online on sites such as:

www.Frightcatalog.com   www.Halloweenishere.com
www.Halloweenartexhibit.com   www.Art.com
www.Halloweenartgallery.com

Look for pictures that range from 5×7" cards to poster-size images to frame and hang throughout your Insane Asylum, dungeon, crypt, monster disco or other Halloween abode.

The Lunatic Picasso in You.

In addition to purchasing Halloween artwork from the lunatic Picassos out there, take off that straight jacket and use your own artistic skills. Let those creative juices flow by drawing and painting pictures that go with your Halloween display theme, whether you've been an artist since you were 2 or you've never even held a paintbrush before.

Think you're not talented enough to enjoy demented craft time? You're probably in for a big surprise: because sometimes, the nuttier it looks, the better. Consider creating these types of pictures to match your party or attraction theme:

• **The Demonic Kid:** Constructing a haunted attraction based on a child possessed by the Devil? Draw basic child-like pictures of houses, trees, birds and people on a large sketch pad with crayons. Then put them in the viewpoint of a tortured soul: set the trees on fire, scribble the sky black, hang people from the trees and give the birds x's over their eyes.

- **An Insane Asylum:** Paint the images you *really* see in your head as a true mental patient. Finger-paint crazy family portraits using dark colors like deep purple, dark blue and black. Scribble psychotic thoughts such as "Voices tell me to kill," or "The clowns made me do it!" across large pieces of sketch paper completely covered in smeared paint.

Eerie Photography.
Photographs can also add a whole new dimension to your indoor décor, as well as your display and event themes. Rather than creating an atmosphere of chaos with scribbly drawings, photography will set the stage for sophisticated insanity with well-placed pictures of anything from eerie portraits to disturbing landscapes.

- **The Family from Hell:** For your haunted mansion attraction, hang portraits of family members so crazy-looking that they make our own look pretty damn good. Use your family as models by dressing them in old-fashioned attire, styling their hair from a different time and using a bare wall for a background. Tell them to wear facial expressions that fit the disturbing characters they're portraying, such as evil, insane, clueless or dead. Develop the pictures in black and white and frame them in large, old-fashioned frames found at your local thrift shop or tag sale.
- **Wacked-Out Funeral Home:** What funeral home wouldn't be proud of its work? Take photographs of the dead for your funeral home display by snapping shots of your family and friends lying on the sofa with their eyes closed and arms crossed over their chest. Dress them in their finest with pale make up and looking as somber as ever. When framing the pictures, attach clear labels to the frames that state the person's name, birth and death date.
- **Home Sweet Home:** Photographs of disturbing-looking buildings also work well for adding gloom and doom. Is there a run-down house, building or barn you've stumbled across on a weekend October drive that just screams *The House of Usher*? Take some pictures and develop the most demented-looking ones in black and white. Hang them so they are crooked, cracked or bleeding on the wall.

Greeting Cards and Photographs.
Another fun and simple method for making Halloween artwork is to frame Halloween greeting cards. Pick out cards that either go with a particular theme you're working with or that will just make some fun Halloween scenery. Place matting around the card and use a slightly thicker frame to make the pictures appear bigger. Space them apart on the wall so that two or three images compliment each other in the hallway or stairwell.

In addition to greeting cards, use the same concept with Halloween images you find in weekly and monthly calendars for September and October, Halloween pictures found in fall magazines, Halloween attraction advertisements and more.

Want to take a stroll down Memory Lane rather than Elm Street? Create some memorable Halloween pictures by framing the monsters you hang around with each October. Look through photo albums for shots taken at Halloween parties, haunted attractions and other events to put up around the Insane Asylum. Show your Halloween adventures throughout the years with the changing displays, costumes and parties you've gone to and made yourself. You can also add mementoes in the frames, such as tickets to the haunting events or shows.

Those Halloween Dummies

No home should be devoid of life-sized monsters and other creatures of the season... especially when you can make them yourself out of simple Halloween dummies. Bring the Grim Reaper to the dinner table or an axe murderer to the closet. Put a killer clown in the window or a 6' ghost in the hallway. Invite your favorite horror icons to your humble Insane Asylum to stand alone or compliment your displays, attractions, parties and other haunting events.

Making the Dummies. Indoor Halloween dummies can be put together in the same fashion as outdoor ones in a scarecrow show, using old clothes stuffed with newspapers. Another method is to use a pillow as the dummy's chest stuffing and only lightly stuffing the arms and legs, or letting them hang flat. Use an appropriate size pillow or just enough newspaper to make your character the size and shape you want. If you're building the Reaper, for example, you don't want him to stand only 4' tall and be as fat as the Stay Puft Marshmallow Man.

You may find that it helps to prop sitting dummies up with a small cushion behind their back or run a thin rod through the back of their shirt so that they don't slump. You can also build the dummies around assembled PVC pipes to make them stand up straight.

The heads of the dummies can be made by stuffing a pillowcase with newspaper and then putting a Halloween mask over the pillowcase. Another option is to use skulls or jack-o'-lanterns for heads, or draping a hood over the head so that the face is not even seen. For the hands, use skeleton hands from your bag of bones, workers' gloves or another style of

gloves that the character might wear, or drape their cape or cloak over the arms so that the hands are not visible.

Adding accessories to the dummies will also help shape their characters and make them appear more scary, menacing, goofy, deranged, or any other profile that works. Use elaborate costumes, hats, gloves, capes, shoes, weaponry and other props. Consider the listing below for different ways to use Halloween dummies in your indoor décor.

Window Dummies. Sit or stand your dummies by the living room window or even the basement windows, staring — or *glaring* — outside. Has an escaped lunatic been seen prowling the neighborhood in your haunted tour story? Place him peeking out the basement window and see which of your guests on the tour spot him.

Create characters such as:
- An eerie mortician waving a skeleton hand
- Witches brewing an overflowing cauldron of frogs
- A fortune teller layered in beads, bones and teeth
- The recently deceased waving from his coffin

Haunted Attraction Characters. You can also place dummies throughout the house as stationary characters in your haunted attraction. Stationary characters work as good decoys since they are what the visitors will see first, distracting them from hiding actors such as that live werewolf hurling itself down the staircase. Place the dummies in plain view, wearing masks or hoods so that they may appear to be live actors, as well.

Create characters such as:
- A werewolf eating a human arm
- A zombie sitting down to dinner of human brains
- An evil clown holding a toy human
- A medieval torturer sharpening his weapon

Dinner Guests. There's always room for another dinner guest or two, so sit a few dummies at the dinner table for your Halloween party. Has the Grim Reaper invited unsuspecting mortals over for an unforgettable evening? His appearance would be expected, of course. Or did someone end up getting murdered at your dinner party... *again?* Place a dummy of the late guest in a seat of honor or in an open body bag for his murder to be solved over the course of the evening.

Create characters such as:
- The Grim Reaper with his scythe
- Other hooded figures with staffs and spell books
- A mummy with a cursed medallion around his neck
- Hannibal Lector with his safety mask

Trickster Dummies. Sit the dummies in ordinary places throughout the house, such as on the sofa, staircase or in the bathtub to see how your friends react at your Halloween party or Halloween story telling and poetry reading when they think the dummies are real guests at first glance.

Create characters such as:

- A lab patient covered in handprints of paint
- A psycho ward doctor with pockets bursting with plastic syringe needles
- An evil farmer splattered with blood

Trick-or-Treat Guardians. Sit a dummy at the candy table on Halloween night as a guardian of the grounds. This monster may look so fake that his pumpkin head shines in the candle light and the kids will still think he's real until they're safely down the street with their goodie bags.

Create characters such as:
- A gravedigger covered in dirt
- An alien with test tubes still attached
- A pirate holding his treasure chest
- An axe murderer holding a head in a basket

Ten Thousand Indoor Props

With the right props, window displays and other displays, indoor attractions and Halloween parties become worlds of their own. And just like the selection for your outdoor creations, the sky's the limit because there are thousands of props suited for all your insane indoor needs.

Go on a hunt for the most authentic yet simple items found right around the corner, as well as objects that can be used in all your Halloween crafting. Open up the cob-webbed boxes around the house and check out second hand shops for items to work into any indoor display.

Autumn Themed Cloth Napkins and Placemats: Drape these accessories across the tabletops and bookshelves to add more autumn colors to the house. Use them as a base for

your centerpiece of candles, pumpkins and Halloween figurines, or as a base for your jack-o'-lanterns in window displays.

Beads and Bead Curtains: Gather all kinds of beads for your window gypsy display and fortune telling parties (discussed in Chapter 8). Fill bowls with beads for the party tables and hang bead curtains in the windows and doorways.

Books and Quills: Stack a bookshelf with old, dusty books, ink bottles and quill pens for your old-fashioned haunted attraction, ghost story shack or tour window display.

Candles, Candelabra and Candleholders: Candles can be used to light up all your indoor attractions and window displays, including black candles to place around the room for your Reaper party and graveyard party.

Clothing: Use old clothes to dress all your Halloween characters, including scarves, belts, hats and wigs. Also use loose cloth for tearing into bandages for injured victims and shredded clothing for random body parts.

Craft and Plastic Pumpkins: Place craft pumpkins along with your real ones in some of the displays so that you can keep your favorite designs year after year.

Draperies and Sheets: Use draperies and sheets for room barriers and backdrops in your goriest indoor haunted attractions, streaking them with blood, bloody handprints or alien slime. Also strip the cloth to use as mummy wrappings and bandages.

Electric Candles: Place electric candles inside props that shouldn't be used with a live flame, such as foam jack-o'-lanterns and skulls. Also use electric candles behind props where you only want a faint light emanating or to light areas of a display where a person won't be present to keep watch, such as an upstairs window display.

Fake Flowers and Plastic Wreaths: Use fake flowers and wreaths in your funeral parlor window display and indoor haunted graveyard. Also scatter black flower petals onto coffins and fake leaves among your indoor jack-o'-lantern display.

Fake Insects: Throw some fake spiders and other crawly critters into jars for your mad scientist experiments, among your trees of the dead and in spider webs in the window displays.

Frames and Canvas: Load up on cheap frames to frame your Halloween pictures and look for blank canvas, sketch paper and poster board for making Halloween artwork.

Halloween Knick Knacks and Figurines: Add Halloween figurines to your Halloween Museum or Halloween village collection (both discussed later in this chapter). Also use them as table centerpieces or place individual figurines by each place card at your Halloween party or Friday the 13th murder mystery party (discussed in Chapter 19).

Incense and Incense Holders: Use incense in your gypsy display and at each table for your fortune telling party. Also create a foggy, forest atmosphere for your interactive haunted forest attraction.

Jars and Vials: Jars and vials are great for filling with odd experiments, potions and strange critters for your mad scientist's indoor display and window display.

Kitchen Supplies: Create a witch's kitchen with wooden bowls and baskets, canisters, large wooden spoons and, of course, a cauldron or two. Also use baskets for storing skulls and body parts in your torture chamber display and for holding utensils at your Halloween parties.

Living Room Essentials: Old lamps, doilies and rugs help create a perfect old-fashioned indoor haunted attraction and also make good backgrounds for your Insane Asylum portraits.

Mirrors: Hang mirrors with messages from the other side written in blood or lipstick for your indoor attractions and murder mystery parties.

Paintbrushes, Paint and Markers: Use second hand art supplies or those you find hidden away in the closet to make Halloween pictures, invitations and for painting props.

Pictures: Use second-hand framed pictures and portraits for indoor décor, painting insane messages over them or tearing claw marks into them.

Ribbon: Tie ribbons around rolled up parchment invitations or wrap them around pumpkins both inside and outside the house. Also use black and orange ribbons in your dead flower centerpieces and in your tree of the dead.

Sheer: Make a ghostly atmosphere in window displays and in your ghost story shack with layers of sheer hanging from the rafters. You can also make floating ghosts by tying sheer around helium balloons taped to the floor.

Spider Webbing: Use string to create huge spider webs covering an entire wall or window, as well as adding webs to your tree of the dead and Halloween pictures.

Stars and Moon Symbols: Hang star and moon symbols from the lamps and ceiling for your fortune telling party.

Toys: Use old-fashioned toys such as dolls, trucks, blocks, games and more for that possessed child's bedroom display.

Trick-or-Treat Bags and Cardboard Window Decorations: The perfect supplies for all your crafting, make Halloween cards and invitations out of old treat bags and window decorations by cutting and pasting them onto blank note cards. Also use them to create place cards for your Halloween party or make refrigerator magnets out of them by gluing the images to a piece of cardboard and magnet.

The Halloween Museum

Is your Insane Asylum just bursting with props, pictures and horrors of every kind of nightmare imaginable? Are your coffins and treasure chests filled with Halloween memorabilia collected throughout the years from haunts, horror theme parks, shows, Halloween shops, parties and other adventures? If so, don't keep them all tucked away. Pry everything from the hands of those skeletons in the closet and put them together in an exhibit of insanity in your very own Halloween museum.

Your museum will tell a story that can't be told or viewed anywhere else: one of your adventures as a Halloween enthusiast, horror buff, monster fanatic and a too-cool freak in a display years in the making.

A Collection of Madness. Make your Halloween museum exhibit one that includes anything and everything related to Halloween, horror and the like that you've made, collected or stolen from the dead throughout the years. Put up that framed poster of the paranormal investigation lecture next to your life-sized killer scarecrow from last year's haunted attraction, seated next to your collection of vampire chronicles and beside your coffin of skulls and bones.

Other items in your exhibit may include:
- Halloween artwork you've made or purchased
- Halloween photos of you and monster friends
- Posters from horror movies and shows on stage
- Spooky photography you've taken or collected
- Halloween props used in displays or attractions
- Life-sized monsters and Halloween dummies
- T-shirts from haunted attractions or horror movie premiers
- Costumes
- Masks and other costume accessories
- Horror, sci-fi or fantasy books and DVDs
- Pamphlets and maps from horror attractions
- Halloween and horror-based board games and card games
- Autographs from Frankenstein, Freddy Krueger or the late Elvis you ran into at horror theme parks
- Halloween collectibles such as figurines, mugs and candles
- Halloween cards and invitations you've made and received
- Halloween packaging collectibles, such as themed cereal boxes and candy bags

The Gallery. Set up your exhibit in any area of the house fit to display your collections (if that's possible). Use the spare bedroom, living room, den, foyer, furbished basement or even hallway. Fill the wall space with posters, pictures and t-shirts on hangers. Fill the shelves and bookcases with collectables and games, the tables with props and accessories and the floor space with characters, coffins and other life-sized props. Put the scrapbooks and photo albums on display filled with Halloween cards, pamphlets and photos, and put out a special guest book (or Book of the Dead) for museum visitors to sign.

Give your Halloween museum its own title, such as The Museum of Horror, so that it becomes a separate entity from your Insane Asylum.

By Invitation Only. Share your exhibit of nightmares with friends at your Halloween party or before heading out on that Halloween weekend adventure. Give them an official tour, as you'll no doubt have a lot of stories to go along with all your souvenirs and creations.

You can even create special tickets for the exhibit to include with each party invitation. Cut out 4×6" pieces of cardstock or scrapbooking paper and write on each: "This ticket entitles you to one free admission to *The Museum of Horror,* presented by the Insane Asylum." You can also make Halloween "business cards" for yourself as a dealer in Fine Arts of the Dark Fancies and the owner of the Museum of Horror. Attach one business card to each party invitation and invite the guests to come browse and/or trade at your museum.

Halloween Villages

Outside your humble Insane Asylum, there are entire worlds of Halloween out there. Ones filled with haunted mansions, dark castles, evil hotels and foreboding graveyards, where every creature of the night comes to life. Sounds awesome, doesn't it? And best of all, you can bring all these horrid landmarks and monsters home with a collection of Halloween villages.

Halloween villages are small models that come out every year from companies such as Spooky Hollow, Collection 56 and Hallmark. You'll find just about every type of Halloween scenery known to the true mental patient, such as haunted Ferris wheels that light

up and play eerie carnival tunes, sinister mortuaries with horse-drawn hearses and haunted covered bridges complete with floating spooks and spirits.

In addition to collecting these miniature worlds of horror just to goggle over them, they can be used in a number of ways to add to your Halloween displays, parties and events. Scan the ideas below to see how you can bring more life and death to your Insane Asylum with an assortment of Halloween villages.

A Centerpiece of Madness. For a fun display at your Halloween parties, set up a large table of Halloween villages as a special showcase. Lay out the castles, houses, bridges and characters as a real village would be. Make paths between the haunted cottages and create hills with fabric draped over shoeboxes to place the castles high above the towns.

Setting Up. Throwing a Halloween story telling and poetry reading where there will be multiple tables set up? Create a different theme for each table with your villages. Make a graveyard table with tombstones, coffins and barren trees and a pumpkin patch table with pumpkins, scarecrows and night critters. Other table themes may include a Halloween parade, hearse procession, haunted circus and any other displays you've got in your Halloween village collection. When sending out invitations to your event, include your guest's table theme on their card.

Set up your village collection in your Halloween museum, either in its own section or stretching throughout the exhibit between the other props and memorabilia. You'll probably start to notice subtle changes in the evolving model themes as you compare them with other Halloween collections each year.

You found that perfect Halloween picture where you least expected it... Take close-up pictures of your village for making Halloween cards, invitations, using in your Halloween newsletter and in advertisements for your Halloween business events (discussed in Chapters 8 and 5).

Set up your limitless Halloween village all throughout the Insane Asylum: along the shelves and tables in your living room, bedroom, kitchen, hallways and staircases. Let the village stretch on and on throughout the house so that wherever you wander, the ghosts, zombies and gargoyles are sure to follow.

Halloween village displays also serve as great models for building your own life-sized displays. Refer to the different tombstone designs, coffins, crypts, jack-o'-lanterns, fences, characters and more for developing looks and patterns for your own props and scenes.

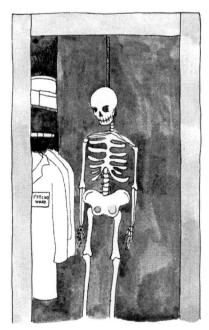

Skeletons in the Closet

We all have our skeletons in the closet... and if we don't, then Halloween is the perfect time to put them there!

Why limit all the creatures and characters in the house to be out on display? A true haunted house wouldn't be nearly as obvious. During the season when it feels like spooks are hiding around every corner, make sure that they are by putting skeletons, ghosts, mummies and other monsters in hiding and ready to scare.

Creeping Demons. No closet is complete without a hanging skeleton or two. And what would a basement be without some ghosts creeping around the corner? Pose a few of these creatures by the doorway into the cellar, along the staircase and down into the dark below. Set up skeletons in the attic, under the dining room table and inside an unused fireplace.

When choosing your demons, you can also work with any display themes you have going. Hide small ghosts in dresser drawers and kitchen cupboards to go with an indoor haunted graveyard (after all, ghosts *do* wander). Or place a vampire behind the bathroom door and hang bats from the back porch for your vampire party. Hiding these creeping ghouls doesn't necessarily have to provoke scares, but creates a haunting atmosphere around every corner so that no one knows just what may be lurking nearby.

Gotcha! Of course, putting skeletons in the closet that *do* provoke scares is always fun, too. Just when your party guests think the only danger in the house is that mummy looking out from underneath the couch, get 'em good with monsters and demons that can be heard, but not seen. Place a motion detector behind the living room curtains for a banshee to let out a piercing scream should any brave soul happen by or set up a detector in the doorway as a heart-stopping welcome for all who enter the abode.

You can also use these skeletons in the closet for your next Halloween party, telling each guest that whoever finds the one-eyed alien or makes the werewolves howl wins a special (and deadly) prize.

The Insane Asylum of Home

Okay, a haunted graveyard has taken over the yard, there's a pumpkin patch in the living room and the Grim Reaper is a nightly dinner guest. Now that your home has officially turned into a chamber of horrors, give it its own special title for the season. Dub your home something that reflects the theme you've been working with in your displays, attractions or other insane décor.

Have you truly turned the place into an insane asylum with escaped lunatics in the window and a dude in a straight jacket on the front porch? Dub your home *The Insane Asylum.* Or did you hang body parts from the kitchen ceiling and splatter blood along the walls? Go with *The Cannibal's Diner* to match the theme.

Make the title official by creating a sign for your front door or mailbox. This way all your party guests (as well as the mailman) will be able to see that they have truly entered another realm when walking onto the premises. You can also change the message on your answering machine or voice mail to sound like the monsters are the ones taking the calls. Let the lunatics in the window rant and rave about their plans of escape or have the cook of the Cannibal's Diner give the breakfast and lunch hours, then grimly ask for ingredient donations.

Don't forget to include your home's new title on those invitations to your Halloween Museum opening, scarecrow set-up party and more, or create special return address labels for all your mailings.

You may come up with a different seasonal name each year to go with your home's evolving themes, or choose a permanent one that reflects your home's marvelously horrid atmosphere throughout the year!

5

HALLOWEEN AND YOUR BUSINESS

Who says that celebrating Halloween has to be confined to home and play? Many of us spend at least 40 hours per week in the workplace, after all. And as scary as that may be in itself, we can make it even scarier by bringing some of our favorite aspects of the Halloween season into the workload.

What good is staring into a computer screen without the chance of a ghost staring back? What fun is getting inter-office mail without a random finger or toe thrown in? In this chapter, we'll explore how Halloween can have a huge impact at your place of business by bringing fun and demented games, activities and events to your co-workers, clients, customers and the entire community.

You just may find that celebrating the season at work becomes one of your favorite Halloween traditions because it brings such a nice, horrifying change to your everyday routine. Read through the following ideas and examples for bringing Halloween to your business for fun, to help your business boom, and just to scare the crap out of your boss. (Well, okay, that's also for fun.)

Bringing Halloween to the Office

Are you feeling stuck in the office this Halloween season? Do you find yourself staring out the window, hands pressed against the glass, dreaming of all those haunts and hayrides, festivals and fun that you just know is going on out there? With so much excitement happening out in the world, it can be difficult for us Halloween enthusiasts to anxiously wait for the weekend to bask in all its evil glory.

But don't despair! After all, the spirit of Halloween isn't something that lingers in a haunted graveyard or skeleton closet. You bring it with you. And you can bring all of the fun elements of Halloween right to the office for some demented celebrations and chaos. Try some of the following ideas (or all of them!) to cruise through the work weeks of September and October, laughing like a banshee and partying like a werewolf.

Friday Night Fever. Get your fellow horror buff co-workers together — because you know they're out there — and plan some Halloween adventures to embark on after work. Head to the biggest and baddest haunted house for a Friday night adventure, see a production of *Frankenstein* on stage or check out the latest horror movie to come to IMAX. Let each person choose a different outing for a couple Friday nights throughout October. You and your monster buddies will have a new haunted happening to look forward to each week!

The Slasher Office Party. Who wants to work when you can paaaaaar-tay?! Throw a costume party or a "costume-optional" party for the painfully shy. Start the fun a little early by putting special invitations of random body parts collected from a dismembered doll in each co-worker's mailbox. Attach a note stating the time and place of the party and ask everyone to contribute one body part or one snack. Throw the party on the day of Halloween or if you're taking the day off (because who wouldn't?) on the Friday before.

The Game of Supreme Knowledge. Have an on-going Halloween trivia game. Come up with a question that only the true Halloween buffs would know the answer to. Email it around, and the first person to guess correctly emails a new question the next day, and so on.

For example:

1. *In what country does the 1935* Werewolf of London *begin?*
2. *What was the name of Freddy Krueger's first victim in* A Nightmare on Elm Street?
3. *Name the only Peanuts characters who didn't dress up as ghosts in* It's the Great Pumpkin Charlie Brown.

Work Flicks. We've all heard the horror stories of murder striking at the office just minutes after everyone has left for the day. Well, why wait? Bring on the gore with an after-hours murderous movie night at the office. Use the conference room or lecture room on a Thursday or Friday night, order take-out and let everyone vote on which movies to watch.

Candy Jar of Doom. Why have a regular candy-counting contest when you can make it demented? Put a jar of Halloween candy on your desk with a select number of eyeballs, spiders or other oddities added to the mix. Email around the office that whoever guesses the correct number of oddities within the jar wins free lunch (everyone playing the game pitches in). Or, whoever guesses correctly gets their ticket paid for at the next haunted attraction outing. Whoever guesses incorrectly is forever doomed.

Skeletons in the Office. In the same way that you hid skeletons and other monsters in the closets of your Insane Asylum, do the same thing around the office. Put a dismembered head in the lunch room fridge (a fake one if you must), spider webs in the supply closet and some hanging ghosts next to your co-workers' computer monitors.

The Desk of Insanity. Come on, you know you're insane and that normal-looking office space is fooling no one. So embrace your insanity by decking it out for the season. Bring in all kinds of objects to create the ultimate work space, such as:

• Monster figurines
• Tombstones
• Black or dead flowers
• A framed picture of a monster from your indoor décor (your long lost Uncle Erwin)
• A skeleton in an office chair dressed for work
• A noose hanging by the window (just in case)
• Skulls and shrunken heads

Treats for the Trick-or-Treaters at Heart. Halloween treat bags are a part of Halloween that adults should never go without. Make each of your co-workers their own treat bag and see their faces light up like the 8-year olds we all truly are inside. Design the treat bags like miniature body bags (made out of a simple black cloth) with each person's name written on them with a white-out pen.

Drawing in the Demons. Why limit your ghostly office activities to those demented within it? Put together a Halloween event or activity that draws them in from the streets. Advertise that any child who comes to the office in costume gets a free Halloween treat bag throughout October. For other ideas on drawing in the demons with a public Halloween event, check out *Letting Halloween Help Business Boom* below.

Letting Halloween Help Business Boom

Now that you've taken your co-workers to the Alien Invasion haunted house, put dismembered limbs in their mailboxes and personalized body bags on their desks, why stop there? Use your passion for the season to create a Halloween business event that draws in customers and clients to become part of the madness. Hold a public event to make your business stand out as one that enjoys bringing fun to the community, as well as providing great service and/or products.

There are all kinds of Halloween events and activities to conjure up and choose from. Some can be geared towards the specific line of work you're in, while others are more general and can be held at almost any place of business. No matter what type of Halloween theme you choose, putting on a seasonal event can help your business gain exposure, bring in new customers and spread the spirit of the season throughout your city or town.

Need to put together some decorations for your Halloween business event? Get the supplies ready for everyone to get their hands dirty with arts and crafts during your slasher office party for making displays, gift baskets, candy assortments and more.

Specific Haunts. To put together a Halloween event that goes along with your specific line of work, consider how you could turn your business into a unique domain of doom, or otherwise bring in the demons to your already-existing sinister dwelling.

For example:

Restaurants from Another Planet: If you're in the restaurant business, choose a theme based on your favorite Halloween icon or horror movie and build an image around it inside

and out. For example, a 1950's sci-fi theme can involve store-bought alien props outside the main entrance, a crashed space craft on the roof, a layer of slime oozing down the sides of the building and glowing footprints leading inside. Put up classic posters throughout the dining area from films such as *The Day the Earth Stood Still* and *The Thing from another Planet*. Create special selections on the menu to go with your theme so that sandwiches, soups, drinks and desserts reflect the characters and scenes of the films.

Enchanted Candy Shops: Turn your candy shop into a witch's house of candy located deep in the woods. Set up smoldering cauldrons on the counters, overflowing with sweets as well as arms, feet, frogs and bats. Scatter spider-webbed broomsticks throughout the shop and use low, colored lighting for a sinister atmosphere. Put together special candy assortments in small cauldrons or witch's hats. Advertise that any child (or child-at-heart) who comes in dressed as a witch or warlock gets a special discount or surprise goodie.

Movie Theater Special Showings: If you own or operate a movie theater, run special horror movie marathons for Friday and Saturday nights throughout October. Range the showings from classics to modern with films like *Creature from the Black Lagoon* and *Curse of the Mummy* to *Sleepy Hollow* and *The Omen*. Put together a special snack combination for the marathons, such as a hotdog, candy bar, popcorn, soda and a plastic eyeball in a Halloween snack box.

Drive-Ins for Monsters on Wheels: Movie marathons are also good events for drive-in theaters. Even if your drive-in closes for the year in September, opening up for each weekend in October with a horror movie marathon could pack the place like it was back in mid-summer. Advertise that anyone dressed in costume gets $1 off admission, free popcorn or soda.

Playhouses — Where Monsters Hit the Stage: If you're involved with a performing arts theatre, putting on a Halloween production in the fall is a sure way to get all the Halloween enthusiasts packed into the house. Advertise that patrons get 1 or 2 dollars off admission price if they come dressed as the main character, such as Dracula, Frankenstein or the Phantom of the Opera.

Haunted Car Washes: Halloween buffs suddenly become drawn to car washes when they're transformed into places of myths and monsters. Turn a hands-free car wash into an after-hours drive thru haunt with workers dressed as witches, vampires, zombies and mummies that haunt the entrance, roam the path of the wash and stagger after customers as they drive away.

Motels from Hell: Learn from the Bates family when it comes to running a good motel. Have a real psycho night with an Alfred Hitchcock costume ball and buffet based on his films and *Alfred Hitchcock Presents* TV episodes. Hang classic film posters in the lobby and raffle off a Hitchcock DVD collection.

Events for All Haunts. In addition to the events mentioned above for specific businesses, there are also a number of Halloween activities that work well for practically any line of work. Consider the list of nightmares below and let them inspire you to come up with your own haunting endeavors to put on with your company.

Monster Displays: Create some Halloween displays both indoors and out that relate to your type of business. It's a real eye-catcher to see a concrete operation with skeletons shoveling cement outside the main entrance or a barber shop with scarecrows getting their hay styled in the front window. Hang disgruntled customers (or Halloween dummies, whichever) in cages from the ceiling or put up pictures of old graveyards and tombstone rubbings around the walls. Customers will be drawn in just to see all your displays and creations and the word will spread like wildfire!

The Halloween Costume Ball: All monsters need a place to party, so why not make it at work? Throw an 18+ costume ball for a night of dancing the night away at your demented lair. Choose a specific theme such as a vampire ball, ghost bash, pirate party and the like. If there are any new horror films being released in the theaters, revolve your costume ball around that while everyone is in the spirit of it all.

The Mad Scientist's Book Sale: A book sale is an after-hours event suitable for just about any business. Talk with your local library and area bookstores to come out and sell a selection of horror, mystery and other haunting books. Create a theme behind the event, such as *The Mad Scientists' Secret Library Book Sale.* Have workers dress as mad lab assistants or other creatures that go with your theme. Set up lab tables of eerie potions and experiments, electric candelabra throughout the rooms and a fog machine outside so that fog emanates around the main entrance.

Halloween Art Show: To get the whole community involved in your Halloween event, sponsor a Halloween art show at your place of business. Advertise that local artists (amateur, professional or both) are invited to sign up a piece of their work that must somehow be related to the Halloween or horror genre. Display the work at your business so that the public may come and view the pieces throughout the timeframe of the contest. For rounding up judges, contact art teachers from local high schools and community colleges to get involved. Awards can be anything from cash, prizes or gift certificates to your place of business.

Home Display Contests: Not all Halloween business happenings have to take place at the office. For another event that gets the community involved, sponsor a contest for the best Halloween yard display in town. Advertise for participants to come to your business to register during the first week of October by filling out an entry slip in the form of a toe tag or death certificate. You and selected employees can judge the displays and choose the top three winners on or around the night of the 31st.

Those Deadly Wheels: Put on a show at your business that's straight from the underworld with hearses from every corner of the grave. Contact funeral homes and hearse rental companies in your state to come put their finest deadly wheels on display for a Halloween event like no other. Make it a day of refreshments and fun, and advertise that anyone who comes to the show in their own hearse gets a special discount at your company for the day.

There are so many different types of Halloween business events to choose from, it can be hard to pick just one! But who says you have to? Let your passion for the season run wild with a haunting display outside your building, a costume ball to start off the season and contests for artists and home haunters to come flocking in throughout the rest of the month!

Choosing Your Insanity. If you're finding it difficult to choose a specific Halloween event to put together, either from the list above or one of your own, fear not. Ask yourself some simple questions that can help you come up with just the right type of seasonal theme that will be fun to put together and will get those new and existing patrons lining up at the gates.

Consider the following:

1. What interests you most about Halloween? Do you enjoy the scary haunted attractions, the elaborate indoor and outdoor displays, Halloween parties or the new movies and shows that come out for the season?

2. Of all your Halloween interests, which would you like to incorporate into an event at your company or an outside event to sponsor? What are some of the ways you can put together such an event?

3. What type of crowd does your business currently tend to draw? Is it a younger crowd? A college crowd? A working age or retirement crowd? Is it one that would appreciate a light-hearted event, such as a costume ball and art display, or a louder crowd that would flock to a Halloween party with a "goriest costume" contest?

4. What new crowds would you like to **bring in** by putting on a special event or contest? Are you looking to reach people from surrounding towns? Patrons who go to your current competitors? How could you advertise your event to reach this crowd?

With these thoughts in mind, you can better assess how to take your favorite Halloween activities and let them help your business boom.

The Smaller Spooks. Not all Halloween business events have to be done on a grand scale. Transforming your greenhouse into the terrain of the Swamp Monster is fun, but not necessary. There are also many smaller Halloween activities to put on for the community that are just as much fun, will help you gain exposure and more customers. For making your business boom in a lighter sense, consider activities that provide entertainment without requiring as much production, such as:

Halloween Raffle: Hold a free or low-cost Halloween raffle. Prizes can be anything from a Halloween gift basket, his and her dress robes for attending the finest costume ball or a gift certificate for a hearse ride on a deadly October evening. Set up a giant cauldron or treasure chest to hold all the entry forms.

Sponsoring a Halloween Attraction: If there's a haunted house, Halloween show or hayride coming up in your area that is looking for sponsorship, support the attraction and be a monster hero. This will also lead to good advertising for your business on the attraction's website, in the newspaper, on the radio and at the location of the haunt.

Monster Tickets: Sell discounted tickets to a local haunted house or horror theme park. In addition to sponsorship, selling discounted tickets will bring in future patrons who follow the trail of the spook. Having a small Halloween display set up will also create more word-of-mouth with each ticket buyer.

Selling the Goods: Sell small Halloween items at your place of business, such as spooky sound effects CD's, books, DVD's, costumes, monster make-up and more. If you have a gift shop, set up a special Halloween section with items that can't be found anywhere else, such as Halloween crafts from local artists.

Stories for Little Monsters: Hold weekly story readings with a different Halloween children's book each week. Schedule the readings for weekday afternoons when kids are home from school and provide snacks for both the kids and their parents.

A Halloween Craft Station: Set up a few tables where parents can bring their kids to make Halloween crafts at your business. Gather all the supplies for making Halloween masks, glow-in-the-dark treat bags, painting pumpkins and more.

No matter what your Halloween event or activity, don't miss the opportunity to promote your products and services along with all the fun. Include your products in the monster displays and advertise your services at each event to catch the attention of all the demons, vampires and other creatures that come to your company for the first time. By drawing new people in for a fun and unique Halloween experience, you'll create future customers who think of your business first because of the great time they had there.

Getting the Scream Out. Putting on a Halloween event will draw in Halloween enthusiasts from far and wide, both those who have been to your business before and those who have not. But make sure you reach them all by advertising in the paper and on the radio, as well as on your company's website. Once your event of madness begins, word-of-mouth will get around that your business is the place to be for a fun Halloween adventure!

In addition to advertising, send out special invitations to the event to friends and family, and ask them to spread the word with their friends, neighbors and co-workers. Check out "Cards and Invitations" in Chapter 8 for some fun Halloween business invitation designs.

Don't Miss the

HALLOWEEN ART SHOW AND CONTEST

Sponsored by HAMPTON BED AND BREAKFAST

Local amateur artists wanted to submit their work in the
Halloween or horror genre for display, art contest and sale
at Hampton Bed and Breakfast!

Show runs October 5–23.

Artists: please come and drop off one piece of work
October 5–7 from 10 A.M. to 3 P.M.

Public viewing hours will be held on Fridays, Saturdays and
Sundays from noon to 6 P.M. beginning October 12.

Judges include Professors Mark Ross and
Lorraine Castner from the Hampton Community College
and Cathy Schultz, curator of the Hampton Museum of Art.

Contest will be judged on Friday, October 23, at 7:30 P.M.

All are invited to a night of refreshments,
art viewing and winner announcements.

Prizes are as follows:

1st place:
$500 and gift certificate to a weekend stay at Hampton Bed and Breakfast

2nd place:
$250 and gift certificate to a weekend stay at Hampton Bed and Breakfast

3rd place:
$100 and gift certificate to a weekend stay at Hampton Bed and Breakfast

See you on the other side!

Did you have an awesome turn-out for your Halloween business event? Why wait until next year to hold another? Put together some monster events in the coming months on full moon nights, Friday the 13th or whenever the maniacal mood strikes you! Advertise your next event while the crowds are still swarming in October. For more ideas of celebrating the season throughout the year at your business, check out Chapter 17, "Full Moon Nights."

The Halloween Business Festival

Another way to get into the spirit of the season with your business is to go all out by putting on a Halloween festival. A festival can run from one day to an entire weekend with Halloween activities for the whole community to enjoy. Rather than limiting your event to one particular theme, you'll reach a broader audience of ghouls, ghoul-lovers and the ghoulie-curious with an event filled with fun, food, merchandise, crafts, contests, raffles and more.

Set up the festival right at your company or somewhere easily accessible such as the town green, a farmer's field, shopping center or other big location. Arrange haunted happenings for monsters of all ages with every type of nightmare imaginable.

Selling the Spook.
When it comes to Halloween events, we enthusiasts are just dying to buy something. Hire vendors to sell all sorts of treats and merchandise that go along with the season, such as:

• **Treats of the Damned:** Candy apples and caramel apples, pumpkin squares and pumpkin pies, hot apple cider and fried dough are perfect treats for a Halloween festival. Contact bakeries and local farmers to come and sell at the event.

- **Hot Foods Straight from Hell:** Fun fall lunches may include soup and chowder in a bread bowl, hot sandwiches and drinks. Contact local sandwich shops and delis to come and join in the madness.
- **Artists of the Underworld:** A festival is a popular event for local artists to display and sell their arts and crafts. Encourage everything from paintings and photography, baskets and quilts to capes and costumes. Advertise for these artists of the underworld in your local newspaper, in the town community center and community colleges.
- **Books of the Dead:** Spell books, craft books and more make great additions to any Halloween festival. Contact used bookstores and libraries in the area to set up a table with a special selection.
- **Halloween Goodies:** Toys and trinkets such as light-up pumpkin necklaces and ghost wristbands are a fun addition to any Halloween event. Contact your local Halloween warehouse and gift shops to come and set up a table full of goodies.

Mad Crafts. Kids and adults alike love to get their hands dirty with arts and crafts. Set up tables for all different types of seasonal mad crafts, such as:
- **The Traveling Pumpkin Patch:** Create a section for kids and kids-at-heart to purchase and paint their own pumpkin. Talk to local farmers about donating pumpkins or to come and sell their pumpkins.
- **Make Your Own Tombstone:** Everyone needs a tombstone, so make a station for patrons to come and paint their own. Contact your local craft stores about donating or selling craft tombstones and paints.
- **Art Gone Wild:** It's the perfect time of year to go wild! Set up a station for kids to make their own treat bags out of paper grocery bags, paints, Halloween cut-outs and glitter. You can also set up different trick-or-treat locations around the festival for kids to get treats for their new bags.

Entertainment. Keep all the monsters happy at the festival with a variety of haunting entertainment. Contact artists, performers and more to bring their talents to the event, such as:
- **Making Monsters:** Have a station where both kids and adults can get their face painted as any kind of demonic creature that roams the night — or if they *insist*, a butterfly. Advertise with the art and theater programs of local community colleges for students to volunteer as face painters.
- **Mystic Tent:** Who wouldn't want their future read... unless the truth is just too horrifying! Look up local fortune tellers to set up a mystical tent for tarot card readings and palm readings.
- **The Ride That Haunts You:** A hearse parked outside the festival makes for an evil eye-catcher. Contact local hearse rental companies to set up their wheels for good advertising.
- **Barkers and Other Monsters:** If anyone in the area is putting on their own haunted attraction or production, invite them to come to the festival with their advertisements, dressed in character or even to put on a skit of the upcoming show.
- **Movies to Die For:** If there is a movie theater in town, tell the manager or owner about your upcoming Halloween festival. They may want to put on a special horror movie

marathon for the weekend to be promoted at the event, creating the perfect after-hours show.

Contests and Raffles.

Everyone loves prizes... especially when it means getting to dress up in costume to win terrifying stuff! Put together a couple different contests and raffles that will let your patrons get into all the fun.

- **Raffle of Insanity:** Put together a Halloween-related package for a free or low-cost raffle. Contact craft stores and Halloween supply stores for donating items in exchange for free advertising. Also look into movie theaters to donate tickets to the next thriller release. You may want to offer two raffles: one with a prize geared towards kids and the other towards adults.
- **The Best Monster:** Have a costume contest for both kids and adults to make sure you get a big array of monsters showing up at the festival. Select Halloween-oriented prizes that are different than those in the raffles, such as gift certificates to a Halloween party store or other Halloween event going on in town.
- **Calling All Scarecrows:** Put together a scarecrow contest where patrons can come and set up their scarecrows right at the festival. You can also hold a contest specifically for all the businesses in town. Make it an invasion of the scarecrows with a contest in which each participating business builds a scarecrow display by their main entrance for the weekend of the festival. Entry fees apply and go towards the first, second and third place prizes.

Don't Miss the

HALLOWEEN FESTIVAL IN CHESTER!

Located on West Main Street

Sponsored by:

HOT CURLS HAIR SALON

J.J.'S MOTORCYCLE SHOP

SIMS CORNER DELI

The Halloween Festival in Chester will be held on Friday, October 9, and Saturday, October 10, from 10 A.M. to 4 P.M. Admission is free and costumes are welcome!

Show Your Stuff at Hot Curls Hair Salon

Stop by the salon to enter a free contest for best child and adult costume. Adult prize is a $30 gift certificate to the salon, a $25 gift certificate to Sims Corner Deli and a special *haunted deli mug*. Child's prize is a Halloween jack-o'-lantern poster and Halloween gift basket of candy, monster make-up and a *haunted deli mug*. Also come and visit our craft tables of jewelry, paintings, clothing and more from Chester's very own artists!

The Dead Ride at J.J.'s Motorcycle Shop

Come and witness skeletons, scarecrows and zombies seat up and prepare to ride away into the dead of night on their Harleys. These displays are works of the Chester Community College's Performing Arts class. Cast your vote on your favorite display. Winner receives a special award from the Chester Community College Arts Department.

Potions and More at Sims Corner Deli

Stop in Sims Corner Deli for special Halloween sandwiches prepared just for the festival. Other menu specialties include pumpkin soup served in a bread bowl, roasted peanuts and a mulled cider of the deli's own recipe. Pick up your cider in an original *haunted deli mug,* a specialty item created just for the season. Wear a costume and get $1 off your order!

The Coven & Mummy's Tomb

Also appearing at the festival will be staff from two of the newest haunted houses around: *The Coven* in Westfield and *Mummy's Tomb* in Chester. These attractions are celebrating their first year of horror! Come see pictures of the haunts, meet and great the monsters in person and enter raffles to win free passes.

Special Showings

Hopwells Movie Theater will be holding a special movie marathon on Friday, October 9, and Saturday, October 10, at 8 P.M. Showings include Alfred Hitchcock's classics *Psycho* at 8 P.M. and *The Birds* at 10 P.M. with a 20 minute intermission. Advanced tickets are recommended and can be purchased at Hot Curls Hair Salon for $10, or $12 at the door.

6

HALLOWEEN IN THE CLASSROOM: LIVING HISTORIES OF THE HOLIDAY

"Okay, class pay attention. Today we'll be putting away our books, dressing up in costume and partying for Halloween like they did in the days when the dead walked the earth." ...Now isn't that what we all hoped our teachers would say at *some* point in October?

If you work in a school, library, day care center or other institution with children, there are many ways to bring Halloween into the classroom so the kids can embrace the season for more than one night of trick or treating. And for a little douse of education, you can put on a series of activities and games that also teach them about the origins of Halloween. This year, take a break from the class party of orange cupcakes and black streamers and throw one that spans back thousands of years to the later days of our great grandfathers.

This chapter covers two types of Halloween party activities, one geared towards a younger crowd of those in elementary school and the other towards an older crowd for those in junior high and high school.

An Elementary Halloween

At this Halloween party for children aged 5–8, the guests of honor are invited to come in their favorite Halloween costume and bring their own trick-or-treat bag. They'll be in for a variety of activities that are similar to how Halloween was celebrated thousands of years ago, including a parade, trick-or-treating for different types of goodies and playing games about ghosts and fortune telling. Each activity is listed below and is followed by a page of short readings at the end of the chapter that relates them to celebrations long, long ago that can be told to the kids before, during or after they take part in the ancient customs.

Halloween Back in the Day. For the first thing the kids see when they arrive at the party, prepare a treat table that goes with the theme of a classic Halloween celebration. Set out cider, nuts, fruits, cake and breads such as pumpkin or banana bread. Decorate the table with pumpkins, gourds, broomsticks and electric lanterns.

At the start of the party, allow the children to take a few treats from the table to enjoy the tastes of Halloween past.

Halloween Parade. To begin their travels back into time, have the kids line up for a parade of trick or treating. Give them each an air horn, party blower, baton, flag or other toy. Play Halloween party music as the kids parade to each trick-or-treat station (described below).

Music for the parade can include any number of Halloween songs, such as:
- "Purple People Eater" by the Big Bopper
- "Ghostbusters" by Ray Parker, Jr.
- "Bad Moon Rising" by CCR
- "Monster Mash" by Bobby "Boris" Pickett
- "Love Potion No. 9" by The Searchers
- "Soul Man" by Drake Bell
- "Super Freak" by Rick James
- "Werewolves of London" by Warren Zevon

Trick or Treating. The trick-or-treat stations can be set up on tables, counters and the like that are spread out around the room or building. Set up anywhere from 5 to 10 stations that each contain the following:

1. A children's Halloween book.

2. A small Halloween display relating to the book. For example, if the book focuses on pumpkins, arrange a few different sized pumpkins, gourds and Indian corn. If the

story focuses on a black cat, put out a few plush black cats, bats and spider webs with spiders.

3. A small bowl or bag of treats. Rather than having fun size candy bars like the kids will be getting on Halloween night, hand out more old fashion treats that resemble what was handed out in Halloweens past, such as:

- Apples
- Plastic gold coins
- Individually wrapped pastries
- Popcorn balls
- Gum

Have one or two specific treats at each station, giving a few to each child when they come by in the parade. Whichever treats you choose, make sure that the kids will have the same types of treats when their trick-or-treating is over, as they will be using them in the game Fooling the Ghost later on.

After giving out treats at each trick-or-treat station, instruct the kids to sit down for a Halloween story telling. To incorporate a broad range of Halloween topics, select titles that deal with all kinds of Halloween icons and activities, such as ghosts, scarecrows, black cats, haunted houses and trick-or-treating. Refer to "Recommended Readings" in the back of the book for some fun title suggestions.

Fooling the Ghost. Once the kids have finished their parade and trick-or-treating at each station, play the game Fooling the Ghost. This is played by kids sitting in a big circle (similar to Duck Duck Goose) with their treat bags in front of them. One child volunteers to be the first ghost and puts on a gray and white sheer shroud. The ghost stands in the middle of the circle and is given a piece of paper that contains one question and answer. The question is one that a ghost may ask to another, such as:

How old were you when you died? (Answer: 100)
How many nights of the year do you return to earth? (Answer: 3)
Is your tombstone flat, round or square? (Answer: Flat)
Do you haunt cemeteries, alleyways or houses? (Answer: Houses)
Have you seen any other ghosts out tonight? (Answer: Yes)

In the game, the children in the circle will want to avoid being confronted by the ghost. They do this by taking one treat from their bag and putting it out in front of them at once. As they do this, the ghost reaches into their treat bag and secretly holds one treat in their hand. Once all the children in the circle have placed their treat in front of them, the ghost reveals which one they have chosen from their bag. They then approach a child who put out the same type of treat and ask them the question on their paper.

If the child gives the answer that is written on the ghost's paper, that child is now the new ghost. They put on the shroud and get their own paper with a question, and the previous ghost takes their spot in the circle. If the child does not give the same answer that is on the ghost's paper, the ghost repeats the action of choosing a treat from their bag while the others switch the treats before them. This is done 5 times, after which time the ghost chooses any child they wish to be the new ghost. (When playing with a young crowd, an adult can help the ghost read their question.)

The Magic Mirror. Another game that relates to ancient Halloween practices is The Magic Mirror. To play the game, set up a large mirror in the center of the room (either a stand up mirror or one placed on a table) with a large cauldron before it. Decorate the mirror with plastic dead branches, black flowers and spider webs. Tape a witch's hat made from black construction paper to the floor a few feet in front of the cauldron and mirror.

Inside the cauldron put small Halloween prizes such as stickers, finger puppets, yo-yos and other toys with a "fortune" tied to each with paper and string. Sample fortunes can read:

You will get what you most desire.
You will try something new today.
You will try a new kind of treat today.
You will dream about what you did today.
You will get the item you hope for on Halloween night.
You will see someone you least expect on Halloween night.

Cover the cauldron with spider webbing or cheesecloth.

To play the game, children dance in a large circle around the mirror. At certain points in the game the music is stopped and whoever is on top of the witch's hat in front of the mirror gets to take a prize and their fortune from the cauldron. (Refer to the music selection under Halloween Parade for some fun dance music.)

A Keepsake from the Past. Finally, make sure that each child will be able to look back at their first Halloween party where they took part in the customs of yesteryear. Suggest that parents bring their cameras when they stop by after (or during) the party for taking their child's picture in front of the divination mirror or at their favorite trick-or-treat station. You may also want to take a picture of the whole class in costume, holding their parade toys and divination prizes to email to all of the parents.

A Teen Halloween

To put together a Halloween party for an older crowd, such as ages 9–16, arrange a series of games and activities that involve a bit more creativity and a bit less dancing, thereby avoiding a crowd of blushing faces — with or without masks.

A teen Halloween party can either involve wearing costumes or coming in regular clothes. In either case, the kids will engage in centuries-old traditions that made Halloween into what it is today, taking them into a seasonal realm different than the gore films and slasher parties for a brief spell.

Halloween Back in the Day: The Stage Performance. Similar to An Elementary Halloween, start the party off with a treats table for kids to sample from when they first arrive. Treats can include apples, pumpkin bread or pumpkin muffins, mini candy bars, nuts and cider.

After picking out their treats, let the kids sit by a type of stage set up for the party, where you or another adult can tell them about the history of Halloween. The stage can be set up in any area of the room with a black curtain backdrop, spider webbing along the walls and pumpkins, Indian corn, broomsticks and witches' hats on the floor. If you have one, place a podium in the center of the stage with torn cheesecloth or other fabrics draped over it and a few mini pumpkins on top.

Read to the kids "The Origins of Halloween" at the end of this section to introduce them to the history of the holiday. You may want to mention that there will be Halloween history trivia and prizes at the end of the party so that more ears will be perked and the information will be more likely to sink in!

Face Painting Contest. Next, let the kids try their hands at turning each other into other-worldly spirits like they did in the times of the Celts. Set up chairs or stools around the room that each bears a small package of Halloween make-up. Tell the kids to split into pairs and take turns painting their partner's face into a spirit, animal or other creation. Set a time limit (for example: 30 minutes) for each pair to apply their make-up.

Once time is up and teams have their faces painted, all the teachers or chaperones of the party can judge the 3 best of the group. Award prizes for first, second and third place, which may include Halloween candy bags or gifts donated from local businesses putting on Halloween events.

Scary Readings. After the face painting contest, tell the kids that they now have their own chance to take part in an ancient Halloween tradition by telling a ghost story. On a table beside the Halloween stage, arrange a selection of readings for the kids to look through. These can include a selection of books or photocopies of excerpts from books that relate to the history of Halloween. (Check out "Recommended Readings" at the end of the book for some fun title suggestions.) The brave souls among them — who are now conveniently masked behind make up — can volunteer to read any Halloween poem or story excerpt at the podium.

Since kids tend to be shy when it comes to public speaking, even when it's a topic they love like Halloween, you may want to give them some extra incentive to do a performance. Set aside special prizes to give to each speaker, each of which may also be obtained through local businesses, such as tickets to a local movie theater, tickets to a local Halloween attraction, gift certificates to a Halloween shop or special Halloween gifts bags. Another option is to obtain one big package of prizes and allow performers to enter a raffle for it at the end of the readings.

The Ghosts of Divination. After the Halloween readings, invite the kids to play a game called The Ghosts of Divination. To begin, split the kids into groups of 5 or 6 and instruct them to sit in small circles on the floor. In the middle of each circle place a plastic or foam carved pumpkin with a glow stick inside, as well as 20–25 black marbles beside the pumpkin. Lower the lights so that there is still enough light to see but dark enough to see the glowing jack-o'-lantern.

Next, distribute a Ghost Card to each player, which they look at but then keep hidden. Ghost Cards can be made out of plain index cards, 1 out of every 5 bearing a ghost sticker and the rest left blank. Lastly, give each player a paper with 5 questions that pertain to what someone who lived hundreds or even thousands of years ago may wish to know about their future. (The same questions can be used on multiple papers.) Sample questions may read:

Will my crops prosper in the coming year?
Will my crops fail in the coming year?
Will my family be healthy in the coming year?
Will any illness strike my family in the coming year?
Will there be any marriages in my family in the coming year?
Will any storms come in the coming year?
Will the weather be fair in the coming year?

To play the game, players asks their question to every other player in their group, who in return answers either yes or no. Those who bear a card with a ghost on it can see the future well because a ghost is helping them, whereas those with a blank card cannot see the future and only make guesses. Once a player has had their question answered by everyone in their circle, they name 2 people who they think are being helped by a ghost (though there may be more or less than 2). The named players take a black marble.

After all players have asked and received answers to one of their questions, those holding marbles move to a new circle, putting the marbles back beside the glowing pumpkin. Those without marbles stay in the same circle. Ghost cards remain hidden, and once again, each player asks a question from their paper to every other player in the circle, then name 2 people who they think are being helped by a ghost. This continues for a total of 5 circle rotations.

After the fifth and final question on the papers are answered by each player in the group, those with the most marbles in each circle take the pumpkin from the center and form a final circle together. (If there is a tie, both kids may join the final circle, but only one holds the pumpkin). The remainder of the players stand outside the circle. Players in the final circle get a new paper with a question to ask the spirits, each of which pertains to darker subjects and cannot be answered by a simple yes or no. Sample questions can be:

What will be the exact day and year when I die?
What will one day cause the destruction of my home?
Where will I be put to rest when I die?
How many men will betray me in my lifetime?
How many people will attend my funeral?
How many in my family will come to harm in the coming year?
How will I know when I am about to die?

This time when players ask the question to each player in the circle, the others must give full answers. After each answer, it is up to the kids outside the circle to say whether or not they think the player is being guided by a ghost.

After all the questions have been asked and answered by everyone in the circle, a final vote is taken from the class as to who is really holding a Ghost Card and in connection with spirits. Any player who is named and holds a ghost on their card gets a prize.

Halloween Trivia. For the final game of ghosts and goblins (and some educational stuff), split the kids into 2 or 3 large groups seated either across from each other or in 3 different areas of the room. Read the trivia questions below and allow any group that had their hand raised first to make their guess. The player in the group who answered correctly gets a piece of candy — which they shouldn't eat yet, as they will be counted at the end of the game!

After all the questions are read, each player in the group with the most candy is awarded a treat bag.

1. Who were the agricultural people who took part in Samhain celebrations? — *The Celts*

2. Spirits that walked the earth during Samhain had died how long ago? — *Within the past year*

3. Why did the Celts engage in parades during Samhain? — *To lead any unruly spirits away from the towns with offerings*

4. What holiday was started by the Romans and took place on November 1? — *All Saints Day*

5. All Souls Day was a day to honor who? — *Relatives who had passed away*

6. Why did the Celts believe spirits were able to walk the earth in late autumn? — *The veil between the living and spirits worlds was at its thinnest*

7. What did the majority of divination questions center on during the time of the Celts? — *Prosperity or destruction of crops and family health*

8. What kinds of spirits were welcomed into people's homes? — *Relatives*

9. How would the Celts dress during Samhain? — *As spirits in animal skins*

10. What were soul cakes made out of? — *Square pieces of bread with currants*

11. What would a person do in return for receiving a soul cake? — *Say a prayer for a member of that family who had died*

12. What did the majority of divination questions center on in America in the early 20th century? — *The identity of one's future husband*

13. What was Halloween night also referred to in the early 20th century when people played pranks and took part in vandalism? — *Mischief Night*

THE ORIGINS OF HALLOWEEN

Halloween Back in the Day

What is known today as Halloween started over 3,000 years ago with a tribe of agricultural people known as the Celts. The Celts lived in the area that is presently the United Kingdom, Ireland and northern France.

In late October, the Celts celebrated the end of the harvest season by lighting bonfires to honor their gods, dancing and playing games. The celebration lasted from October 31 to November 2 and was called Samhain (pronounced Sow-In). At this time, it was believed that the spirits of those who had died within the year could return to walk the earth one last time.

Samhain later merged with two other holidays started by the Romans: All Saints Day on

November 1 as a day to honor the saints, and All Soul's Day on November 2 as a day to remember relatives who had passed away.

Halloween Parades

Other festivities for Samhain included dressing in animal skins and taking part in parades. In the hopes of keeping any malicious spirits away from their homes, the Celts carried offerings of food and drink as they paraded to the edge of their village. The offerings were then left outside the towns to keep these unruly spirits away and prevent them from causing mischief.

Trick-or-Treating

The Halloween tradition of trick-or-treating started as a European Christian custom called souling. On November 2, All Souls Day, the poor would walk from door to door begging for soul cakes, which were square pieces of bread made with currants. For each soul cake a beggar received, they would say a prayer for a person who had died in that family. This was believed to help the soul of the dead enter heaven more quickly, and also ensured that the less fortunate had more to eat during this time of year.

Trick-or-treating did not begin in America until the early 1900's. Before that time, it had become a common tradition for both children and young adults to perform vandalism on Halloween night, which had since taken on the name Mischief Night. Kids would perform pranks, vandalism and even destroy public property. To try to move the holiday into a better direction, advertisements began to appear in magazines and newspapers that encouraged adults to hand out treats to any children who came to their door on Halloween night.

Ghost Stories

The Celts believed that the shortest day of the year during Samhain was when the barrier between the living and the dead became thin, which is why spirits were believed to be able to walk the earth during this time. The Celts would ask the spirits to aid them in divination, or foretelling the future, in the attempt to foresee prosperity or destruction of their crops, health and family in the coming years. The prophecies that the Celts received through divination were passed down from generation to generation and are the earliest forms of Halloween ghost stories.

Years later as European immigrants came to America, they continued this tradition of telling ghost stories on Halloween night. In addition to those passed down of spirits that roamed the earth, ghost stories had come to involve any number of ghouls, goblins, witches and demons.

Fooling the Ghost / Spirit Offerings

Spirits of relatives who had passed away were welcomed into people's homes during Samhain, and offerings of food and drink were set out for them. Offerings were also left outside the door to appease unruly spirits and keep them from coming in. When not at home, Celts dressed in masks and furs in the attempt to resemble spirits themselves and avoid being confronted by them.

The Magic Mirror / Divination

Fortune-telling was revived as a Halloween tradition in the early 1900's in the United States. However, rather than inquiring about family health or livelihood, traditional adult Halloween parties consisted of trying to see one's future husband through tarot cards, mirrors, runes and palm readings.

7

YOUR HALLOWEEN ADVENTURES

Okay, now that you've turned your home into a full-fledged Insane Asylum and your office morphed into a completely different kind of torture chamber than it was before, you've got both burial grounds covered. The tombstones are in place, the skeletons hanged and Friday night is fast approaching... it's the time you've been waiting for! Time to head out on those weekends of horror to party, scream and run for your life, only to hope you'll survive in the end.

But just when you thought it couldn't get any better than the list on your Halloween calendar, it turns out there's even more in store. Such as hidden Halloween treats that only the sneakiest shape-shifters can uncover and ways to become the monster you've always wanted to be without having to chain yourself to the basement. In this chapter, we'll discover them all and more by embarking on adventures that test your true psychosis while extending those planned outings to haunts, shows, tours and more from your researched Halloween happenings.

And who knows: with each adventure, you may be changed forever. You may find yourself entranced within a vampire castle thousands of miles from home or wandering more sinister dwellings just minutes down the road. But there's no turning back now... and who would want to? All your Halloween adventures await for a season like never before.

Extending your Halloween Adventures

The weekend is here! You've preordered your Saturday night tickets for the Bleeding Coffin Theme Park and packed your bag with all the essentials: camera, spending cash, glow-in-the-dark pumpkin necklace and vampire teeth. But suddenly the minute-hand on your recently-decaying grandfather clock moves slower and slower, until practically reaching a stand-still... and it's only 3 pm! Will nightfall *ever* arrive??

But wait! With so much autumn magic in the air, there are a hundred other uses for it than wishing for an early sunset. The Halloween season is short, and there's so much to be enjoyed while it lasts. So before you head out on those weekend adventures, plan on extending them a little further by adding an extra nightmare or two before or after that haunted house, ghost tour or horror stage show.

Ride of the Dead. Need a ride to the airport for that Halloween weekend getaway? Why use an ordinary car when everyone can be chauffeured in style? Surprise your friends by showing up in a hearse for a deadly send-off. Check out hearse rental companies in the area that rent hearses in the same fashion as limos: to transport parties to their destination

of choice for an hourly fee. Many chauffeurs will even dress the part in gothic attire and give you the option to buddy up with a fellow traveler, such as a skeleton in his coffin. Request special party music for the ride such as the classic "Monster Mash" or the latest Midnight Syndicate album while you sit back, relax and enjoy a view that many never get to speak of.

It All Began with the Pumpkin. Before you head out to that hypnotist and magic show, invite your friends to your place for an afternoon of carving pumpkins. Make a group trip to your local pumpkin stand so that everyone can pick out their own. Back home, whip up some Reaper's Delight and Butterscotch Potion (both recipes can be found in "The Halloween Menu" in Chapter 8) while carving your creations. Take pictures of everyone carving as well as all the jack-o'-lanterns together once they're finished.

Want a picture that will look great in your Halloween museum? Take a photo of everyone holding their jack-o'-lanterns after dark, removing the lids so that the light shines up on their faces.

Applying the Monster. If you're going to a Halloween destination that involves dressing up in costume, have everyone apply the monster together. Invite your friends to your place for a group trip to your local Halloween warehouse for picking out costumes. You can also load up on hair coloring, monster make-up and a few bags of candy to keep everyone going throughout the night. Or if everybody already has their costumes, tell them to come by an hour or so before the event to help each other with make-up, wigs, etc. Put on some Halloween tunes and take pictures of everyone in their monster characters.

Grave Beginnings. An awesome place to stop along the way to your haunted attraction is an old graveyard. Head to one with the oldest stones around to stroll the grounds, take pictures and look at the inscriptions and carvings. If there is a graveyard that has any type of haunted history, go to that one and tell its story. If the cemetery is well kept, it can also be a good place to have a picnic before your event. Bring a picnic basket of goodies or stop to pick up something along the way and you have the perfect atmosphere for a haunting supper.

And They Were Never Heard from Again... Rather than taking the highway home from your haunted ghost tour outing, drive the back roads to get a new take on some seemingly innocent suburbia. See how the dark country roads suddenly develop a menacing atmosphere after a night of spooky tales. What was the story the tour guide told about a woman in white who suddenly appeared by the roadside? And what was *that*?

Drive the countryside and you're also sure to pass by houses with glowing jack-o'-lanterns and Halloween displays for the perfect October drive. Keep an eye out in your local newspaper for homes that have put up especially big and elaborate Halloween displays (in addition to your own, of course), and make sure you hit those roads, too.

Living It Up with the Undead. After your night of haunted hayrides and monster discos, invite everyone over for a party at your place. Make a couple Pizzas from Hell and indulge in some Desserts of the Dead (described in "The Halloween Menu" in Chapter 8). Watch scary movies and see if they compare to the live nightmares you all just barely escaped.

PARTY NIGHTS

Want to throw a Halloween party with a demented theme all its own?
Check out "Party Nights" in Chapter 8 for some truly insane ideas.

Hidden Halloween Treats

When most of us think of Halloween treats, we envision a giant pumpkin pail overflowing with chocolate bars, popcorn balls, gum and enough sugar to keep us flying until New Years. But not all Halloween treats come in fun-size candy wrappers. Some of the best treats are small-town original recipes such as cookies, pastries, candies and specialty drinks that can only be whipped up in a true mad scientist's laboratory. And when the pickin's good, you can load up on a cauldron-full of these delectable treats found right around the corner... if you know where to look.

For another fun and tasty addition to your Halloween adventures, head to some of the following locations for uncovering all kinds of hidden Halloween treats.

Ice Cream Shops, Bakeries and Sweet Shops. From early September, ice creams shops come out with seasonal flavors for the fall, such as pumpkin, pumpkin pie and even ginger ice cream. Stop by your local ice cream shop on the way home from costume shopping for a pumpkin waffle cone or sundae, or grab a pint to bring back for the whole family.

We can smell them a mile away and for good reason... Bakeries are drool-inducing spots for picking up treats like pumpkin muffins, pumpkin donuts and even pumpkin whoopee pies. Bring a dozen to your slasher office party or back home for a mouth-watering weekend breakfast.

Candy stores and sweet shops not only make specialty items for Halloween, but oftentimes entire gift baskets of seasonal goodies. Pick up a basket filled with all kinds of home-made Halloween candies, cookies and more for treating your special someone, using as a prize at your Halloween business event and, of course, one for yourself!

Farm Stands, Country Stores and More. Farm stands are a sure winner for Halloween treats, and the fact that they're often surrounded by a field of pumpkins doesn't hurt, either. In addition to picking out your pumpkins, gourds and Indian corn, you'll probably find selections such as pumpkin bars, apple crisp, pies, candy apples, pumpkin cookies and other home-made recipes.

Small mom and pop country stores and markets thrive on their specialty items that just can't be found anywhere else. Look for home-made pumpkin and banana breads, chocolate and fudge with special fall flavors, pumpkin butter and more to pack up that picnic basket for your graveyard picnic.

What better place for an October breakfast than a pumpkin patch? Check out your local berry farms and small, area restaurants that are set in the countryside. They may be holding special Sunday breakfasts of pancakes and waffles served outside, followed by a hayride through their pumpkin patch or berry fields.

Halloween goodies aren't limited to foods alone. Check out the coffee shops in your area for seasonal flavors of coffee and tea, including pumpkin spice, pumpkin pie, hot cider and ginger. Coffee shops also tend to have an assortment of goodies that go well with these seasonal drinks, such as flavored biscotti and scones.

Volunteering with a Local Haunt

If you find that you want to get involved with a haunted attraction but you're not quite sure about building one yourself, you're in luck. Because for every haunted event out there, there's a need for people crazy enough to work it. Volunteering with a local haunt is a fun Halloween adventure and a good first step for entering into the haunt world. You'll meet people who share your interest and passion for Halloween while learning various skills to apply back at the Insane Asylum.

If you know that you want to get involved with some kind of Halloween event but you're not sure which kind, refer back to the list you made in Section 1 of all the Halloween happenings in your area. Scanning the list, think about what catches your interest the most. It may be anything from monster theater, haunted houses, tours, parades or any other type of madness going on for the season.

There are several ways to bring out your true monster by volunteering with a haunt. Read through the categories below and see which ones spark your morbid curiosity. And if you find a few that you just can't resist, don't wait! Contact those running the show early, since many Halloween events are planned months in advance.

Be a Monster! Like acting? Be the monster you've always wanted to be. Live actors are the key to bringing haunted attractions to life, acting scary, goofy, deranged, mysteries or dead. You'll get to dress in freakish attire, wear horrendous make-up and run around acting crazy... who could ask for more? If you don't have any previous acting experience, don't worry. Just find out when the attraction is holding auditions and if they're looking for specific types of characters. Practice ahead of time as being a vampire on the prowl, a zombie just crawled up from the grave, a mad scientist on the verge of a ludicrous discovery, a werewolf sniffing for fresh meat, an escaped lunatic, a lost ghost, an enraged mummy or any other type of creature they suggest or you think up.

If you don't like the idea of having to scare people, remember that not all monsters in haunted attractions jump out at people or run after them. There will also be a need for monsters to work as greeters and line entertainment.

Design and Build Sets or Make Props. Like working with your hands? Small haunts often need help in setting up everything from the base walls to the "Thank you for coming" sign. No matter what your skill level, you can be trained to help with sets in a variety of areas. Construct a haunted castle from the ground up, put up draw bridges, town ruins and circus scenes. Haunt owners may also be looking for new ideas to keep their attraction changing with each season. You could share your insane insights to help put a new spin on a house of chaos.

Want to share your stone-cutting and coffin-making skills with the world? Haunters often build most of their props themselves rather than buying them, and a lot of help is needed to fill three floors of a haunted prison. Volunteer to help with prop building and you could learn about making props such as guillotines, jail cells, elaborate character props and more. Or if you would rather volunteer for something that's more low-key, there may also be help needed working with smaller props, such as carving jack-o'-lanterns or putting together Halloween gift bags.

Publicity and Other Work. Do you like writing and photography? You're already a natural with those display storylines and pictures of the undead. Volunteer to write articles on the upcoming attraction and take pictures of the actors in dress rehearsal for their website, local magazines and press releases for the newspaper. You could also help to write and design brochures and pamphlets for the haunt as well as ticket and poster designs.

Do you want to keep your inner monster hidden but still get into all the action at show time? Work the nights of horror as a ticket seller, merchandise vendor or directing cars where to park. You could also be a secret psychopath in the gift shop or craft station or volunteer to bring in baked goods to sell. You'll get a front-row view of all the mortals who come running out of the event screaming for their lives, followed by the ones who never made it out of line before running away with them.

MONEY TO BURN

Want to earn some extra cash while turning yourself over to the dark side? Look into working the bigger haunted attractions, such as theme parks and zoos, that are putting on an after-hours Halloween show. Working these bigger haunts will pay a small wage so you'll have some dough to burn on all of your other Halloween adventures!

Gifts for the Season

Everybody loves getting a gift for the season... especially when it's got a grinning skull or half-crazed jack-o'-lantern on the card. If you're holding some Halloween business events or throwing a Halloween party at the Insane Asylum, you may be looking for just the right types of gifts and prizes for all your raffles, drawings, games and more.

Some of the best types of gifts for events such as these are Halloween assortments, since it will most likely be the Halloween buffs attending. Just about every shop and retail store has their own selection to choose from for costumes, collectables, movies and other merchandise for celebrating some nights of terror. But with so much to pick from, where do you start? The bleeding hand candle or the Frankenstein door bell? The skulls and bones party platter or the shrunken heads necklace?

For putting together Halloween gifts and prizes that work well in any haunting event, consider the following gifts to die for.

Horror Tickets. Tickets to an additional night of terror are what every Halloween buff craves. Pick up a pair of tickets or coupons to other haunted happenings going on in the area, such as:

- A horror theme park or haunted house
- A monster stage production
- A public Halloween party
- A ghost or graveyard tour
- A horror museum exhibit
- A night's ride in a hearse rental
- Opening night tickets to the latest horror movie

Include an additional haunted item or two with each pair of tickets or coupons, such as a flashlight and ghost hunting book with ghost tour tickets or a package of monster make-up and colored hair spray with tickets to a Halloween party.

Halloween Gift Sets. Halloween gift sets are fun to give, receive and put together. What monster could resist an assortment of skulls, Halloween books and other oddities to add to their collections? Assemble gift sets for a variety of Halloween hobbies, such as:

Decorator's Halloween Set. An indoor and outdoor Halloween décor set could include props and special effects such as a Styrofoam tombstone, small coffin, bag of bones or skeleton, body parts, spider webbing, plastic insects or a fog machine.

Collector's Halloween Set. For the Halloween village collector, a gift set of their dreams can include a miniature haunted house, dark castle or witch's cottage or smaller accessories such as a wooden fence, evil trees, tombstone collection or pumpkins. For the collector of Halloween books, movies and music, make a collector's set that includes a horror movie DVD, paperback novel or horror soundtrack CD and a package of popcorn and candy.

Crafter's Halloween Set. A Halloween set to satisfy any monster crafter can include everything for their Halloween scrapbooking and card-making, such as scrapbooking paper and cardstock, Halloween stickers and cut-outs and framing supplies for making Halloween pictures.

Child's Halloween Set. A nice Halloween gift set to use for a children's costume contest can include a Halloween book and coloring book, Halloween cartoon DVD and a plush black cat, ghost, or vampire. You could also make a trick-or-treating gift set with a package of monster make-up, costume accessories such as a hat, wig or cape and a new trick-or-treat bag.

A Coffin Full of Goodies.

A coffin full of goodies works as a great prize at any Halloween festival. Line a small coffin with fake autumn leaves and fill it with treats to satisfy any sweet tooth: fun-sized candy bars, candy corn, ghost pops, popcorn balls and gum. Also throw in some Halloween confetti, vampire teeth and rubber eyeballs.

Putting together these types of gifts and prizes will spice up all your parties, event games and raffles with just the right type of poison. And if you're a big fan of gift giving (and getting!), start a new Halloween tradition of a horror gift exchange with your fellow enthusiasts.

If all this talk about Halloween gifts is making you want to put together a special something for just about *all* your loved ones this season, then go for it! Although, not everyone out there is a Halloween buff (...it's true, people are strange) and you may have a few friends or family members who just wouldn't appreciate the beauty of a bloody mansion for starting a Halloween village or a coffin full of vampire teeth. But as weird as these people are, we still love them (kind of) and there are other seasonal gifts to put together that don't center on the ghosts and goblins we love so much.

The Gift of Pumpkin.

Who doesn't love getting a pumpkin, just for the occasion of it being the pumpkin season? Sugar pumpkins make great gifts for those who like to make their own breads and pies, cookies and soups, and bigger pumpkins are fun gifts for those who like to use them as decorations and carving jack-o'-lanterns. Mini pumpkins and Indian corn also make nice Halloween gifts. Put together a festive gift basket with mini pumpkins, Indian corn and home-made pumpkin muffins wrapped in orange ribbon.

Halloween Recipes, Memories and Treats from Afar. Did you create or find a seasonal recipe that you just know a friend would love? Make a copy of the recipe and paste it on the back of a Halloween postcard. Put the postcard in a gift basket filled with all the ingredients they'll need for making the recipe, as well as a Halloween oven mitt or pot holder... just to get them in the spirit!

Have some fun pictures of you and friends from a past Halloween event? Put the photo in a black frame using Halloween craft paper as matting for a fun gift. Framed photos also make perfect gifts for family members. Take a few pictures of you and the family picking out pumpkins or surrounded by colorful foliage for a special autumn gift for your mother or grandmother.

Does one of your friends live in an Insane Asylum in a far-off land of chaos? If so and you've discovered some hidden Halloween treats that aren't available in their area, fill a gift basket or Halloween box with one of each treat and pop it in the mail for a delivery of sweet surprises.

A Halloween Story Telling and Poetry Reading

Oral traditions go back centuries. Long before lovers of the supernatural ran to double features and horror theme parks to become captivated in a world of dark fantasy, they gathered around the fire to listen to spookster tales passed down from generation to generation about spirits, curses, enchantments and magic.

The tradition of storytelling can also be put into an imaginative and theatrical event for the Halloween season. How many times have you read your favorite short story, novel or poem in the early fall because the tale puts you into the perfect Halloween mood? Stories of dark creatures prowling the night and thrilling stanzas of silent graveyards transport us into a world we seek out and try to create right at home. If engaging in these kinds of stories and poetry is one of your favorite pastimes for the season, share it with others who have the same passion. Bring those legendary characters and mythical worlds to life with a Halloween story telling and poetry reading.

A story telling and poetry reading is an event you can put together for an adventure like no other. After going to all those horror shows and productions, it's now *your* turn to take to the stage. You can either make the event one that includes the whole community or hold a private gathering with a small group of friends.

Monster Productions. Whether you decide that your event will be big or small, the structure can be the same: a series of short presentations that each delve into the world of Halloween, horror, mystery and the like. Presentations can consist of participants reading a poem, short story, excerpt from a novel or piece of writing they have done themselves to the audience. The selections should be made before coming to the reading.

Choosing material for the event can be as simple as going to your own Halloween collection (see Chapter 8) and picking out your favorite book. If you don't see anything there that fits the type of performance you'd like to make, head to your local library or cruise the bookstores in the poetry section, sci-fi/fantasy, horror, Occult or New Age section.

To make each reading more like a theatrical performance, encourage participants to dress in a costume that fits the theme of their reading. They may also bring a small prop or two to set up and add to the scene. For example, doing a reading from Washington Irving's *The Legend of Sleepy Hollow* may include the performer dressing up like someone from the late 1700's and setting a lantern and skull on the podium. A reading of Edgar Allan Poe's *The Raven* may include the reader dressing up in an old evening jacket, holding a pipe and putting a large, leather bound book on the podium for a better visual of the speaker's surroundings. Whatever attire and items the readers choose, just let them know they should be able to set up and remove their props promptly when making way for the next performance.

Monster Theater for the Masses. To make the story telling and poetry reading a grand affair, hold it in a public place such as your town library or community center. Advertise at least six weeks in advance in your local paper as well as at the location where the event will be held. You can either require that everyone attending take part in a performance or allow guests to attend without participating. In either case, participants doing a reading should submit their piece to you at least three weeks in advance so that you can set up a schedule.

You may also choose to make programs for the event that list each story or poem by order of presentation. These make great souvenirs and also give everyone a new collection of Halloween readings for their home library. Don't break the bank on making them, though: ask for donations when handing them out!

The Small Group of Poet Monsters. To hold a story telling and poetry reading with a small group of friends, use the same structure as for a public event back at your Insane Asylum or other intimate location. Set the date and send out invitations well in advance, giving everyone enough time to choose their writing piece and prepare their presentation. Begin the night with a pot-luck spread and follow with the series of readings.

Just like you would do for a public event, create programs that list all the presentations of the evening. You can also make more personalized programs by taking a picture of each performance and then inserting the photos by the listings to print out after the event.

Check out "Recommended Readings" at the end of the book for some great titles for all your Halloween story telling and poetry readings.

Friends of Slater Library's Annual
HALLOWEEN STORY TELLING AND POETRY READING
FRIDAY, OCTOBER 2

Welcome to the Friends of Slater Library's 1st Annual Halloween Story Telling and Poetry Reading!

Tonight's performances include avid poets, poetry-lovers, writers and art buffs, each having selected one of their favorite poems, excerpts from literature or their own original work. Each performance is unique in that it involves either costume, props, music or lighting to truly capture the essence of the reading.

Please refrain from any questions or comments until the conclusion of the show. There will be a 15 minute intermission at 8:30. Refreshments will be provided in the lobby.

Please consider making a donation to help support the mission of Friends of Slater Library and bring future educational and cultural programs like this one to our community.

Enjoy the performance!

PERFORMANCES:

1. Spirits of the Dead
By: Edgar Allan Poe
Performed by: Joe Wheeler

Thy soul shall find itself alone
'Mid dark thoughts of the gray tombstone-
Not one, of all the crowd, to pry
Into thine hour of secrecy.

Be silent in that solitude
Which is not loneliness, for then
The spirits of the dead who stood
In life before thee are again
In death around thee, and their will
Shall overshadow thee; be still.

The night, tho' clear, shall frown,
And the stars shall not look down
From their high thrones in the Heaven
With light like Hope to mortals given;
But their red orbs, without beam,
To thy weariness shall seem

As a burning and a fever
Which would cling to thee forever.
Now are thoughts thou shalt not banish-
Now are visions ne'er to vanish;
From thy spirit shall they pass
No more — like dew-drops from the grass.

The breeze — the breath of God — is still,
And the mist upon the hill
Shadowy — shadowy — yet unbroken,
Is a symbol and a token,-
How it hangs upon the trees,
A mystery of mysteries!

2. Excerpt from *The Legend of Sleepy Hollow*
By: Washington Irving
Performed by: Janet Wallace

But all these were nothing to the tales of ghosts and apparitions that succeeded. The neighborhood is rich in legendary treasures of the kind. Local tales and superstitions thrive best in these sheltered long-settled retreats, but are trampled under foot by the shifting throng that forms the populations of most of our country places. Besides, there is no encouragement for ghosts in most of our villages, for they have scarcely had time to finish their nap and turn themselves in their graves before their surviving friends have traveled away from the neighborhood; so that when they turn out at night to walk their rounds they have no acquaintance left to call upon. This is perhaps the reason why we seldom hear of ghosts except in our long established Dutch communities.

The immediate cause, however, of the prevalence of supernatural stories in these parts was doubtless owing to the vicinity of Sleepy Hollow. There was a contagion in the very air that blew from that haunted region; it breathed forth an atmosphere of dreams and fancies infecting all the land. Several of the Sleepy Hollow people were present at Van Tassel's, and, as usual, were doling out their wild and wonderful legends. Many dismal tales were told about funeral trains, and mourning cries and wailings heard and seen about the great tree where the unfortunate Major Andre was taken, and which stood in the neighborhood. Some mention was made also of the woman in white that haunted the dark glen at Raven Rock, and was often heard to shriek on winter nights before a storm, having perished there in the snow. The chief part of the stories, however, turned upon the favorite specter of Sleepy Hollow, the headless horseman, who had been heard several times of late, patrolling the country, and, it is said, tethered his horse nightly among the graves in the churchyard.

3. What Shall I Sing
From the film The Innocents
Performed by: Rudy Carter

What shall I sing to my lord through my
     window?
What shall I sing, for my lord will not stay?
What shall I sing, for my lord will not lis-
     ten?
Where shall I go, for my lord is away?

Whom shall I love when the moon is arisen?
Gone is my lord, and the grave is his prison
What shall I say when my lord comes a' call-
     ing?
What shall I say when he knocks on my
     door?
What shall I say when his feet enter softly,
Leaving the marks of his grave on my floor?

Enter, my lord, come from your prison,
Come from your grave, for the moon is
     arisen...

4. Excerpt from *Dracula*
By: Bram Stoker
Performed by Mike Danton

14 August —

...The setting sun, low down in the sky, was just dropping behind Kettleness; the red light was thrown on the East Cliff and the old abbey, and seemed to bathe everything in a beautiful rosy glow. We were silent for a while, and suddenly Lucy murmured as if to herself: —

"His red eyes again! They are just the same." It was such an odd expression, coming *apropos* of nothing, that it quite startled me. I slewed round a little, so as to see Lucy well without seeming to stare at her, and saw that she was in a half-dreamy state, with an odd look on her face that I could not quite make out; so I said nothing, but followed her eyes. She appeared to be looking over at our own seat, whereon was a dark figure seated alone. I was a little startled myself, for it seemed for an instant as if the stranger had great eyes like burning flames; but a second look dispelled the illusion. The red sunlight was shining on the windows of St. Mary's Church behind our seat, and as the sun dipped there was just sufficient chance in the refraction and reflection to make it appear as if the light moved. I called Lucy's attention to the peculiar effect, and she became herself with a start, but she looked sad all the same; it may have been that she was thinking of that terrible night up there. We never refer to it; so I said nothing, and we went home to dinner.

Travel

Traveling takes us beyond our everyday lives. Whether we're out joy-riding down some new country roads or journeying across an ocean, exploring new areas can create a whole series of adventures in which we see new landscapes, meet new people and try new things. And what better time to explore the unknown than during the season that thrives on the idea of it all? Halloween-themed travels can include journeys to areas that helped shape the culture of Halloween into what it is today, treating yourself to one of the top horror destinations in the country or just taking some time to marvel at the seasonal changes going on all around you.

In this section, we'll embark on even more Halloween adventures for local travel, distant travel and even foreign travel in some fun out-of-the-way and out-of-the-ordinary endeavors. So grab some snacks, the camera bag and your appetite for adventure and head out there into the beyond.

Local Travel. If you like taking long day trips to see what the world next door has in store and possibly step into your own private twilight zone, you may find that the spinning spiral is closer to home than you think. For traveling on a local level, indulge in Halloween adventures that are just a short trip away to party with zombies, relax down a country road or meet some unruly spirits somewhere in between.

Events and Attractions: Using the same method you did in Chapter 1, do a search to see what's going on for the Halloween season in your surrounding states. Focus on areas that would require a drive of just a half day or so and look for events such as big costume parties, horror theme parks, Halloween shows on stage, festivals and other activities. You'll probably discover attractions and productions that you've never even heard of before, even though they've been around for years! When you head out on your travels, remember to keep an eye out for those hidden Halloween treats along the way.

Foliage and Other Autumn Scenery: Even monsters love a scenic drive. Plan some foliage travels by taking out your road map and looking for sections marked as scenic roads in your state or surrounding states. Set some time aside to admire the changing seasons by spending an afternoon or even the whole day just driving from one country area to another for a fun and relaxing October outing. You may also come across an out-of-the-way restaurant that has put together a special monster theme or a costume shop with original designs you won't find anywhere else. Keep an eye out for billboards and banners of Halloween attractions that aren't being advertised in your area.

Places with Strange or Haunted Histories: Odds are that there are many areas in your state known for strange histories and legends (how else do you explain the way *you* turned out?) and are worth exploring. Do an online search of haunted locations and strange histories in your state. You may discover a town with a history of vampires that reportedly returned from the grave to take the blood of their family members, or another that once held witch hunts, has a history of spacecraft sightings, alien abductions or other unexplained phenomenon. Areas such as these also make great destinations for stone hunting and ghost hunting (discussed in Chapters 15 and 16). Check out the local bookstores during your travels for locally-published books that go into the strange history of the town.

In addition to towns filled with strange events, look up specific destinations that are known for being out-of-this-world. You may find a forest that's reportedly the home of an unidentifiable creature, haunted cemeteries and fields, or even a stretch of road that defies gravity!

Remember that taking the road less traveled doesn't have to be limited to the weekends and vacation days. Do some exploring during your lunch break in an area not far from where you work or take a country road home that has always caught your eye.

Essentials for Local Travel:

Road map	Notebook and pens
Lunch, snacks and drinks	Extra cash
Camera and extra batteries	A light jacket or sweatshirt

Distant Travel. If you're feeling even more adventurous and you want to take an overnight trip, weekend trip or week-long vacation, there are many places across the country known for having the biggest Halloween celebrations around or for being focal points in Halloween legends.

Some destinations that no Halloween buff should miss are:

Salem, Massachusetts: It's the ultimate destination for every Halloween enthusiast. Salem is most widely known for its infamous witch trials of 1692, but it's become a town that once you enter, you never want to leave. See how its history has shaped its culture with witch museums, haunted houses, tours both day and night, specialty shops, theatre, festivals and much more. For more info: www.hauntedhappenings.org

Sleepy Hollow, New York: Step into Sleepy Hollow, the home of Washington Irving's *Legend of Sleepy Hollow* and see how its residents have taken the story and galloped with it. Embark on cemetery tours and haunted hayrides and stay for the Halloween parade and annual reading of the town's famous tale. For more info: www.sleepyhollowny.gov

Headless Horseman Haunted Hayride, Ulster Park, New York: This top-rated haunted attraction by *Haunted Attraction Magazine* is a must-see haunt. Dare to embark on a mile-long haunted hayride where the characters are larger than life, try to survive three haunted houses, incredible stage performances and monstrous gift shops. For more info: www.headlesshorseman.com

Halloween Horror Nights, Universal Studios, Florida and California: If anyone knows how to do Halloween, it's got to be Universal Studios: the production company of so many classic horror films. Halloween Horror Nights is an after-hours event that prides itself on its level of scariness to keep the true horror fans coming back for more. The monsters are ruthless and the shows are screaming: just the way we like it! For more info: www.halloweenhorrornights.com

Fright Fest, Six Flags Theme Parks: Fright Fest has the ultimate combination of shows, haunts and roller coasters... who could ask for more? Since Six Flags is open all day and Fright Fest is included in admission, this park is also a great deal for your dollar. Spend the day screaming on the rides and the night running from the monsters that lurk behind every corner. For more info: www.sixflags.com

The Greenwich Village Halloween Parade, New York: The world's largest public Halloween celebration takes the holiday to a new level with a parade like no other. Artistic puppets, floats and tens of thousands of die-hard costumed Halloween buffs fill the streets in a celebration that the whole city embraces each year. For more info: www.halloween-nyc.com

Eastern State Penitentiary, Philadelphia, Pennsylvania: 177 years after its construction, the Eastern State Penitentiary now lies in ruins... but do you dare enter at night and see just who or what resides inside? This haunted attraction takes place in Philadelphia's former prison and was ranked America's #1 haunted house by AOL City Guide. For more info: www.easternstate.org

Terror on the Fox, Green Bay, Wisconsin: Terror on the Fox just may be the most intense and fright-filled haunted attraction you'll find this side of the netherworld. Step onto an antique passenger train, dare to walk through the haunted forest maze and graveyard and keep your sanity in the 3-D haunted house. Want to have a party of the dead you'll never forget? Hop a hearse and book Terror on the Fox for a private party to see just who survives. For more info: www.terroronthefox.com

House of Shock, Jefferson, Louisiana: You have to be a brave soul to enter the House of Shock, where "you haven't lived until they've scared you to death." Nationally acclaimed for being one of the most intense haunted houses in America, the House of Shock also includes live concerts, a full bar and Hell's Kitchen for a meal to die for. The attraction was partially founded by Philip Anselmo from the group Pantera and has gladly been terrorizing those who dare to enter its gates for the past 15 years. For more info: www.houseofshock.com

Howl-o-Scream, Busch Gardens Theme Parks: In October, Busch Gardens becomes a horror theme park that has it all. Embark on up to 5 haunted houses and mazes, join in the Monster Stomp party for a real "rockstravaganza" and see if you can survive the scare zones where zombies and other monsters are just dying to see you. And if you find the creak of the coffin a little too much to take, just refer to the park's scare guide to see which attractions and locations are for the death-defying-and-ready and those better suited for the easily spooked. For more info: www.howloscream.com

In addition to partying the night away on one of these vacations, big Halloween events can serve as great inspiration for putting together your own displays, Halloween business events and new party themes. You'll also come across the best gift shops around to load up on souvenirs, costumes and collectables for your Halloween Museum.

You may choose to combine a few of these adventures into a week-long trip to make the most of your Halloween getaway. Wherever you decide to go, look up additional activities going on in the area, such as Halloween hotel parties, ghost walks, tours, smaller haunted attractions and more. And if you can't seem to locate any online, ask the locals once you get there. You may get an inside tip on a monster-themed club, special horror exhibit or other awesome event.

Additional Essentials for Distant Travel: Maps of the areas and parks that you can get a hold of beforehand. Familiarize yourself with the area and plan out your route so you'll have more time to enjoy it when you're there.

As your list of Halloween destinations continues to grow, is the season suddenly becoming all too short? Well don't worry, because you can also find Halloween excursions that are conveniently open all year for future adventures in the off-season. Check out Chapter 13, "Future Events and Your Next Halloween Vacation."

Foreign Travel. The U.S. isn't the only country having monster celebrations this time of year. Halloween may not be celebrated everywhere, but many countries hold histories, folklore and other superstitions that have contributed to what the holiday is today. Venture forth on a vacation abroad for some spooky sights and exciting adventures that may not even be specifically aimed at the Halloween community... though we're happy to explore them just the same.

Castles of Transylvania: Visiting Dracula's Castle and the Fortress of Vlad the Impaler in Transylvania, Romania is like stepping into a Halloween enthusiast's fairy tale. Make it a Halloween you'll never forget by traveling to a land rich in gothic history and imagination. Look for special tours and hotel packages to accommodate a Halloween vacation Bram Stoker-style.

Pyramids of Egypt: Okay, Halloween isn't so big in Egypt... but with the history they've contributed to its culture, we can forgive them. For a mythical adventure, take a trip to the pyramids that inspired classic horror tales of mummies and curses... just try not to uncover any while you're there!

Haunted Castles of Great Britain: What good is a castle if it's not haunted... or at least has a good story? In Great Britain, you won't be cut short of castles from Northern Ireland to southern England that contain tales and sightings of ghosts throughout the centuries. Take pictures of every nook and cranny and remember to smile for the camera... because you never know who may be smiling next to you!

Streets Where Jack the Ripper Roamed: For all you mystery buffs, go on an adventure of the serial killer "whose file will always be marked unsolved." Tour the locations where Jack the Ripper's victims were found, read the story of the Whitechapel murders and see if you can uncover who Jack the Ripper *really* was.

Catacombs of France: Go on a tour in the catacombs of France where up to six million people were buried in underground quarries during the 18th century. Check out the skulls and bones that line the walls of these giant graves which were originally removed from above-ground cemeteries to avoid overpopulation. Next year's torture chamber display may be the next best thing!

Day of the Dead in Mexico: Make sure to visit Mexico on November 1st and 2nd to celebrate the Day of the Dead. You'll encounter exuberant, artistic parades and city-wide celebrations honoring past ancestors. One of the most celebrated holidays of the country, Day of the Dead festivities include processions of ghosts, mummies, skeletons, coffins and more carried throughout the streets. Embrace this festival of worldly culture that shares the images and imagination of Halloween.

Additional Essentials for Foreign Travel: Travel books or website print-outs about the country and its customs. The more you know beforehand, the more you'll appreciate all your discoveries once you're there!

The Solo Monster. Concerned about being a monster traveling alone? Well, fear not. No matter what kind of demented destination you have in mind, look for travel packages online specifically catered for those traveling solo. You may find a special deal that includes airfare, hotel stay and meals all with other monsters out cruising the spook. Whether you're traveling a few states away or across six time zones, you never know when some fellow ghoulies are just a few graves behind.

More Vacation Time Please! With so many places to go, don't you wish you had endless free time to do it all? Well, your vacation may be limited, but you can use some tricks of the trade for getting more out of that precious time to stretch out the Halloween season.

• **Stretching the Weekends:** Use a vacation day or even a half-day every Friday in October, making those weekends of horror even longer. Many Halloween events and attractions are open during the day on Fridays as well as Thursday nights. Taking Fridays off will also give you more travel time for those longer trips.

• **The Big Night Adventure:** Use additional vacation time for October 31, as well as the day before and even the day after to make a long Halloween vacation. This way you won't be as concerned about the drive or flight to and from your Halloween destination, but will be able to just sit back and enjoy your adventure with ease and insanity.

8

HALLOWEEN IN YOUR INSANE ASYLUM

Ah, the good old Insane Asylum of home. With the comfort of the glowing gargoyle eyes in the graveyard and the silent stare of the Reaper in the dining room, there's truly no place like it.

Your Insane Asylum is the perfect place for engaging in some of your favorite aspects of the season. Set the stage for a Halloween party that has murder written all over it. Fire up the cauldron for delicacies fit for a true cannibal's diner. Let the lunatic Picasso in you take over by creating delirious Halloween invitations and a newsletter of nightmares straight from the underworld.

In this section, we'll delve into all kinds of ways to live it up in the comfort of your own chaos with party themes, crafts of madness and kitchen experiments gone horribly wrong. You've already transformed the place into the ultimate horrific dwelling, and now it's time to enjoy it from luring unsuspecting mortals down into the dungeons to cackling the night away by your loony lonesome.

Party Nights!

What's the Halloween season without a party? The gang back at the office may still be sitting stunned with their dismembered body part presents, but now you've got your whole homestead to work with. The moon is out and your closet banshees are posed... let the party begin!

But before you start blowing up the balloons, consider throwing a party with its own unique theme. And when it comes to Halloween party themes, anything goes. Options are limited only to your personal level of psychosis. Maybe you want to center your party on a particular display you've put together or are currently working on. Or how about taking your favorite Halloween character that's visiting for the season and making him or her the host for the evening?

In this section, we'll go into different party themes that include games, prizes, crafts and just

enough suspense to prevent sudden death... because anything less would just be a shame. Try a few of these parties out for yourself and let them inspire you to come up with your own epiphanies for some unruly party nights.

Grim Reaper's Party. It's the last party you may ever throw... This Halloween party is hosted by the Grim Reaper, who has decided to invite all your friends over for what may be their last meal. Each invitation, appropriately resembling a death certificate, states that the Reaper has asked for the guest's presence for a special evening. Refusal to appear is futile, as they would surely not prefer his personal visitation.

For the Reaper to give his appearance at the party, make a life-sized Reaper figure and sit him at the head of the table, watching over the band of mortals in their last hours on earth. Place a gold medallion around his neck and set before him four objects: a large black box filled with small pieces of paper, a large, rolled up parchment containing a secret riddle, a platter of gold coins and an hourglass. For additional Reaper décor, put up life-sized tombstones around the room and hang pictures of the dead from Chapter 4 and graveyard photos along the walls.

The game of the party is "Life and Death." The Reaper has guaranteed all the guests one thing: they will remain safe for the night... except for the one who has to die. And for a little fun, he has decided to let everyone guess who will be the one to go. It will be the person who is the most foul, and has committed the most atrocious acts. Guests are asked to attend the party looking like the vile creatures they truly are, dressing as axe men, serial killers and other vandals.

In the box before the Reaper, small pieces of paper contain a bit of information about each guest, such as "Ran over their neighbor's cat," "Robs graves in rich cemeteries," "Killed

a man in Texas," and so on. (All the information is fictional... hopefully.) In addition to the vile acts, a certain number of skulls are drawn on each paper: 1 skull for crimes that are not too hideous, and 5 for the most evil. (As the creator, it will be up to you to decide which acts are worthy of 1–5 skulls.)

The game is played by each guest taking a paper from the box and revealing their shameful deed to the group. This continues until each guest has 4 or 5 horrific crimes out in the open. The number of skulls listed, however, players keep to themselves. Once all the secrets are out, the guests must decide who has the most skulls, and is therefore the one the Reaper wants. It could be because that person is the most monstrous... or the most pathetic. Either way, who needs them? In the end, the victim must fess up and those who guessed correctly each get a gold coin from the Reaper's platter as a reward for their damning nature. But it's not over yet...

The victim has one last chance to be pardoned by the Reaper. He or she must take the rolled up parchment by his side (don't get too close, you don't want to touch him!) and read the riddle it contains. A sample riddle could read:

> *I carry your name*
> *I know when you died*
> *With only your wealth*
> *Could you in me reside*
> *There's still room for friends*
> *And family inside*
> *Who visit me often*
> *But have no where to hide*
>
> *What am I?*

The answer: A tomb

(Note: when writing the riddle for the game, don't include the answer on the paper!)

The hourglass is turned while the victim ponders the riddle. If he answers incorrectly, he's doomed: the death deal is done and he must now bear the gold medallion from the Reaper's neck. If he answers correctly, however, the Reaper has not only pardoned him but has given him a special treat: to decide who will be the one to take his place. The choice is made and a new victim is cast. If the new victim had previously won a gold coin from the platter, it is forfeited and the gold medallion is taken as its replacement.

Fortune Telling Party.
Fortune-telling is a tradition that epitomized Halloween parties in the 1920's and 30's. Adults from every walk of life would gather together to tell each other's fortunes in a series of games that are just as much fun to play today as they were back then.

To throw your fortune-telling party, set up four small tables in your living room with a different game at each one: tarot cards, fortune-telling dice with an interpretation chart, a dream interpretation book and a guide on palm reading. Create an area that's fit for true mystics with sun and moon bead curtains in the doorways, purple, blue and gold fabrics draped over the game tables and window curtains, dimmed lights and burning incense throughout the room.

For a twist on your fortune-telling party, make an additional game to play through-out the night that involves trickery and prizes. Once everyone has arrived, have each guest pick a piece of paper from a magic bag. One paper reads "Fortune Teller," while the rest read "False Reader." Tell guests not to reveal what is written on their paper.

Throughout the evening, players break into groups to partake in each of the fortune telling games. But as each game is played, guests must consider whether the one telling their fortune is the genuine fortune teller or a false reader. The roles they have been assigned may cause them to go all out and act their part accordingly... or far from it. Once every-one has had a turn telling fortunes and having their own told in each game, votes are cast on who everyone thinks is the actual fortune teller. Whoever guesses correctly wins a small prize, as does the person who played the fortune teller.

Looking for ideas for your party game prizes? Refer back to "Gifts for the Season" in Chapter 7 for gift ideas to make any Halloween buff drool.

Crazy Project Parties.

It's a party in an art class from hell! Throw a party that involves all the creative aspects of putting together your Halloween display, haunted attraction or other Halloween event you're working on. Whether it's an endeavor for your home, busi-ness or commercial Halloween attraction, getting friends and family involved makes a crazy project party that's a lot of fun and will also help move your endeavors along.

Tell your friends to come dressed as true lunatic Picassos with smocks and clothes they've long-since damned for an evening of sloppy mess. Make it a night of prop build-ing, painting, carving, costuming, and any other components of setting up your attraction or display. Let everyone get messy carving pumpkins, painting tombstones, drawing deranged pictures, making scarecrows, dressing skeletons, painting signs and more.

Have all the essentials you need for your crazy project party so that everyone can dive right in when they find a project they like. Use your deck, yard, shed or if you're truly brave (or *mad*) your living room to set up carving tools, paints, brushes, costumes and drawing pads. Give everyone ideas of the looks and styles you're going for in each project that will match the event's theme. Let them discover their own insane, artistic talents in an arts and crafts session they'll never forget.

Get your creative juices flowing early by making special invitations that foreshadow the madness of the party. For example, take a picture of a coffin filled with blank tomb-stones, shovels, skulls, body parts, carving tools and paints to use as invitations for a haunted graveyard project party.

Attraction Parties.

If you don't need any help setting up your displays or attractions but want to save all that fun for yourself, throw a Halloween party once the project is com-pleted, revolving the party theme around your new creation.

Throw a costume party where everyone comes as the types of characters that would be found in your display. For example, throw a haunted graveyard party where guests must come as gravediggers, grave robbers, zombies, skeletons, ghouls, insane morticians and the like. Use your haunted graveyard as a "prop" of the party by burying skulls and body parts in random graves. Put a couple shovels of in the graveyard and tell guests that whoever finds enough body parts to make their own live monster becomes the mad scientist of the year and wins a special prize.

For a scarecrow show party, invite guests to come as scarecrows, demented farmers, zombie farmers or even farm animals! Let your guests name each of the scarecrows in the show, writing the names on small signs to hang around each scarecrow's neck. Use the same method for building party themes around your pirate walk-through, medieval torture attraction, killer klown haunt and other display themes.

Horror Movie Parties. Don't miss the opportunity to have a horror movie party during the height of the Halloween season. Why get scared watching your favorite films all by your lonesome when you can have a bunch of friends over... and scare *them*? Pull all your couches, loveseats and recliners together in a circle of protection surrounded by candles and jack-o'-lanterns. And, oops, did you forget to shut off the motion detector on that skeleton behind the curtain? Well, that's what happens when people insist on going to the bathroom with killer zombies on the loose.

Of course, not all Halloween movie parties have to consist of horror movies. You can also have a showing of dark comedies with movies like *Clue, Ghostbusters* and the like for the truly timid (and wimpy). Just don't shut off that motion detector.

For the true movie buffs, you can even start a tradition of throwing a movie party once a week throughout October. Having your movie nights on a weeknight is also a great way to add some extra adventures during the week without taking time away from those horror theme parks on the weekends. Check out "Collections and Libraries" later in this chapter for some dark and demented genres and titles to get your Halloween movie parties started.

For planning your horror movie parties ahead of time, send out special invitations that include a horror season schedule. For example:

You are invited to attend this year's

HALLOWEEN SEASON MOVIE NIGHTS

Held every Wednesday night at
THE CANNIBAL'S DINER, October 1–29

FILMS AND DATES INCLUDE:
October 7: *Amityville Horror*
October 14: *Poltergeist*
October 21: *The Others*
October 28: *Texas Chainsaw Massacre*

MURDER MYSTERY PARTY

Want even more party ideas for a night of fun and screams? Check out Chapter 19,
"Friday the 13th and Murder Mystery" for writing your very own murder mystery party!

Cards and Invitations

With all that you've got going on for the season — and that's quite a lot, doesn't it rock?— there's a lot of who, what, when and where that you'll want to get out there: family to invite to graveyard openings, friends who need their messages from the Grim Reaper and the whole town to tell about your company's mad scientist's secret library book sale. That's where your Halloween cards and invitations come in.

Invitations serve as the first impressions of your events. They set the mood and foreshadow the madness with a design all their own for a night of horror, fun, suspense, silliness or strength of mentality. Your friends all got a clear picture of what your Reaper's party was all about when they got their personalized death certificates in the mail. Invitations also serve as a fun piece of your event that friends can keep as souvenirs. Remember that weekend of ghost-hunting up the coastline? Well, who could forget with the plush ghost invitation still hanging in the rear-view mirror?

You can create just the right effect for all your haunted happenings. Consider making cards and invitations for all your activities, such as:

- Haunted Attraction or Display Party
- Grim Reaper or Fortune Telling Party
- Halloween Museum Opening
- Halloween Office Party
- Halloween Business Event
- Halloween Story Telling and Poetry Reading
- Horror Movie Nights
- Halloween Weekend Getaway
- Full Moon Night Events (see Chapter 17)

Crafty Invitations. Let's get crafty! Create Halloween invitations of your own design with a variety of Halloween-themed paper and images, small props and even old t-shirts for your Insane Asylum parties and Halloween office parties. Try your hand at some of the following to express your true mentality.

Crafty Cards: *For Your Halloween Museum Opening*

Fill your lab table with an assortment of card-making supplies for these hand-made invites, such as:

- Halloween scrapbooking paper
- Light-colored cardstock
- Halloween add-ons and stickers
- Lettering stickers
- Black and red markers
- Fine black marker
- Double-sided tape

Take a sheet of scrapbooking paper and fold it into quarters so that it becomes a 6×6" card. Use double-sided tape to seal the backsides of the paper together. On the cover of the card, tape a Halloween ad-on image of a werewolf, vampire or other creature. Write a message underneath such as "Happy Halloween," "You're Invited..." or "You're Doomed..." using lettering stickers or black and red markers.

On the inside of the card is where you'll list the horror to come. Cut out a 5×5" piece of cardstock and write the date, time and location of your Halloween Museum opening or other insane event with a fine black marker. Use double-sided tape to attach the cardstock to the left flap of the card, leaving 1" of scrapbooking paper on each side. Cut out a second 5×5" piece of cardstock and paste a Halloween sticker or other Halloween ad-on in the center and write an additional message, such as "RSVP or be eaten." Tape the cardstock to the right flap.

Prop Invites: *For Your Halloween Office Party*

Say it all with a small piece of horror. Get your co-workers excited about the up-coming slasher office party by making invitations out of actual props that go with the theme. For example:

The Body Part Invitation: Get a doll from your local second-hand shop and ever-so-gently pull it to pieces. Use each body part as an invitation to the "Mad Scientist Reveals All" Halloween Party. Attach a piece of paper toe-tag style to each body part, giving the what, where and when of the party.

The Cemetery Plot Deed: Create 8×10" cemetery plot deeds out of light gray cardstock. Using a calligraphy pen, write each guest's name and assigned plot number, all of which were paid for by "a friend." Include the what, where and when of "The Fresh Cemetery" party.

Parchment Invites: *For Your Pirate Walk-Through Display Party*

Arrr...! This be a treasure map, I'd wager...! For the perfect invitation to your pirate walk-through display party, make treasure map invitations out of cloth.

To create the texture of a real map, cut out an 8×10" piece of material from an old light-colored t-shirt. Stretch the material and pin onto a piece of Styrofoam or nail down to a piece of plywood to remove any slack.

Using acrylic paints, apply a base coating of brown or tan as the background color of the map, leaving 1" of visible cloth on all sides. Let dry a few hours. Once the base coat has dried, paint a simple treasure map over it that resembles (if ever-so-slightly) your pirate walk-through display. Mark one end of the trail to the other using symbols and images such as an island, ship, compass, mountains, trees, skulls and an "x" for the location of the treasure.

Once the parchment has completely dried, roll it up with the story of your display and tie with a black ribbon to hand-deliver to your guests.

Cards and Invitations from the Computer.
You can also create an assortment of mad invitations right on the computer using online images (for personal use only) and your own photos. Choose from different styles of cards and flyers to get just the right look for party invitations, weekends of horror and for your Halloween business events.

Postcards: *For Your Jack-o'-Lantern Light Show Halloween Party*

Create cards that make you look like the ultimate graphic designer, using postcard cardstock from your local craft store or office supply store. (This type of paper can be used in any printer that accepts cardstock.)

To make postcards for your light show party, take a picture of some (or all) of your jack-o'-lanterns lighting up the night in your show. Insert the picture into a plain Word document and paste a text box over the image to write your message, such as "You're invited to a showing of *Monsters!*" and print out onto the cardstock paper. For the opposite side of the card, create a separate document that lists all the information of your party, including the theme or storyline used in the display. Flip the cardstock over in the printer and print out. Mail the invitations out as regular postcards.

Note Cards: *For Your Weekend of Horror Getaway*

Another type of card you can create on the computer is a note card. These can be printed on note card cardstock and made in either a design program or Microsoft Word.

The advantage of making note cards as opposed to postcards is that you have a lot more space to work with, so you can use a couple different images and write about the coming horror in more detail. If you're making invitations to a weekend of horror that includes more than one haunting destination, use a picture of each event from their website, such as:

- An image of the haunted house you're going to
- An image of the monster play you'll be seeing
- An image of the haunted bed and breakfast where you'll be staying

Write brief descriptions of each event over the images and print out onto the cardstock. If you're working with a printer that doesn't accept cardstock, fear not. Simply print out the images on a plain sheet of paper to cut and paste them onto a blank note card.

Flyers: *For Your Halloween Business Event*

Another fun invitation that's easy to make on the computer is a flyer, such as one you might see in a shop window. Flyers make great advertisements for your upcoming Halloween business events, such as your vampire costume ball or midnight movie showing, and can be posted at your place of business or mailed out to customers as personalized invitations.

To make the flyers, simply use a Halloween picture you've taken yourself, such as one of your Halloween displays at the office, a customer being put into the stocks, etc., and insert it into a blank document. Write the information about the event around it, using spooky font and adding a Halloween border. Print out the flyers onto either colored paper or Halloween-themed paper. You can also make smaller, half-page flyers to display at your business for customers to take home with them.

Madness Galore.
Whichever type of Halloween cards and invitations you choose to make for events at work, the Insane Asylum or a getaway to the Bleeding Coffin Theme Park, include a few surprises with them to add to the coming gloom, such as:

- Brochures to the Halloween events you'll be going to
- Specially-made "tickets" to your Halloween Museum opening, display or party
- Printed web pages of the events
- Coupons for the attractions
- Party favors for the show, such as newspaper, confetti and toilet paper for *The Rocky Horror Picture Show*
- Subtle trinkets of horror, such as an eyeball, finger, or "the black spot" that go with your party theme

In addition to making invitations to Halloween events, you can also use the designs above for creating general Halloween cards just to say "Happy Halloween My Fellow Ghoul." Send out your event invites at the beginning of the season and Halloween cards just a few days before the 31st to give your friends two haunting surprises in the mail.

REMEMBER THIS!

Whatever type of Halloween card or invitation you create, make an extra one for yourself or make photocopies of each to put in your Halloween museum or scrapbook.

Costumes

Dressing up is one of the best parts of Halloween. In costume, we can transform *ourselves* as we so elaborately did with our home-front and office. The arising insanity brought on throughout the season can be expressed with costumes that alter our appearance to one almost unrecognizable. We suddenly become an escaped mental patient, a lustful vampire, an evil clown or an innocent mermaid. The personage we held just a month or so before becomes a distant dream as we change into the scariest, funniest, and weirdest characters imaginable that could be a direct contrast from our former selves, or possibly more in tune with our truer selves.

You may find yourself taking part in a variety of seasonal activities that involve dress-

ing up in costume, as well as dressing props, characters and actors in your displays and attractions. But that doesn't necessarily require spending an arm and a leg (unless you wanted to get rid of them anyway). Because for all the ways there are to use costumes for the season, there are just as many ways to get them.

The Grand Scheme. First, let's go over everything that you may have going on throughout September and October that includes using costumes. Some wonderfully demented projects and events may be:

- **Halloween Parties and Costume Balls:** For that costume party at home, when this is the year you're finally going to dress as your childhood hero: Freddy Krueger. Also, for that vampire costume ball at the horror hotel, and don't forget about the Halloween convention with its best murder victim contest!
- **Window Displays:** The monsters in the living room window display can't exactly go naked... if they did, it would totally ruin the effect. Consider costumes for your ghosts, mad scientists, alchemists and haunted funeral parlor workers.
- **Haunted Attractions:** Are you transforming into an alien killer klown for your interactive haunted attraction? Consider the types of costumes for you and other live actors to become the deranged circus performers from distant planets. Consider stuffing an over-sized costume to look like one who has eaten a few too many teenagers, or getting fake teeth or fangs to better take on the look of the clowns from the film.
- **Outdoor Displays:** That grave robber in the haunted graveyard needs the perfect costume to look his shabbiest. Also, think about costumes for the zombies, hearse drivers and scarecrows that will be taking to the stage.
- **Halloween Dummies:** For those Halloween dummies peaking out of the basement windows, resting on the staircase and seated at the dinner table. Create costumes for your Grim Reaper figure, witches, warlocks and electric chair victims.
- **Haunted Tours:** For all those characters prowling the night in your trick-or-treaters' haunted tour. Dress characters such as your cemetery watchmen, hangmen and other corpses, demons and devils.
- **Halloween Story Telling and Poetry Reading Performances:** Doing a reading from *The Legend of Sleepy Hollow*? Get the perfect costume for your performance as Ichabod, Katrina, or even the horseman himself. Or if you'll be reading a poem where the character is up to interpretation, let your imagination go wild with the image of who you envision as the speaker.
- **Halloween Business Events:** Are you and the gang at work dressing up for the 1950's science fiction theme you've got running throughout October? Step back in time with costumes that reflect the films, from 3-piece suits (appropriately covered in slime) to silver jumpsuits.

Stores and Your Creations. For some of the costumes on your list, it's fun to treat yourself to the store-bought selections. Particularly for costumes you'll be using at special events such as parties, Halloween business events and that Halloween story telling and poetry reading performance. For these events you'll most likely be dressing up in costumes that you'll want to hang on to for a long time, so go all out. Head to specialty shops and

Halloween warehouses that have a huge range to choose from, as well as all the accessories you could ever need like hair spray coloring, wigs, party hats, fake nails, monster make-up and much more. Also check out the store websites for an even bigger selection.

For costumes that involve a few rips and tears such as those zombies emerging from the haunted graveyard, getting them cheap means getting to destroy them without guilt. Check out second-hand shops, flea markets and tag sales to get a coffin-full of costumes for all your indoor and outdoor displays and Halloween dummies. Pick up some old suits for your zombies, plaid shirts and faded jeans for scarecrows and axe murderers, old shoes, hats, coats and just about anything else to fit your characters. You'll find materials to rip, tear, paint, roll in the dirt, splatter with blood and even burn to suit your displays without wasting quality clothing or giving a hoot if they get damaged by heavy wind and rain.

Sometimes to get just the look you want it's better to take matters into your own strangling hands. By making costumes yourself, you can be as creative as you want with designs, patterns and size. Can't find a cloak to dress that ten-foot warlock in your conjurer's circle display? Get the materials and make it yourself with a fire and bones image for the perfect crest. Become a fashion designer from hell by making capes, cloaks, robes, shawls, dresses and more. If you need a good starting point for ideas, watch a few movies that have the types of characters you're making, or browse the craft stores for sample costume patterns.

Getting It Right. Just like you would try out different costumes before putting on your haunted attraction, use the same concept of experimentation with all your monster creations. Practice with costumes, accessories and make up for your outdoor displays, Halloween party costumes and after-hours business event costumes. Would a psycho killer look more realistic with his shirt covered in dirt or blood? Or what if you dumped a whole bucket of blood over your head for the ultimate effect? It's always best to know the results of these things ahead of time. This way you won't be running around soaked to the bone an hour before curtain call.

Other accessories to add to the charm of your character creations can range from goofy to deadly, using:

Fake noses	Ropes	Mutilated teddy bears
Bow ties	Chains	Spider webs
Monster heads	Balloons	Bandanas
Skulls on a rope	Weapons	Jewelry
Rags	Dead flowers	Tattoos

The Cave of Wonders. With your new and overwhelming pile of costumes, your Insane Asylum may start to look like a bargain truck drove in and exploded. To avoid this dilemma, both during the in- and off-season, keep all the costumes, make-up and accessories together in your own cave of wonders. Convert a small closet into a storing place where any horrific creature imaginable could go to look just fabulous. Hang the costumes on hangers, display your masks and party hats on hooks and fill trunks with all your monster make-up, hair coloring, and wigs.

This cave of wonders just may turn into a place you visit often in future celebrations throughout the year! Stay tuned...

The Halloween Menu

You can sure build up an appetite during a season that never stops. And what better time to experiment in the kitchen of your Cannibal's Diner for whipping up some treats as devilish and mysterious as the banshee behind your living room curtains?

Each of your Halloween undertakings calls for a different delicacy that tastes great, goes with the season and doesn't tie you to the cauldron when you could be stuffing others into it. To indulge in a Halloween menu fit for any monster, go wild with the snacks, drinks and meals below, designed to accommodate all your Halloween activities so you can create the perfect dish, jump into your hearse or plop into your coffin and not miss a beat.

Recipes

The Experiment Gone Wrong: *Appetizers for Halloween parties at the Insane Asylum*

For a tasty and loony appetizer at your mad scientist party or Night of the Werewolf party, create a series of experiments fresh from the lab.

What you'll need:

  3–4 flavors of spaghetti sauce
  1 loaf of Italian bread
  An assortment of shredded cheeses

Fill small bowls with 3 or 4 of your favorite spaghetti sauces and heat in the microwave for 2–2½ minutes. Slice the loaf of Italian bread in half and sprinkle different shredded

cheeses over different areas. Put the bread in the oven for 5–7 minutes at 350 degrees. Let cool and cut into pieces just big enough for dipping.

Set out the Experiments Gone Wrong on your lab table for all to enjoy.

The Addiction: *Snacks for Your Slasher Office Party*

The Addiction is a snack so good your co-workers will be drooling like zombies and begging for more weeks after the slasher office party.

What you'll need:

　　12 pretzel rods
　　½ cup melted semi-sweet chocolate chips
　　½ cup melted butterscotch chips
　　½ cup creamy peanut butter
　　A variety of candies to crush

Cover approximately ⅔ of pretzel rods with melted chocolate, butterscotch or creamy peanut butter. Roll the pretzels into your favorite crushed candies such as Reece Pieces, Heath bar or Butterfinger. (To crush the candies most efficiently, pour them into baggies and then crush with a pot.) Lay the candy pretzels flat on wax paper and put in the fridge for 15–20 minutes.

The Butterscotch Potion: *For warming Up While Building Outdoor Displays*

This deliciously haunting drink makes for the perfect break while setting up your outdoor displays on those chilly October weekends.

What you'll need:

　　3 cups skim milk
　　½ cup butterscotch chips
　　1 tbsp caramel
　　½ cup mini marshmallows

Bring the milk to a boil over medium heat. Add butterscotch chips, caramel and mini marshmallows while stirring constantly. After the chips and marshmallows have completely melted, remove from heat and whisk for 30 seconds. Serve immediately in your favorite Halloween mugs. Serves 2.

The Dessert of the Dead: *For Full Moon Nights*

No full moon frenzy is complete without a killer dessert. For a sundae that will make any werewolf come running, indulge in one of these Desserts of the Dead.

What you'll need:

　　1 package of ready-to-go sugar cookie dough
　　Vanilla ice cream
　　Caramel

Bake a fresh batch of sugar cookies from ready-to-go cookie dough mix, saving a heaping tablespoon of dough per person in the fridge. Once the cookies are out of the oven, let them cool for 5 minutes. Make the sundaes by scooping vanilla ice cream onto 1–2 fresh cookies, then applying the leftover cookie dough and drizzling caramel on top.

To make this Dessert of the Dead in chocolate, use the same technique with brownies, vanilla ice cream and brownie batter.

The Reaper's Delight: *For Your Halloween Business Event*

For a light treat that's perfect for your Halloween business event, mix up some Reaper's Delight to accompany your Halloween art showing or hearse show.

What you'll need:

    4 large Macintosh apples

    2 cups Chex Mix

    2 tbsp cinnamon

    1 cup mixed nuts

    ½ cup raisins

Place 4 cups of peeled and diced Macintosh apples in a 9×9" ungreased casserole dish and sprinkle with 1 tbsp cinnamon. In a separate bowl, mix together Chex Mix, mixed nuts, raisins and 1 tbsp of cinnamon. Pour mixture over the apples and bake at 350 for 30 minutes. Cool for 10 minutes before serving. Makes 6–8 servings.

Grave Hunter's Nosh: *The Grave Hunter's Power Snack*

Whip up some Grave Hunter's Nosh for a true monster's snack to keep you going as you explore the many stones, crypts and statues in graveyards across the state.

Mix together in a large bowl:

    2 cups mini pretzels

    1 cup honey-roasted peanuts

    1 cup dried pineapple

    1 cup dried apricot

    1 cup banana chips

    ½ cup M&M's

    ½ cup Reece Piece's

Pour mixture into individual sandwich baggies. Makes 6 servings.

The Pizza from Hell: *For Your Horror Movie Marathon*

Great horror movies require great food that's as deadly in appearance as it is excellent in taste. For your next horror movie night, create the Pizza from Hell that's specifically tailored for a night of blood and guts.

What you'll need:

    Pre-made pizza dough

    1 jar sausage-flavored spaghetti sauce

    2 Italian sausage links

    ¾ cup shredded mozzarella cheese

    1 red pepper

    1 large tomato

    1 onion

Roll out pizza dough on a pizza baking dish and apply a happy and heavy dosage of shredded mozzarella cheese. Over the cheese spread sausage-flavored spaghetti sauce and top with cooked sausage links, red peppers, tomato and onion. Bake at 400 degrees for 35 minutes, or the time listed on the pizza dough package.

The Alchemist's Theory: *A Lunch for Prop Building*

Building some killer props can take hours, and in between all the painting, carving, hammering and drilling, sometimes you just don't feel like making a big lunch. Instead, put together The Alchemist's Theory with a bit of everything from the alchemy table to keep you going like a madman.

Create a smorgasbord with:

   1 chopped up Macintosh apple
   1 container of vanilla yogurt for dipping
   1 handful of red grapes
   2 slices of Muenster cheese
   1 slice of buttered Italian bread
   1 handful of dried apricots

Spread out your selection for a tasty lunch by the coffin.

The Sandwich to Die For: *A Breakfast Sandwich Before Your Traveling Adventures*

Before you head out on that day trip of foliage drives and exploring haunted lighthouses, power up with a breakfast sandwich to die for.

What you'll need:

   1 whole-grain bagel
   2 tablespoons butter
   1 egg
   2 slices of ham
   1 slice American cheese

Butter a toasted whole-grain bagel and pile on 1 fried egg, 2 slices of ham and 1 slice of American cheese. Compliment with a cup of the Butterscotch Potion or your favorite tea.

Collections and Libraries

When we learn about the world around us, we are changed forever. Exploring such subjects as history and sociology, philosophy and religion can open our minds (and possibly induce nightmares) in ways we never could have imagined. Not too surprisingly, the culture of Halloween holds many secrets to be discovered, as well. As we learned in *Halloween in the Classroom* in Chapter 6, what we know of today as Halloween traditions are actually thousands of years worth of cultural rituals, stories, beliefs, legends and lore.

These ever-evolving celebrations can be explored in many areas. This section focuses on indulging in them through literature, film and music. The Halloween season is the perfect time for curling up with a good book to take you away to a land where 500-year-old vampires dwell in ancient castles, or for throwing in a DVD to watch Alfred Hitchcock introduce his weekly "play." It's also a time to escape into your wildest imagination through the entrancing sounds of instrumental horror music. Through all forms of literature, movies and music, we can step into a world beyond our own reality (as we know it) and experience all that it holds in store — which for some, is what the spirit of Halloween is all about.

If you haven't already, start your own Halloween collection and library for those relaxing nights by the fire, taking out at your most deranged Halloween parties and for every horrific night in between.

Literature. Literature has a way of opening our eyes through novels, short stories, plays and poems, allowing us to see the world from many different points of view. Through fiction, we become the characters and creatures we fear and love, hate and sympathize with. Dr. Jekyll and Mr. Hyde may cause us to ponder human nature and morality. Vampires that have lived throughout the centuries may make us question our true feelings of immortality. Through non-fiction, we are able to explore subjects that may have always captured our interest, such as fortune-telling, hauntings, UFO studies and the history of witch trials. With each journey through the pages of countless titles, pieces of the puzzle come together about different aspects of Halloween, where they came from and what they mean to us today.

To begin or expand your Halloween library with tales and traditions throughout the years, look into a variety of topics, such as:

The Classics: *Frankenstein, Dracula, Dr. Jekyll and Mr. Hyde, The Legend of Sleepy Hollow,* tales of Edgar Allan Poe and more. Reading the classics takes us back to a time before Halloween was what it is today, when eerie stories were told in a style and language that has all but been lost over the years. Reading through the classic tales of forbidden experiments, intrigue and seduction, do you pick up subtle hints of the foundations of modern-day Halloween?

True Hauntings: What better way to celebrate the season than to read about the real haunted houses that the Halloween attractions can only hope to imitate? Reading the stories of reported hauntings that occurred hundreds of years ago to present day may

take us away from the comfort level of our own lives as we enter the nightmares of others.

Local Eerie Happenings: Have you ever wondered if your *own* town was haunted? There may be some spooky secrets lurking in the cemeteries, abandoned homes or even bed and breakfasts just down the road. Books that focus on hauntings in specific towns are often locally published and not found at the bigger chains, so check with your library and local bookstores. You may find that your favorite spot around the corner has a history you never would have believed.

Tales of Fantasy and Magic: With so much magic in the air already, the Halloween season is a great time to indulge in tales of fantasy and magic. Books like *Harry Potter, The Lord of the Rings, The Chronicles of Narnia* and other enchanted tales can take us to places where anything is possible. Also check out publications that go into detail with the magical studies, creatures and even the real-life people who shaped and inspired these stories.

Ghost Hunters: If you're a Halloween enthusiast of a scientific mind, going through the research of real-life ghost hunters may be right up your alley. Try to uncover the mysteries of the supernatural with those who have spent years working in the field, conducted investigations around the world and come across just about every type of specter imaginable.

Experiences with Unexplained Phenomenon: Are we alone on this planet? Have some people really been visited by aliens and lived to tell the tale? There are many beliefs and theories on the subject, but reading about UFO sightings and other unexplained phenomenon from across the globe may leave you looking out into the night to wonder, *What is* out *there??*

Vampire Tales: Tales of vampires vary greatly from century-old legends to modern-day novels. A young and handsome monster in one tale could be nothing more than a ragged, insane bloodsucker in another. Reading the different interpretations of these figures may not only keep you up at night but can serve as great inspiration for creating your own costumes, displays and vampire Halloween tours.

The History of Halloween: It's been said that until we know who we were yesterday, we cannot know who we are today. This goes for humans and monsters alike. Learning the history of Halloween from the spirit parades of the ancient Celts to the stylish costumes and parties of the 1930's may have you looking at the holiday of horror in a whole new light.

Witch Trials of Salem and Europe: Humanity has long hunted out what they fear and do not understand. Prime examples can be found in the witch burnings throughout Europe that spanned centuries and the witch hangings in Salem, Massachusetts of the late 1600's. These legendary atrocities are informative and fascinating, and can also serve as inspiration for your Halloween artwork, displays and story telling performances.

The Evolution of Gravestones and Graveyards: If making tombstones and graveyard displays is what keeps you crawling out of your coffin each morning, reading up on the history of both is a great way to expand your knowledge on the subject. Learn the meanings of gravestone symbols, graveyard rituals and how the beliefs and cultures throughout the centuries are reflected in these outdoor museums. You can also find books that list epitaphs carved on stones throughout the country that are insightful, humorous and even spiteful!

Dream Studies and Interpretations: The world of dreams is difficult to understand, where anything can happen and we seldom know why. Sound like the culture of your favorite holiday? Many titles out there serve as handy guides for theories in dream symbolism and interpretation, answering those lingering questions while still leaving you swirling in the mystery of it all. These books also come in handy for all your fortune telling parties.

Collections of Horror Fiction: Novellas and collections of short stories often come out around Halloween for reading around the campfire or in bed at night, daring you to try to fall sleep afterwards. These make fun additions to your library each year and also work well for Halloween story telling and poetry readings.

A MONSTER BOOK CLUB

Want to get your friends involved with all your monster readings? Start a monster book club throughout the season or even throughout the year!

The Movies. We tend to lose ourselves in films when we want a story that's larger than life. The images, music, characters and plots transport us into a world of thrills and suspense that we need just to keep us going in an otherwise horror-free existence.

For the ultimate Halloween film collection, include a variety of titles to go with Halloween activities of every kind, such as horror movie nights, Halloween parties, to have running in the background while you work on props and crafts and for keeping the season alive all year. Build a collection of horror, thrillers, classics, sci-fi, dark comedies, foreign films and history, including:

The Classics of Horror: *Dracula, Frankenstein, The Wolfman, The Mummy's Tomb* and countless other films have shaped the horror genre that we know and love today. If it's been a while since you watched some of the old black and whites or if it will be your first time with them, make it a Friday night of monster culture and see how the masters of horror brought their creations to life before the use of high-tech special effects.

Creature Features: The creatures of science fiction have also inspired many horror theme parks and haunted attractions we know and love. Sit back and scream with *The Creature from the Black Lagoon, Them!, The Thing from Another Planet* and *The Blob.* These films are also great to have running in the background of your Halloween party and for listening to while you stitch up those deadly costumes.

Films of Vincent Price: *House on Haunted Hill, The Fly, House of Wax, The Last Man on Earth* and more are films that inspired future remakes, but can they hold up to the originals? Throw a marathon of the movies centering on one of the most famous horror movie legends of all time, choosing from over 150 titles!

Slasher Films: *A Nightmare on Elm Street, Friday the 13th, Halloween, Texas Chainsaw Massacre* and other slasher films may have been some of your first encounters with Halloween in your post trick-or-treating era. These more modern classics are perfect for reminiscent horror movie nights, for playing in the background while making Halloween pictures and even for making your own haunted attraction soundtrack.

Classic TV Episodes: *Alfred Hitchcock Presents, The Twilight Zone, The Munsters* and *The Addams Family* are fun shows to have running at Halloween parties. These older episodes set the Halloween stage for future generations just as much as classic films did. Step back in time before the days of IMAX theaters when spookster enthusiasts turned to their television sets for their weekly dose of doom.

Recent TV Episodes: How do modern day stories of aliens, ghosts and monsters in shows like *The X-Files*, *Supernatural* and *Medium* compare to the older shows of the 1950's and 60's? Do demons in *The X-Files* seem more real than they did in *The Twilight Zone* because the story is set in our own time period? Combine more recent TV episodes with your classics on the same movie night to see how the storylines, scenes, costumes and acting has changed throughout the decades, and see which style you prefer.

Dark Comedy Films: *Ghostbusters, Beetlejuice, Clue, Haunted Honeymoon* and countless others are great Halloween movies for those who would rather laugh than scream, taking the strange and spooky and putting it on the lighter side of the grave. Some Halloween-enthusiasts relate to Halloween more on a humorous level than they do with horror and gore, so have these films running during your mad scientist project parties as well as while you make your Halloween cards and invitations.

True Accounts of the Unexplained: Documentaries on UFO's, legendary monster sightings and other unexplained phenomenon are perfect shows for the season. These tales from real people, not actors, may be the true essence of Halloween come to life. Check out The History Channel, the Discovery Channel and The Travel Channel for these types of documentaries to play on horror game nights.

Films of Demons and Demonic Possession: *The Exorcist, The Omen, The Exorcism of Emily Rose* and others are films we may watch behind covered eyes. Devils and demons creeping around — or *in* — the most innocent of people provides a different sort of scare than killer klowns ever could. They may make us question what's real versus what's based on interpretation while also serving as inspiration for your own props, tours and costumes.

Stories from the Master of Horror, Stephen King: Stephen King has contributed to horror what the pumpkin has contributed to Halloween. Set some of your horror movie nights in the small towns of Maine with *It, Pet Sematary, The Shining, Cujo* and other unforgettable films. You may also get ideas for new Halloween business event themes with each twisted tale.

Dark Musicals: Some musicals are just as bloody and gruesome as horror films, and that's exactly why we love them. Include titles like *Sweeney Todd, Little Shop of Horrors* and *Phantom of the Opera* to your collection. And damn it, Janet, don't forget about the show that taught us all to do the Time Warp: *The Rocky Horror Picture Show* is a must-have for any Halloween movie collection for throwing all those Rocky parties.

Halloween Cartoons: We could have just celebrated our 40th birthday and The Great Pumpkin will get us just as excited as when we were 5. Include Halloween cartoons to watch while carving pumpkins like *It's the Great Pumpkin, Charlie Brown, Garfield's Halloween Adventure, Scooby Doo's Spookiest Tales, The Legend of Sleepy Hollow* and *The Halloween Tree*.

Films That Shaped the Insane Asylum: If you've watched a horror film, creature feature or other movie that inspired you to build your home display or attraction, add the movie to your collection as one you have now brought to life. You may have consulted *Pirates of the Caribbean* for your pirate display, watched *Sleepy Hollow* and knew you had to have a Headless Horseman theme or ate cotton candy during *Killer Klowns from Outer Space* while taking notes for your clown attraction. Including these films in your collection will also come in handy for showing them at your attraction parties.

Music. In addition to literature and film, Halloween-themed music is another great way to relax and lose yourself in your own world of insanity. Music has the power to move the soul and depending on the style, a Halloween music collection can move your soul away from the land of the living and straight into the depths of the underworld.

With the start of each Halloween season, you can expect to find all kinds of new music for your Halloween parties, haunts, events and background music throughout your Insane Asylum. Look for the following types of tunes to suit every spooky occasion:

Horror Instrumental Music: Horror instrumental is music that creates a world all its own and can be used at your Halloween parties, walk-through displays, haunted attractions and just to put you in the right frame of mind while you paint Halloween pictures and carve tombstones. Look for albums by groups such as Midnight Syndicate, Virgil and Nox Arcana.

Halloween Party Music: Halloween party music is lively and upbeat so you can keep on boogying while hiding those skeletons in the closets. Since it isn't scary-sounding in the way that horror instrumental can be, Halloween party music can be a better choice of tunes for your Halloween business events, festivals and work parties.

Creepy Sound Effects: Creepy sound effects compliment any Halloween display, setting the mood of your haunted graveyard and emanating from the windows for your alien display. Mix and match a variety of albums to get just the right sounds that go along with your theme.

Movie Soundtracks: Movie soundtracks from films in horror, thriller and sci-fi genres are a must-have for any Halloween music collection. With every movie marathon you attend or throw, notice if the music in the films have sounds you're looking for to incorporate into your next haunt. Soundtracks to movies such as *Sleepy Hollow*, *Halloween* and *Friday the 13th* make excellent music for the season, as well as soundtracks to monster musicals like *The Phantom of the Opera*, *The Rocky Horror Picture Show* and *The Nightmare before Christmas*.

Your Own Spooky Sound Effects CD: You don't have to be a renowned harpsichord player to put together some spooky sounds for your haunted displays. Get the speech and effects you need from your own monstrous vocal chords and by using everyday objects. Record the screams and torments of your stationary characters in the Cannibal's Diner display, use sounding alarms for your alien haunt spaceship countdown and record the maddening movements of torture devices in your torture chamber attraction.

The Halloween Newsletter

Are you just dying to share all your Halloween goings-on with everyone you've ever come into contact with? Well, who could blame you with all the monstrous creations you've put together, parties you're throwing and outings and adventures you're going on? It's all so exciting... so momentous... who's going to believe all of this? And as much time as you may have to make 20 phone calls at 25 minutes per call in between those axe-murderer costume fittings, there's also another option. Get your quill pens, snap shots and sealing wax ready for creating a Halloween newsletter: the ultimate resource for sharing all the haunting happenings going on in your neck of the underworld.

A Halloween newsletter can either be made on the computer with a simple software program like Microsoft Word or you can get crafty and make it by hand. Write articles on your macabre adventures, announcements of events you've discovered that just can't be missed and horrific invitations for all your friends and family.

Give your newsletter a seasonal title, such as *Haunted Happenings* or *The Reaper's Edition*. Write articles on the topics below, as well as other Halloween info that you've got to share or you'll just explode. Include pictures, Halloween stickers or even sketches with the different articles and listings.

Halloween Events, Sights and More.
Write brief descriptions of all the Halloween events going on in the area that no one should miss under the October moon. Include your favorite haunted houses, hayrides, horror theme parks, monster productions and other events

of the season. Write a short article about each one or put them all under one heading of "Nights of Fright." If you're planning trips to some of the events, include the dates you're going, the location of each and ticket prices. Who could resist?

Get the word out: your Insane Asylum is the place to be! In place of sending out individual invitations, write an article about each event you've got going on at home, such as your killer klown interactive attraction party, Halloween story telling and poetry reading and Halloween museum opening. Tell guests to RSVP fast because seats are filling up! You can also include the storylines to your outdoor displays or a sneak-peak of one of your Halloween pictures or museum exhibit.

Have you discovered some out-of-the-way Halloween sights that monsters of all walks of life would love? Write an article about these secret spots, such as houses in town with awesome Halloween displays (besides your own) or a stretch of road with beautiful fall foliage. Include hidden Halloween treats you've come across and how to find them and local businesses with special Halloween displays and seasonal events.

Share your plans of dressing up as a vampire hunter and staking out cemeteries the night of the 31st, or anything else you've got going on for the big night. Write about your future trick-or-treat station (discussed in Chapter 9), special goodies you'll be making, Halloween-themed games you'll be playing or scary movies you'll be watching—*before* you start out on that vampire hunt. If you and the family will be dressing up, talk about your costume choices and any crazy stories behind them.

You've made your own tombstone and coffin, who wouldn't be proud? Write about the props, characters, costumes and sets you've put together around the Insane Asylum, at the office or volunteering with a haunt. Include pictures of your creations to show that you're on your way to becoming that mad scientist you always told people you were.

A good snack should always be shared... at least in writing. List a recipe or two that you've created or discovered in your Cannibal's Diner. Did you unlock a key ingredient for making the ultimate pumpkin pie, cookies or cake? Pass it on for friends and family to try out and experiment with... but, damn it, you get rights!

THE OPEN GRAVE
A Halloween Newsletter
A Printing of THE CANNIBAL'S DINER

• Come on a Weekend of Horror! •

Mark your calendars for the upcoming *Weekend of Horror*! This year's getaway will run from Saturday, October 10 to Sunday, October 11.

Events are as follows:

Saturday:
- *Frankenstein* production at the Bradley Playhouse in Torrington, Connecticut, on Saturday at 2 P.M. Tickets: $17.50
- Fright Fest at Six Flags New England in Agawam, Massachusetts, at 7 P.M. Ticket with coupon: $25
- Overnight stay at Lizzie Borden Bed and Breakfast. Rooms from $175 to $250

Sunday:
- Brunch at Witch's Brew Cafe in Salem, Massachusetts, followed by a fun-filled day of haunts, museums and more! Prices vary.

Please RSVP for the *Weekend of Horror* to Chris by September 25. We are also in need of one additional vehicle and driver (hearse preferred).

• Halloween Poetry Night •

Attention poets and poetry buffs: Phoenix Library will be holding its annual Halloween Poetry Reading on Friday, October 2, at 7 P.M. Come for a night of poetry of the dark, creepy and unusual genres.

Tickets are $10 per person and are available in advance at the library's front desk. To enter as a speaker, contact Ruthie at 555-2324.

Phoenix Library is located at 5 Main Street in Essex.

• Scarecrow Party! •

Calling all scarecrows! You're invited to a Halloween party for scarecrows, farmers and other strange (or evil) creatures of the farmer's field. Come celebrate the best night of the year with a dance party where the hay will fly! The scarecrow Halloween party is in honor of our friends in the field who will be the first to welcome you when you arrive!

Held Saturday, October 17, at 7 P.M., and lasts until the cows (or crows) come home. RSVP to Chris at 555-1013. Please bring one snack or pumpkin.

• Movie Nights! •

This year's Halloween Movie Nights have been scheduled at the Cannibal's Diner! Come Thursday nights throughout October for some good scares and great food! The schedule is:

October 1: *The Wolf Man* with beef stew and buttermilk biscuits

October 8: Bram Stoker's *Dracula* with small steaks, baked potatoes, and asparagus

October 15: *The Frighteners* with home-made pizza

October 22: *Poltergeist* with Alfredo pasta and garlic bread

Please RSVP the Monday before each showing.

9
SETTING UP FOR THE BIG NIGHT

You made it! It's here! The day you've been waiting for: October 31! And you could spot it a mile away: there's that crisp smell in the air that some may attribute to the scent of fallen leaves but also carries with it the aroma of lit jack-o'-lanterns and monster make-up, candy corn and glow-in-the-dark spray paint. It emerges with the setting sun on this most anticipated of nights, and although the excitement may make you faint or explode, as long as you survive, you're going to have fun!

Halloween night is one to be celebrated in any number of ways, from a highlighted haunted attraction on your Halloween calendar to the ultimate Halloween party at the Insane Asylum. It's the night to go all out with a grand finale, concluding a season of insanity you'll never forget.

But perhaps what makes Halloween night the most exciting of all is that celebrations are going on not just with the Halloween enthusiasts, but with so many others, as well. The spirit of the season comes alive to all who seek it, including those hanging a plastic skeleton in the window for the first time and filling up candy bowls by the front door, and of course to the caravans of miniature vampires, super heroes, scarecrows, and butterflies that journey around the neighborhood in their exciting quest for treats.

This chapter is dedicated to these faithful trick-or-treaters who we all salute; the short, special Halloween buffs who we all were at one time in our lives. For many of us, Halloween has been an entire season of partying and playing, discovering and creating. But for these up-and-coming enthusiasts, Halloween night may be their only

night to delve into that realm of fantasy, entering exciting worlds of haunted graveyards, jack-o'-lantern light shows and deadly pirate displays. Here, we'll go into different ways of creating Halloween adventures, stories and treats to bring lasting memories to these future Halloween enthusiasts of the world.

The Ultimate Trick-or-Treat Station

Do you remember that special house you discovered trick-or-treating as a kid that you'll never forget? The house that really brought Halloween to life and kept you racing back each year to once again step into its fun and frightening realm. What was it that made the place stand out as the ultimate trick-or-treat station? Was it a certain kind of display set up throughout the yard? The hideous monster that opened the front door and handed you a treat bag through its long, twisted fingers? Whatever it was that made it stick out in your mind, it created a lasting impression of Halloween like never before.

What kids want today is no different. They seek out adventure and excitement in their trick-or-treating travels just as much as getting a good haul of candy. And you can make their adventure into the gates of your Insane Asylum an experience they won't soon forget... and without even using chainsaws.

Despite whether or not you've set up elaborate displays or haunted attractions in the yard, you can put together some original creations, treats and souvenirs just for Halloween night to build the ultimate trick-or-treat station of your own. So start the morning with a hearty Breakfast Sandwich to Die For and indulge yourself into a day of making madness for the masses.

The Haunted Pathway.
Create the ultimate first impression with a haunted pathway to the house. Line the path with jack-o'-lanterns and strings of orange and green lights wrapped around staked skulls and standing lanterns. On either side of the walkway, construct a graveyard from ancient times. Make old grave markers by nailing together sticks in the form of crosses, then stick each marker roughly four or five inches into the ground.

Make it a graveyard of nightmares with skulls and skeleton hands emerging from the ground and reaching out for the trick-or-treaters.

If you have already put together an outdoor display that's set at a distance from the walkway, place candles or spot lights within it so that it can be seen after sundown.

The Hidden. In addition to the pathway and ancient burial ground, set up creatures and images that remain hidden. Place small, hiding Halloween dummies throughout the yard and walkway so that they are not entirely visible and may even be missed completely by those not keeping a sharp eye. Set up a grave robber crouching behind a large tree away from the candlelight and a zombie creeping around the porch steps. Other subtle images may include a message written in blood on a stone step and glowing eyes (using reflector glass) up in the trees. Setting up hidden creatures and images throughout the walkway will ensure that not everyone sees the same show as they travel through and can pick out things they may have missed on their journey back.

The Watching. If you have window displays set up, make sure they're visible after dark by using candles or a string of lights around them. You can also put the lights on a timer so that they go on and off every few minutes. This way the display will suddenly appear out of no where to those approaching it at just the right time. If you haven't set up any window displays, write secret messages on the glass with window paints, such as "Get out while you can!" or "Don't trust the clown!" to also appear every few minutes.

Picking Your Poison. For setting up the ensemble of monstrous delicacies, create a lab table or witch's kitchen display on the front porch. Fill a few cauldrons, wicker baskets and wooden bowls with different types of treats surrounded by candles, potion vials, spiders and a body part or two. Allow each trick-or-treater to take a couple goodies so they can pick their own poison. In addition to candy, have at least one bowl filled with Halloween toys, such as monster finger puppets, vampire teeth or eye balls floating in a bucket of water.

The Monster That Lived There. Don't forget to include the *real* monster that lives there: get yourself involved in the action by dressing up as a character you envision living in your Insane Asylum, Cannibal's Diner, or other theme you've created. Be a humble mental patient who politely asks the visitors to untie the straps of his straight jacket, a gypsy who tells fortunes by gazing into her crystal ball or the Grim Reaper who makes foreboding, silent gestures with his scythe.

Signed in Blood. Who wouldn't want to leave their mark in the Devil's book? He needs *something* to read, doesn't he? In addition to your lab table of goodies, construct a small podium out of an upturned crate or two to hold a leather-bound guestbook for the trick-or-treaters to sign. Supply a quill and red or black ink for them to leave their permanent mark in the Asylum's maddening history.

For Their Travels. Before the kids begin their journey back past the hidden zombies and ancient burial ground, make sure they leave with a token of good luck for their travels. Hand out small magical items to use as protection against warlocks and demons, such as black candles tied together with a silver ribbon. Other tokens of good luck may include some gems from your treasure chest to pay off any murderous pirates that come their way or two coins from the Reaper's platter to pay Charon, the ferryman, should they happen across his river to the Underworld.

Making the ultimate trick-or-treat station will not only create a monstrous world for the trick-or-treaters, but for the whole neighborhood. The fun of it all just may spark the creativity and Halloween spirit in your neighbors to build displays and characters of their own next year!

The Trick-or-Treaters' Haunted Tour

Want to be a tour guide from hell? There's no better kind! Another fun and creative Halloween adventure to put together for trick-or-treaters is a haunted tour. A haunted tour differs from a walk-through or haunted attraction in that its story is told by an actual guide, as well as through various outdoor displays.

A tour can involve a written script or you can ad-lib the story as you go along. Since the tour relies mostly on storytelling, you can also limit the amount of props to as few (or as many) as you like around the yard and windows as well as using the barn, shed or garage. So grab a lantern and light the way on a tale that's just got to be seen to be believed.

Tour Storylines. For coming up with a storyline for your tour, think about a tale that would best be told through a narrative, as well as through a series of displays. The story can be completely fictional, written by you or one you've read, or it can be based upon an urban legend, myth, or actual occurrence that you want to bring to life.

Begin brainstorming ideas with a character or set of characters to set the story around. If you've already got an outdoor display or window display set up, you may want to base

the tour around the characters you've made. Don't focus on the specifics of how the tale can be made into a tour until you have an outline that you like.

For example:

1. An Accused Witch. An elderly woman was accused of witchcraft in the early 1700's and was secretly killed by her neighbors deep within the woods. Not long afterwards, it was discovered that the woman actually *was* a witch. Enraged at the townspeople's evil doing, she sought revenge and cast spells upon them all after her death. The tour centers on the woman's murder and the effects of the curse.

2. Remains of a Mad Scientist. A crazy alchemist spent years concocting deadly experiments in his lab. One day, one of his most dangerous experiments was stolen and the scientist fled in panic. The stolen chemicals produced a vast outbreak of insanity, which quickly spread throughout the entire town. The tour focuses on the different ways people were affected by the experiment.

Tour Displays. When thinking about where to set up the displays of the tour, consider which areas of your yard best match the background of the story. Does one part of the tale involve a large stretch of field for the crumbling remains of an old village? If so, create a display in a section of the yard to be viewed at a distance. Placing props far from the tour path will also allow you to get away with using less of them, since they are meant to be only partially visible and to compliment the story, not create it.

You can also make the path of your tour around the parameter of your house, using solely window displays viewed from outside. Putting displays in the first story windows can be beneficial in that you can include small and detailed props that are better seen in good lighting, such as an open notebook with scribbled notes, small framed pictures and so on. You can also create window displays in the second story windows, making scenes with Halloween dummies and other large props that can be seen from a distance. Window displays also work well in stories that take place inside, such as in a mad scientist's laboratory or haunted mansion. To get the best effect, make sure that the rooms with window displays are the only lit rooms in the house.

As the tour guide, light the way of your tour with a lantern or flashlight. Whether you set up your displays in the windows or throughout the yard, make sure they are in areas where there won't be a lot of light from streetlights or neighbors' houses. This way the displays will be almost completely hidden until they are approached, or, if at a distance, until you shine your light on them.

Tour Outlines. With a basic story idea and different areas of the yard and house to work with, write out the story using a series of displays to accommodate it.

For example:

Witch Accusations
A haunted tour traveling through the side and backyard.
Tour guide leads the group with a lantern.

First stop: (Front porch display: an old-fashioned kitchen table covered with basic cooking supplies — cauldron, vials of ingredients, books and candles.) "In 1705, Elisabath Wintergood, a quiet, elderly woman, lived alone in the small town of Black Rock. She was accused of witchcraft during an unusually dry summer when the crops failed all over town due to lack of rain... all the crops, that is, except Elisabeth's. The townsfolk had long been suspicious of the woman because they knew little about her, as she had always kept to herself. One July night, they kidnapped Elisabeth and hanged her from a tree deep in the woods. They then burned her house to the ground, hoping to rid the town of any evil it contained."

Second stop: (In the distance of the yard: an open field with the image of a face in ashes.) "After Elisabeth's death, the drought ended, rain returned and crops flourished. However, over a period of just a few months, each of the men who had taken part in the woman's murder had his field burned to the ground by an unseen fire, with an outline of Elisabeth's face eerily formed in the remains. A few days after the field fires, the men's houses burned down, as well, each of which consuming the families in the fire. Those residents of the village who had no part in the Elisabeth's murder (and coincidentally had also had been threatened with witchcraft accusations) suffered no harm."

Third stop: (Up in trees a short distance from the trail: hanged dummies with lit lanterns beneath them for additional lighting.) "After the men had lost their families, homes and crops, they too were soon to perish. One by one they went missing, and were all found weeks later hanged deep in the woods. The same image from the fields had been etched into the bark of the trees they were hanged in."

Final stop: (Side of the house: A small, ancient graveyard set up at the end of the path, lush with flowers and bushes.) "Many people left Black Rock for good, believing it to be cursed, but others remained. Those who stayed eventually prospered, buying the newly available land which produced large and flourishing crops. They converted Elisabeth's land into a small graveyard, laying her to rest as well as the men responsible for her death and what could be found of their families. The townspeople named the burial ground Wintergood Gardens, and planted various flowers throughout it. But some say that the grounds are haunted to this day, and that seeing the ghostly appearance of Elisabeth is nothing short of a warning of the pending doom and destruction that will soon befall them."

(The tour ends with a woman dressed as a ghost emerging from behind the graveyard, carrying a wicker basket of treat bags for the kids to choose from.)

Tour Treats. To give the kids their ultimate treat — *candy* — distribute special goodies at the end of the tour that keep with the theme. For example, to conclude a Frankenstein haunted tour, an emerging monster may stagger out from behind a tree with a platter of sewn, mismatched gift bags. Or to go with a pirate story, fill a wooden chest with black sacks or chocolate coins.

In addition to a treat, you can also give out a few "supplies" that go along with the tour's story. For example, conclude a werewolf tour by giving out a handful of wolfsbane (herbs) and magical stones (painted stones) to serve as counter-curses against turning into a werewolf in the event they encounter one on their future travels.

The Ghost Story Shack

It was a dark and stormy evening just like tonight... when you picked up your chainsaw and tore your neighbor to smithereens! ... No? Well, how about just telling a story that you did.

Telling ghost stories is a Halloween tradition that predates trick-or-treating, back when relatives would make up tales to keep their children, nieces and nephews awake all night before they branched out to terrify the neighbor's kids. You can work with this kind of campfire storytelling tradition by set-ting up a ghost story shack for your trick-or-treaters.

A ghost story shack is your own parlor of intrigue for telling a variety of spookster tales to a small group. Unlike a haunted tour, telling ghost stories in your shack involves one central indoor location which provides advantages such as being able to use all indoor props and not having to cancel the show due to bad weather.

A ghost story shack can be set up in areas such as your barn, shed, garage or anywhere else on your property that's safe for visitors.

Introducing the Horror.
One way to use your ghost story shack is to tell the background story of your outdoor displays, window displays or haunted attraction. Before sending the trick-or-treaters on their way through the Island of Hell's Bounty, tell them the story of crazy Captain Robert the Lion and the cruel acts of torture he unleashed onto all those who dared attempt to steal his treasure... or maybe his Halloween candy! With the story told beforehand, the kids get an extra show all in itself before going out into the haunted world where it actually takes place.

If you would prefer not to work with the theme from one of your displays but want to set up a completely different type of horror, use your ghost story shack to tell a tale from any number of ghost story books. Choose one that's fitting for Halloween and only takes a few minutes to tell, since trick-or-treaters may have low attention spans in the midst of a high sugar rush. You may also choose to tell a story that you've written yourself or use the spooky reading you performed during your Halloween story telling and poetry reading event. Just make sure the story isn't *too* scary or you may have some younger audience members start crying!

Setting Up the Shack.
Set the stage for whatever story you choose with the right décor and props throughout the shack. As the storyteller, you can also dress the part as the unusual character who is telling the tale. For example, if the storyteller is an aged pirate who was around during the black days of the Island of Hell's Bounty, dress up as an old, one-legged sailor, pale and ragged, wearing an eye patch and exposing yellow teeth. Set up the shack like an old sailor's shack with ropes and anchors on the walls, old trunks and barrels on the floor and a wooden leg on a dusty shelf.

Or if you tell the tale of a 1930's haunted mansion, dress as the long-dead resident of the house and build a scene using the old furniture you picked up at those second hand shops. Drape long layers of sheer throughout the banisters, doorways and windows for a ghostly effect. Light the shack with a series of electric lanterns or electric candelabra (since real flames could be a fire hazard).

Latecomers, Beware! Put on the story-telling performances in your shack in whatever fashion you like, such as one show at a specific time (later in the evening so that the kids can come back after they've finished trick-or-treating), or a couple different times throughout the night. Post the performance times on the shack's front door in addition to spreading the word to the trick-or-treaters as they come by throughout the evening.

Just like you would for a haunted tour, give out candy at the end of the story so that it goes along with the theme. Tell the kids to search the shack for the hidden key that unlocks the large treasure chest of treats for your pirate tale, or to look behind every ghost to find where the spirits of the story are trying to hide the candy for themselves.

The Haunting of the Jarrabecks
A Story for the Ghost Story Shack

(Shack is set up with long, sheer fabric draped throughout the room from the rafters to the floor with mats placed in between for the kids and parents to sit on. The narrator, an old caretaker, tells the story by lantern light.)

Some ages ago, in a house not quite unlike this one, a couple by the name of Jarrabeck shared occupancy with a most unusual visitor. Not a visitor they could ever see, but who made his presence known well enough. It was not at all uncommon for the doors of the house to forcefully open and slam shut as the Jarrabecks would step out for the day, or for random objects to disappear one night and reappear the next morning. Other times unknown bells would begin to sound in all corners of the house when the couple would return home for the night, while a high-pitched, hysterical laughter would mockingly echo. And on some occasions, the couple could even make out a tall, thin silhouette in an upstairs window, which would suddenly disappear into no where.

The Jarrabecks referred to their unruly houseguest as Huntley, as the name had mysteriously appeared on their bathroom mirror by an unseen hand. As it seemed Huntley only cared to play these small innocent pranks, and only when the couple would leave and return home again, the Jarrabecks dealt with the spirit and lived in relative peace.

But when the Jarrabecks started to invite guests into the house, these unruly episodes turned dangerous. Rugs would suddenly be pulled out from under the guests' feet or their drinking glasses would suddenly shoot out from their hands and smash against the walls. Other times a faint, ghostly image would appear to them when their hosts would leave the room.

And every time this happened, the guests would run screaming out into the street, not speaking to the Jarrabecks again. Eventually, the couple had enough of these episodes, and after their fifth pair of guests had run away from the house — leaving their coats and hats behind them — the Jarrabecks took hold of their courage and demanded to Huntley that he never again cause any trouble when visitors were present.

The Jarrabecks didn't know what the spirit would do in retaliation, and for days, they waited tensely. However, Huntley seemed to stop his childish pranks all together from that day, even when the couple would leave and return home. And for six months the house stayed quiet.

So then, one night, thinking that all their worries were over, the Jarrabecks invited some friends over for a dinner party. Dinner went undisturbed, and everyone retired to the parlor. After an hour or so, in the middle of much conversing, one of the guests turned to Mrs. Jarrabeck and asked, "So... is it true that your house is haunted?"

Mrs. Jarrabeck sat quiet for a moment, looking anxious. She didn't want to say the wrong thing in fear that she might tempt or even anger Huntley into acting up once again.

After a few moments hesitation and seeing the intrigue in all her guests' eyes, she said, "There are no ghosts here, and as far as I know, there never have been."

"And besides," Mr. Jarrabeck added slowly, "We plan on moving soon. We have buyers from a few towns away coming in the morning, so this may be one of our last nights here." As he said this, he looked discretely about the room. The guests all sensed a certain tension and sat frozen, wondering if the Jarrabecks were truly looking for an unseen force... But still, all remained quiet.

And then suddenly, something strange *did* begin happen. A large, white haze appeared from everywhere around the room: from the windows, the doorways, the banisters, the fireplace. The white fog rose up and engulfed everyone in a thick mass of cloud. In just a few moments, no one could see an inch before their faces. The windows slammed open and shut until all the glass had shattered. The coffee table could be heard being thrust into the fire, the flames soaring hot before them.

The guests gasped and screamed, reaching out for each other. "What's happening?" they shouted. "Is it truly the ghost?"

The Jarrabecks didn't know what to say, perplexed and embarrassed. "Please, stay calm!" they pleaded. "Huntley, stop this at once!"

The guests wanted to run for their lives, but to where? They couldn't see the way out, and they didn't want to be separated from the others, possibly to run straight into a ghost!

Quick flashes of horrid images flew past everyone: transparent faces with maddening grins. The faces came from behind them, below them, above them; all laughing in a high-pitched scream which billowed throughout the room. A hysterical voice mocked, "Is it true, the house is haunted?"

The guests screamed out to the Jarrabecks, "What do we do? Why won't it stop?" But nothing was heard in reply.

And just as suddenly as the mist appeared, it disappeared without a trace. The noises stopped, the fire went down, and all was once again quiet. The guests looked around in fear, unable to believe what had just happened. But in the place where the Jarrabecks had been, was nothing.

Of course, no one was going to take even a moment to ponder the disappearance of their hosts, but rather flew from the house all together, without looking back. None of them would ever mention the dinner party again.

But no one ever discovered what happened to Mr. and Mrs. Jarrabeck, nor did any of the townspeople dare to come near the place to look for them. The house stood empty for years, never being sold or shown but slowly slipping into decay, its tale becoming nothing but a myth.

And though none ever dared enter the gates, there are some who claim to have seen two silhouettes standing motionless in an upstairs window, looking out. The lights would often flicker and windows slam open and shut on the floor above, a high-pitched, maniacal laughter emanating from the grounds.

(Tour ends with a high-pitched laughter coming from the rafters of the ghost story shack, with two silhouettes visible in a window above.)

The Treasure Hunt

Another fun activity to put together for trick-or-treaters is a treasure hunt. Some treasure hunts include maps and clues for kids to follow through a series of trails until finally discovering the hidden treasure. However, a hunt for Halloween night can be made into an activity that goes along much quicker. Rather than using a map and scouting out a vast area, this hunt can involve simple clues to follow in a short amount of time that lead to one or two locations of hidden treasure.

The hunt can also involve either elaborate displays or simple props set up in a few different locations throughout the yard. Since the goal will be for kids to look for the hidden treasure or candy, the main objective in setting up the grounds is to make sure the display items can hide the secret stash effectively and not give away its location at first glance.

If you can, set up the treasure hunt in an area of the yard that the kids won't see when they first arrive. If kids usually go to your front door for candy on Halloween night, set up the treasure hunt in the backyard, or vice versa. However, you'll still want the kids to come to your door first to give out the items they'll need to start the hunt. This will also keep the treasure hunt a secret and surprise.

The Story. As with all good displays and attractions, come up with a story to base your treasure hunt on. Most hunts tend to revolve around pirate stories, but this doesn't always have to be the case. You can make a treasure hunt from just about any story you put together. All you need is a stash of treasure (or candy) and a reason why it has been hidden.

Think about what other characters would hide treasure other than pirates. A wealthy old man who kept every penny he ever earned? A thief who robbed a bank but died before he could spend a dime of it? Consider qualities that would make the main character in the

story unique to make it a tale all your own while also serving as a good basis for what to use as props and displays in the hunt.

For example:

The Secret Stash of Jerry Jerpie

Jerry Jerpie, the town gardener, finally reached his end at the ripe old age of 104. Jerry was a most unusual man. He had been gardening since he was 14 years old, and was rumored to have kept almost every dime he ever earned from taking care of the trees, bushes, flowers and other shrubbery of the town.

It was believed that Jerry kept his money hidden throughout both his house and yard. This way he would still have access to his fortune if the house suddenly caught on fire and the money within it burnt up, or if a terrible storm were to come and the money outside were blown away.

After Jerry died, payment was needed to cover expenses for his burial. Since he had no remaining family or friends, his house was investigated and enough money was found to pay for the services. Ever since that day, Jerry's spirit has been angered because his money was taken, and any who come on the property feel themselves being lifted up into the air by unseen hands and then thrown far down the street. The house and property have now been abandoned for the past 50 years. However, the yard was never combed for the remainder of the money, and some believe it still remains hidden within the trees and shrubs.

During the last full moon, a brave young man was hurrying past the property on his way back from town. He suddenly saw a small piece of paper carried by the wind land in front of him in the road. He picked it up and saw that some clues were written on it which seemed to lead to something hidden and secret. The man believed it was the location to old Jerry's remaining fortune, and has offered to give the clues to any brave soul who would dare try to hunt it out on Halloween night.

Within the story, try to include a type of item that the kids will need to use as payment or safe passage to begin the hunt. For example, hand out gold coins, pennies, magic stones or other items at the front door so that the kids may enter without being forced away by evil spirits. In the case of Jerry Jerpie, kids may have to pay the ghost of Jerry one penny so that he allows them access onto the grounds and doesn't hurl them down the street. When they arrive at the location where the hunt begins, the kids can then drop their item into a chest, bucket, pail or other container.

Setting Up the Hunt. Once you've got the story behind your hunt thought out, you'll have some good ideas on what kinds of items to set up throughout the yard to bring it to life. With the case of Jerry Jerpie, set up old plants and shrubbery (either real or fake) throughout the yard. Hang vines from trees, use thin wire and fake black flowers to create rose bushes and other shrubs. Set up flower pots and urns of old, withered plants of all shapes and sizes, as well as gardening tools such as rakes, hoes and shovels, bags of soil and gardener's gloves.

To add more gloom to the grounds, especially if the atmosphere is one long abandoned, add stretched spider webs, plastic spiders and other bugs to the props. Other additions can include plastic rats and hanging bats. Create glowing eyes that look onto the treasure seekers from all angles by carving eyes into jack-o'-lanterns and posing them all over the grounds. Additional lighting can include small spot lights or jars and tin cans with candles inside.

Don't forget the most important character of the tale: the ghost himself. If kids will want to look for his hidden treasure, they'll have to get past Jerry while keeping their feet firmly on the ground. To do this, set up a ghost at the gate, fence or other marker serving as the entrance to the hunt. Make the angry spirit out of a skeleton sprayed with glow-in-the-dark paint, a Halloween dummy or even a purchased monster prop. Set before him a large container (such as a large flower pot in Jerry's case) for kids to pay one penny and appease the spirit.

The Treasure and the Clues. The treasure that the kids will seek out on the hunt can be either regular Halloween candy or chocolate coins that resemble actual treasure. You may also choose to put the candy in separate treat bags or even brown paper lunch bags with a large dollar sign drawn on them.

To make the clues for kids to follow in seeking out the treasure, use small pieces of paper to give out at the front door along with the penny, coin or other item they'll need for safe passage. Hide the candy or treasure in different locations to make the hunt more challenging and allow room for more goodies. This will also be beneficial in that you won't have one group of kids totally giving away the secret location of the treasure just as another group arrives. Create a different series of clues for each treasure spot, writing only 1 set clues on each paper.

In the case of Jerry Jerpie, clues may read:

First Set of Clues:

10 steps from the gate	*Look there to the left*
A quarter turn round	*Where shadows won't cast*
3 steps toward the trees	*Hiding back from the moon*
Crouch low to the ground	*Just under the grass*

(The treasure or candy can be hidden inside a bucket buried in the ground. Another bucket lies on top of it above ground, concealing the one below.)

Second Set of Clues:

Keep the hanging vines	*Beside a lantern burning*
Away to the right	*A soft subtle hue*
Pass the bush of thorns	*That is not like the rest*
That scratch, cut and bite	*With its flicker of blue*

(The treasure or candy can be hidden behind a lantern that is a glass jar with blue construction paper taped around it.)

When writing the clues, you may also choose to keep each set in a separate container for handing them out. This way you can distribute them by the ages of the children rather than giving them out at random. For example, clues that focus primarily on taking a certain number of steps in different directions would be better for younger children, and clues that contain riddles are better for older children.

For Those Who Dare to Enter. When the trick-or-treaters come to the door on Halloween night, hand out the two items they'll need to begin the hunt: the paper of clues and payment they'll need for entering the grounds. Invite the parents to go on the hunt with their kids as well, especially for the younger kids who may need their clues read to them. You may also choose to have a small amount of candy ready at the door to give to those who choose not to take part in the haunt, or if you have a large crowd of trick-or-treaters and decide to reserve the hunt for a select number at a time.

Don't forget to invite family and friends to come take part in the treasure hunt challenge as well. Mail out the story of Jerry Jerpie or other tale you've worked with along with your Halloween cards so that nieces, nephews and other special visitors can stop by on Halloween night either before or after their trick-or-treating.

The Best Treats Ever

No matter what you've got going on for the trick-or-treaters on Halloween night, from skeleton shows, witchcraft tours, haunting stories or books of blood, we all know what *really* lights up their faces after all the horror: the candy! And who can blame them? Being given your own personal, overwhelming selection of sugar in all its forms is pure happiness at just about any age.

And to make sure the goodies you give out are as exciting as your murderous axe men, try one of the following ideas that the kids will call the best treats ever.

Themed Treats and More Goodies.

Base your treats on the theme of your outdoor décor, ghost tour or other monstrous display. Fill a coffin with candy body parts to go with your haunted graveyard, guarded by a gravedigger who means business. Or fill a bucket with bags of gummy worms and Swedish Fish to go with your haunted shipwreck front porch display. Set up the treat buckets, coffins and cauldrons so that they are a part of the display that the kids get to reach into.

Full-Size candy bars can never be beat! Compared to the average fun-sized candy bars, full-sized candies look like Everest. Fill a gigantic cauldron with an assortment of Crunch, Hershey, Reece Peanut Butter Cups, Heath, Butterfinger and more and watch the occasional trick-or-treater pass out into the pumpkin patch.

The perfect variation (or addition) to chocolate is a soft, yummy pastry. Individually-wrapped Little Debbie and Drake's snacks are fun surprises to find inside a spider-webbed wheelbarrow for your scarecrow show. Build a heap of Twinkies, Fruit Pies, Ho-Ho's, Funny Bones and more next to Farmer Fritz being attack by killer crows.

Treat bags are the ultimate gift of mystery. They could contain as endless supply of goodies to last FOREVER! ...Or they at least look like they could. Include a Halloween toy in the treat bags as well as a candy bar or two and set them up beside one of your displays. For a Reaper display, place black treat bags on a large platter beside the Reaper on his throne. Next to the treat platter, set up a silver platter in which each trick-or-treater must place a gold coin (which they pick up along the haunted pathway) in exchange for their treat bag.

Warning: Once you deliver the best treats ever, there's no going back. Trick-or-treaters will come flying past the staggering zombies and fight off your killer clowns to get their next pail-full of the ultimate treat next season. This will become an annual tradition until they reach at least age 30.

10

THE COMPLETED CALENDAR AND HALLOWEEN SCRAPBOOK

As the night of the 31st comes to a close, take a moment for monster reflection. Sit back in your electric chair next to your good pal the Reaper and think back on all those Halloween adventures that really made the season one like never before: putting that first tombstone in the ground, finger painting the Insane Asylum pictures, driving three hours to that horror theme park so you made the very last hayride, raiding the costume warehouse until your car reached its weight capacity. It's been a couple of months of Halloween mania filled with memories that will last a lifetime. And with your faithful Halloween calendar and a coffin of souvenirs, crafts and pictures, you've got everything you need to keep the nightmares and memories alive.

The Completed Calendar. Looking at your Halloween calendar, how has it changed and evolved from when you first made it back before the season even started? In addition to all those original weekend outings you planned, how many other activities took their place on the page? Did you remember to include activities such as making Halloween invitations and stuffing the Halloween dummies? Did you mark the afternoon when you stopped at the pumpkin stand and held that all-night movie marathon?

Make sure you've included even the tiniest tid-bits, writing them down now before you forget just when you did what. With this keepsake of all your Halloween

events, parties, gatherings and adventures, you have a great reminder of all the fun you had and new things you tried with each passing week. Your Halloween calendar will also serve as the perfect starting point in making a Halloween scrapbook.

The Halloween Scrapbook. Is every desk, end table, dresser and shelf of your Insane Asylum covered with Halloween memorabilia from the season? Everywhere you look do you find enough haunted attraction ticket stubs, monster stage production catalogs, cemetery deeds, toe tags and party photos to make your own book of the dead? If so, tackle that mound of proud souvenirs from every nightmarish adventure you survived and create your own Halloween scrapbook.

To make a Halloween scrapbook, purchase a blank scrapbook and include all your 2-dimensional treasures of the season, such as:

- Your completed Halloween calendar
- Ticket stubs from haunted attractions, horror shows on stage, movies you saw in the theater, Halloween-themed exhibits and Halloween festival raffle tickets
- Pamphlets and advertisements from Halloween attractions and events (including those you made yourself for home attractions), Halloween business events or attractions you worked
- Halloween cards and invitations you were given, as well as copies of the ones you made yourself
- Storylines of your outdoor displays and attractions, trick-or-treaters' haunted tour and pictures of the displays
- Floor plans of your displays and attractions
- Pictures from your Halloween business events
- Pictures from all your Halloween adventures: exploring graveyards, eating at haunted diners, carving pumpkins and riding in a hearse
- Your Halloween story telling and poetry reading program
- Pictures of your Insane Asylum events: the Reaper party, trying out different axe murderer and killer clown costumes and make-up
- Your Halloween newsletter
- Halloween recipes you made
- A list of the movies you watched throughout the season and/or added to your film collection
- A list of new books you read and/or added to your Halloween library
- Names and numbers of monster friends you made throughout the season
- Return address labels of your Insane Asylum and the written message of insanity from your answering machine

Make your Halloween scrapbook truly psychotic by using different designs of scrapbooking paper, cardstock, lettering stickers and Halloween stickers throughout it.

In addition to the pictures, crafts and storylines you want to remember, include all the happenings that took place during your adventures, as well. Next to each photo, pamphlet or ticket stub, write a short description of what took place that made the trip an adventure like no other. Did one of the mad scientists in a haunted lab attraction say something that made you crack up rather than scream? Did a zombie accidentally fall on you during a hayride, completely covering you in blood? Write all these experiences down so that you'll remember them in years to come.

Future Spooks. A Halloween scrapbook is your very own book of the dead to share your experiences with friends and family, but it can also inspire ideas for future spooks. Looking through your scrapbook in the coming months, you may develop new ideas for display themes, attractions, business events, party themes, costumes and future travels for next season.

But hey, who says your scrapbook has to be for September and October events alone? It can also be for storing memories of Halloween-related events you engage in throughout the year. So sit tight in that straight jacket, because a variety of ways to celebrate the spirit of Halloween in the off-season will soon be discussed in *Section III.*

11

THE HALLOWEEN WEBSITE

With the Halloween scrapbook you just put together in Chapter 10, you created a collection of Halloween memories that can be shared with friends and family. But by creating a Halloween website, you can post your adventures to share with *the world*. And more than that: you can share Halloween experiences past, present and planned adventures yet to come with your seasonal displays, haunted attractions and all other events you bring to life.

If you already have your own website, create a link to a page that's dedicated to your seasonal endeavors. If you don't have a website, you can go to browsers such as Yahoo or Google to create one for free or for a small yearly fee, as well as get step-by-step instructions on how to set it up.

Your Haunt. Dedicate the main page of your website to the display or haunted attraction you put together at your Insane Asylum. For example, if you put on a killer klown interactive haunt, post a picture of one of your party guests armed with his or her Nerf ball gun and stepping onto the demented circus space ship. Insert the picture so that it fills the entire screen and over it write *Killer Klown Interactive Haunted Attraction!* as the title of the page. Below the picture, insert the storyline for the attraction so that visitors (as well as the party guests who were there) can read the background of the all the horror behind it.

In addition to the main page that will give a quick glimpse of your haunt, set up links

that list additional chapters of the story, inside information and more. These chapters may include:

- **Attraction Party:** Set up a link that shows everything that happened the night of your attraction party. Post pictures of the killer klown sneaking up on the townspeople, the fight scenes and the journey back through silly string and bleeding balloons. Give a summary of what happened throughout the adventure: how did the townspeople battle the klown or klowns? How many times did the klown get shot before it was successfully hit in the nose? Or did the klown manage to wipe out the townspeople completely and save all his cotton candy for himself?

- **Elsewhere in the Circus:** Set up a separate link that shows any additional scenes of the attraction, such as a window display or indoor display. For your killer klown attraction, create a link of the window display with the menacing neon sign. Write an additional chapter that goes along with this extra scene... could another killer klown be out there that got away, possibly to return next Halloween?

- **Character Bios:** Set up a link that tells the biographies of all the characters in the attraction, both for the killer klowns and each of the battling townsfolk. Where do the klowns come from? What do they want? How old are they? For the bios of the townspeople, let the party guests make up their own character info, such as their name, how they first encountered the klowns and if they'll ever go to a circus again. Post a picture of each character with their bio.

- **In the Works:** Another link on your haunted attraction site can discuss future displays or attractions you're either currently working on or will be starting on soon. This could include an attraction for next Halloween or possibly one you plan to have during the off-season. Write a brief scenario of the future event and post any photos of props or scenes you already have for it as a quick glimpse of what's to come.

Other Haunting Adventures.

In addition to posting all the information of your haunted display or attraction, you can also post the haunted happenings of your other Halloween events. List a separate set of links from the main page for events and displays that you put on both inside and outside the Insane Asylum.

For example:

- **Halloween Business Events:** Create a link that lists the Halloween business events you held, including outdoor displays that were set up, contests that were held, festivals and after-hour parties. Post pictures for each event and write about all that took place, such as games played, contest winners and more.

- **Story Telling and Poetry Readings:** If you put on a Halloween story telling and poetry reading, either for the community or right at home, create a link that gives a brief summary of how it went. Post the program of readings as well as any pictures of the presentations.

- **Halloween Weekend Outings:** Create a link that lists all the weekend outings you ventured on throughout the season, such as to horror theme parks, Halloween parades, magic shows and more. Post your most hilarious and horrifying pictures and tell the stories of each adventure.

Other links on your site can include the tales and happenings of your haunted tour and ghost story shack, Halloween museum, Halloween dummy bios and Halloween newsletter.

The Inside Scoop. You can also use your Halloween website as a source for giving all your friends and family the inside scoop of your upcoming endeavors. Use your "In the Works" link to post your upcoming killer day trips and haunting weekend adventures you plan throughout the year (see Chapter 13), Halloween and horror conventions you go to (see Chapter 14), home and business events during the full moon and murder mystery parties you throw during the off-season.

When sending out invitations to each event, make sure to include your new web address so that everyone can log on and get all the horrific details.

SECTION III

KEEPING THE SEASON

Is Halloween a mentality? Just as much as life is. We've discovered through our many endeavors that what made Halloween all that it was, was ourselves. The passion, the excitement, the ideas, the planning and the fun were all what turned a Halloween season into the ultimate adventure.

Throughout the passing weeks, we may have also changed, somehow. With each new chapter, we engaged in our monstrous talents and brought out new, demented sides of ourselves, allowing our inner monster to run free without rules, expectations or explanations needed. And now, is there any going back? We made Halloween come alive and thrive, but that doesn't mean it has to go anywhere. The spirit of the season comes from right within us, and — if we choose — it can be seen and experienced throughout the entire year.

What was it that you enjoyed most about the season? Making displays of the dead? Throwing killer parties for killers only? Going on haunting adventures? Changing into a demonic character? Chances are that no matter what it was, it can be found and brought to life any time of year. It doesn't have to be autumn, it doesn't have to be dark and foreboding outside, and there doesn't have to be a werewolf staring out your window (though it helps). And if you're up for the nightmare, you'll probably find that it brings more fun, excitement and horror to everyday life: the perfect combination.

In this third section of Making a Monstrous Halloween, *we'll explore a number of ways to delve into your favorite aspects of Halloween and celebrate them in the off-season. From travel, parties, haunts and exploring the unknown, the world around us can hold limitless fun and insanity while keeping the spirit of Halloween alive all year.*

12

THE HALLOWEEN FUND AND HALLOWEEN SALES

With October come and gone (don't cry), are you starting the off-season by scrounging for pennies? Where the heck did all that money go that you swore you had tucked away just last month? Maybe it disappeared somewhere between the haunted attraction gift shop and the hearse parade at the drive-in's creature feature.

And just think of all those plans you had for next year! How will you even afford the paint for your next tombstone if you're still paying off that life-sized haunted castle you bought on an impulse buy?

Well, don't jump into the moat just yet because next year can still be a go. There are many ways to prepare during the off-season by slowly saving up cash and pouncing on the right supplies while they're cheap. With a new Halloween fund and taking advantage of post-season sales, you can be floating on air with the graveyard ghosts with all the dough you'll have to spare next October.

The Halloween Fund

First things first: with the official Halloween season over, now is the perfect time to start a Halloween fund for next year. This fund doesn't have to be anything major — just a few dollars per week (or however much you allow yourself) can boost your spending limit big-time for next year's creations and activities.

Need some inspiration? Think about a particular item or event you put off this past season because it was just a bit too "millionaire serial killer" while you were rather "flat broke raging lunatic." With a Halloween fund, you'll be able to snatch that special something next year and run off cackling into the night with it.

Create your Halloween fund for goodies such as:

- **Dressing in Style:** Get that Halloween costume to die for from the specialty shop without running like hell from the price tag.
- **Partying the Night Away:** Load up on all the essentials for your next Halloween party, including life-sized character props, game supplies, decorations and the lab table buffet.
- **Haunting Weekends:** Don't let one weekend be void of Halloween adventures such as

haunted attractions, shows, theme parks, parades and concerts, or treating yourself to an RIP pass to your favorite outing.

- **A Monster Vacation:** Go all out on that long getaway to the ultimate Halloween spectacular. Save up for everything you'll need such as plane tickets, hotel (or castle) stay, car rental, food and fun money.
- **Future Creations:** Go to the hardware or craft store to stuff the shopping cart with all the supplies for your next outdoor displays, haunted attraction and indoor décor while sparing no expense.
- **A Dream Collection:** Go on a shopping spree for your dream list of books, movies and music for your Halloween collections and library.

Where and how you keep your Halloween fund can have a big impact on how much you contribute to it. Keep the fund in something that reminds you of Halloween so that each time you look at it, you'll remember all your future, sinister plans and be less likely to empty it out half-way through the year. Use your favorite cauldron, treasure chest or pumpkin pail to store the savings beside your Halloween library or monster DVD collection. Another good place to store your fund is inside a Halloween card or invitation you saved from last year, or even a plain envelope with a Halloween sticker on it to tuck amongst the monthly bills.

Another easy way to make a Halloween fund is to save all your spare change. Empty your pockets each night into one of your alien experiment jars and include the change that builds up in your car and sofa. Small change adds up fast, and you'll be surprised at how much you have after ten months of saving it!

Halloween Sales. Okay, enough dilly-dallying: it's November, you've started your Halloween fund, now what are you standing around for? Grab your last stack of pennies and hit the stores to take advantage of all those post–Halloween sales!

Every shop under the full moon including Halloween warehouses, department stores and craft stores will have a crypt-load of leftover merchandise that they want gone fast. That means big sales on anything and everything left over from Halloween: collectibles, costumes, make-up, props, crafts and everything you were drooling over last week will have their prices slashed and gutted.

But hey, when it comes to making a killing, always think long-term. In addition to loading up on stuff for next Halloween, you can get everything you need for all those Halloween-themed events you'll be putting on in the off-season, as well. You'll have a heck of a time finding glow-in-the-dark spider webs in February or fake blood and vampire teeth in March unless you want to pay the shipping costs of buying them online. Get it all now for a final Halloween blow-out of the year! Don't wait too long or the other monsters will beat you to it.

Get your paws and claws on items such as:

- **Party Supplies:** Nothing makes a party better than knowing you got everything you needed for it at 50 percent off. Pick up a new party music CD, Halloween-themed party-ware, tablecloths, monster party favors and more, both for Halloween parties next season and full moon parties in the coming months.
- **Props:** Clean house for next year's haunted attraction, getting all your tombstone supplies, body parts, skeletons, craft pumpkins, nooses and fake blood. Loading up on these supplies early also means you can work on building props and displays throughout the year for a whole new look next season.
- **Costumes:** You were good last season and only bought one costume from the Halloween warehouse even when you saw ten you liked. But now, that mad scientist's lab coat is calling out to be worn by a true psychotic. And wouldn't you know it... the crazy wig and glasses are on sale, too!
- **Craft Supplies:** Halloween craft supplies tend to disappear with the rising moon on November first. Load up on Halloween-themed paper, cardstock, stickers, add-ons and cut-outs. These craft supplies are perfect for making invitations to your full moon events, murder mystery parties and haunting vacations throughout the year as well as for next Halloween.
- **Toys:** You can never have enough Halloween toys... because they're just so *cool!* Fill up your cauldron with vampire yo-yo's and mummy finger puppets, rubber eyeballs and severed fingers for next year's body parts invitations and trick-or-treat station. You can also use these Halloween toys in treat bags for your next ghost story shack or as prizes at parties and Halloween business event games, both during the on- and off-season.

Can't find those leftover piles of Halloween goodies in some of the stores? Ask the sales associates if there are any items left over from the season. They may have been put in areas that you would never see, like on a bottom shelf tucked away between the hair gel and shower curtains.

November 1 Shopping List
Supplies for: *Howling Dance Party*
January Full Moon
Bobby's Cafe

- ✓ Monster Make-Up
- ✓ Furry Hands
- ✓ Hair Color Spray (brown and black)

✓ Prize for Scariest Costume: *The Howling* DVD
✓ Prize for Goofiest Costume: *Van Helsing* DVD
✓ Fun Size Candies
✓ Halloween Party CD
✓ Black and Brown Streamers
✓ Fake Blood
✓ "Monsters Welcome" Sign
✓ Werewolf Window Decorations

13

FUTURE EVENTS AND
YOUR NEXT HALLOWEEN VACATION

After embarking on so many Halloween day trips and weekend excursions throughout September and October, are you feeling down, thinking that the fun's over? What happened to all those horror theme parks and haunting stage shows? Where did the mad scientist's library book sales disappear to? Why won't they come back??

Travel

Well, don't fall into a slump just yet, because the travels aren't over. There are many Halloween-themed destinations to visit that are fun, frightening and may possibly cause a psychotic meltdown no matter what the season. After all, not every creepy spot on the map needs a jack-o'-lantern lighting the way. If traveling to explore the unknown is one of your favorite Halloween activities, keep that road map handy and gear up for as many adventures as your sanity allows with future nightmares throughout the year and planning your Halloween vacation for next season.

Killer Day Trips. How many places did you discover during the Halloween season that you couldn't squeeze into those two months of mayhem? Did it turn out that some of them were actually open all year? Perhaps while taking part in a graveyard tour you heard about a nearby restaurant that's supposedly haunted, or in a fall tourism guide you read about a witch museum and 3-D haunted house that stays open all year. Future events: discovered!

If you're drawing a blank because you're still recovering from one too many pumpkin pastries, refer back to all the places you researched in Chapter 1, "Researching Halloween Happenings." Notice which destinations you held off going to because you discovered they would be open even after the haunted hayrides had come and gone.

Some of these life-saving areas may include:

Haunted Locations: Ghosts know no season and we love them for it. What better place for a haunting day trip than to an area that's reportedly the home of those from the other side? Do a search for area restaurants, taverns, inns, mansions and more with a haunted history and check out Chapter 16: *Ghost Hunting* for some great ways of getting out into the spook.

Monster Shops: In some shops the monsters are there to stay. On some of your travels you may have come across restaurants, bookstores, hobby stores and more that have an entire horror, sci-fi or fantasy theme. The next time you're in the mood for a day of shopping or fine dining, go straight to where the spirit of Halloween lives and thrives.

Killer Exhibits: Killer culture is invaluable... not to mention cool. Check out museums that may be showing exhibits you won't want to miss, such as Egyptian displays, human bodies and skeletons, UFO studies, ancient weaponry, dark artwork and objects of the paranormal. Now who ever said that museums couldn't be fun?

Monster Productions: When you scanned the theatre and playhouse schedules in your area, did you remember to look at the upcoming shows for the remainder of the year and into the next? Monster productions like *Little Shop of Horrors* and *The Phantom of the Opera* can run anytime, and make for the perfect off-season horror show.

Themed Events: Are you so sure that the vampire costume balls are over until next year? Check back with businesses that put on pirate parties, Hitchcock nights and more. They just may be planning a future chaotic event to throw during the full moon, Friday the 13th or to accommodate the next horror movie release!

These are just some of the local killer day trips you can embark on to keep things spooky throughout the year. Keep your eyes and ears open for all other kinds of horror that may be creeping your way in the coming months.

Monster Excursions. Any excuse for a vacation! In addition to day trips to areas close by the Insane Asylum, you can also venture forth on Halloween-themed events that are more than a hop, skip and jump away. Heading to these nightmarish events in the off-season provides an extra bonus in that they probably won't be as heavily busy — or in some cases, expensive — as they are in October. Such events open all year include:

The Tower of Terror, Disney's Hollywood Studios, Florida: This free-fall ride is themed after the classic *Twilight Zone* episodes and is a haunted house and adventure ride all in one. As sure as the series, The Tower of Terror takes you away from the world you think you know and into the furthest realms of your imagination. For more information: www.waltdisneyworld.com

The Haunted Mansion, The Magic Kingdom, Florida: The Haunted Mansion was one of Walt Disney's most exciting visions, and once you experience it, you'll see why.

Narrated by Vincent Price, the Haunted Mansion is a ride that has inspired many professional haunt builders and horror film directors and is a must for any Halloween enthusiast. For more info: www.waltdisneyworld.com

Classic Monsters Café, Universal Studios, Florida: Don't you just wish that all the cafes in your town were inhabited by monsters? Universal Studios understands. So they've made a monster's café themed after some of our favorite horror classic films, including *Dracula, Frankenstein* and *The Wolf Man.* For more info: www.universalstudios.com

Haunted Houses in Niagara Falls, Canada: Halloween is not only growing in Canada, they even realize that we need it year-round! Five haunted houses that are open in all seasons include Ghost Blasters Dark Ride, The House of Frankenstein, Castle Dracula, Screamers and the Haunted House. For more info: www.visiting-niagara-falls.com

Salem, Massachusetts: In addition to the array of Halloween events that open for October, there are many happenings in Salem, MA that stay open all year for the die-hard fans. Explore haunted houses, witch museums, tours and stage performances while avoiding the mass crowds of the peak season. For more info: www.salem.com

Jekyll and Hyde Club, Greenwich Village, New York: Sometimes you just need to escape to a place where insanity is as appreciated as it should be. The Jekyll and Hyde pub and club each hold displays, shows and the perfect atmosphere for personal transformation. And don't miss their spookiest neighbor, the Slaughtered Lamb Tavern located just a block away from the pub. For more info: www.jekyllandhydeclub.com

Zombie Crawl, Philadelphia, Pennsylvania: Zombie Crawls can be found throughout the country and allow you to be the staggering, drooling monster that you tend to resemble in the mornings. Zombie crawls include dressing up as one of the undead and "crawling" from one bar to another after sundown... after having your fill of brains for the evening. For more info: www.phillyzombiecrawl.com

The Stanley Hotel, Estes Park, Colorado: *Heeeere's Johnny!* The Stanley Hotel is a trip for anyone who has ever seen *The Shining* and thought, "Oh I would handle it *way* better than that." Stephen King based one of his most spine-chilling thrillers at this hotel that has some truly spooky history of its own. The owners and operators have since put together special ghost tours throughout the year to commemorate their eerie place on the map. For more info: www.stanleyhotel.com

Cemeteries of New Orleans, Louisiana: The above-ground cemeteries of New Orleans are world renowned for being as beautiful and mesmerizing as they are creepy after hours. Ghost tours and cemetery tours are still in operation, just make sure to call in advance as some have closed down since the devastating destruction of the city. Roaming the grounds in a tour is always much safer than going alone, as the cemeteries have unfortunately been known for high crime rates. For more info: www.hauntedtraveler.com

Gettysburg, Pennsylvania: If you're in the mood to step out into the spook, Gettysburg is the place to go. What better place to start your ghost hunting than what's known as the most haunted place in America? Grab your camera and tape recorder to explore the battlefields and maybe even its long lost residents as you step back into history.

Now don't you feel silly for thinking all those haunting adventures were over? And you don't even need a post-season Halloween calendar to mark all your new outings to come (unless you want one). Just throw a Halloween sticker on your regular monthly calendar as a ghoulish reminder of these future excursions.

Vacations for Next Halloween. Another fun way to keep you cackling into the night is to brew up your next Halloween vacation for the coming fall. The off-season is a great time to buy tickets for those big Halloween shows and parties, some of which get promoted up to a year in advance. Buy tickets as soon as they go on sale and book the best hotel room right in the midst of all the haunts, parades, festivals and more that will be going on in the area.

Refer to Chapter 7 as well as all the Halloween happenings you researched last season. While the other horror buffs are resting in their coffins, you'll be getting the best airfare, car (or hearse) rental rates and admission prices. You'll also have plenty of time to get any days off work you need, handle any baby-sitter, pet-sitter or creature-sitter needs and all the while look forward to that monster getaway.

14

HALLOWEEN AND HORROR CONVENTIONS

Have you ever looked out your window at night and wondered about the other Halloween enthusiasts of the world out there? The tens of thousands of monsters dry-brushing their tombstones and building the perfect torture chamber, scattered throughout the country from California to the New York islands?

Wouldn't it be great if they could all get together and share their passion of haunts, horror and all things insane in one big extravaganza? Well, dreams really do come true, even for those who prefer nightmares. There are actually two types of such monstrous events that take place all around the country and at all different times of the year. For the ultimate Halloween-fix during the off-season, attend a Halloween or horror convention specifically tailored for haunters, horror fanatics and the rest of us weirdoes to gather from far and near to see the latest in the spookster world.

Halloween Conventions

Halloween conventions are geared towards those putting together a home haunted attraction, corporate haunt, and for those selling Halloween merchandise at their place of business. They generally involve everything you need for setting up haunts, learning the tricks of the trade and quite often parties and shows. You'll find showrooms stuffed with props, special effects, costumes and more for attractions of all levels and sizes. Get a life-sized headless horseman for your haunted tour, an entire wardrobe of bloody aprons to sell at your late night murderous business ball and even a castle lined with corpses for that theme park you're just inches away from buying.

Halloween conventions are typically held in the off-season so that haunters can load up on supplies and begin building and preparing well before October. The timing also works out great because it makes for a perfect Halloween getaway of haunted houses, monster parties and shows just when the withdrawal of it all was starting to take affect. You can look forward to partying with Halloween buffs from around the globe, learning different aspects of the trade and trying out the latest additions in the world of the spook.

The parties and events going on at Halloween conventions may just get your head spinning like Linda Blair. Prepare for a vacation of:

- **Boogying Down:** Special shows at conventions may include concerts, costume fashion shows and after-hours parties that you won't find anywhere else. Boogie the night away as a mad scientist with that new lab coat you got at the post-season sale and see how your fellow enthusiasts transform into all kinds of crazy characters.
- **Killer Field Trips:** Take special tours of haunted houses and other attractions located close to the convention. It's a field trip into the underworld where you can go backstage and see how these corporate haunts were put together by haunting professionals and continue to evolve with new additions each season.
- **Contests and More:** If it involves Halloween gifts and prizes, you gotta go for it. Enter contests for best costume and make-up design, bid in silent auctions filled with Halloween collectables and memorabilia and enter raffles to win all kinds of free merchandise.
- **Monster Buddies:** Perhaps the best thing about attending a Halloween convention is the sense of community: meeting fellow monsters from around the world and making friends with those as passionate about the season as you are. Where else can you find hundreds of people discussing the best ways to provoke scares and screams, build 10-foot scarecrows and perfecting zombie make up?

In between the parties, you might as well learn something. And you'll be dying to do just that from the pros who can answer any questions you may have about the world of haunting.

- **Seminars:** Attend a broad range of seminars to learn how to improve your Halloween business event or corporate haunt. Hear about different methods of costuming and special effects, marketing and improving sales, adding vendors and expanding your attraction from those who have been in the business for years.
- **Halloween Artwork:** Get the ultimate dose of monster culture. Check out Halloween artwork and photography to see how different visions and designs reflect the psychosis of others. Compare posters, pamphlet and website designs, t-shirts, ticket designs and more used at big and small haunted attractions around the country.
- **Props Galore:** Just when you were thinking about a new look for your torture chamber, you come to the place that has it all. Browse the selection of hundreds of vendors specializing in props and special effects from electric chairs to thunder and lightning. You'll see the latest in building materials, backgrounds and backdrops, lighting, sound and more.
- **Evil Epiphanies:** Another big bonus of attending a Halloween convention is that cruising through the props, sets and attractions, both at the convention and those set up around it, can lead to all kinds of ideas and inspiration for your own future displays, attractions, parties and business events.

Don't hold back when you can dive right in! Here's one thing you won't get from your typical Halloween outing: the chance to touch, sample and try on just about every prop, attraction and costume you come across.

- **Into the Nightmare:** Go inside a hallway of claustrophobia before it's ever put into a haunted house. Hop into a coffin simulator ride that may just be your last. Put on a 10-foot tall troll costume that would look awesome in next year's conjurer's circle display and get your face painted from stage make-up professionals.
- **I'll Take Ten!** Your wallet just may come flying out of your cloak. Order everything you need for your haunt or business event right at the convention, from a few body bags to a bulk order of coffins. Test the squishiness of eye balls before you buy them, listen to different horror soundtracks before choosing the right ones and watch a variety of prop-building videos before adding them to your collection.

Admissions and Fees. Admissions and fees for Halloween conventions vary and often depend on the size of the event. Smaller conventions may last one day and have a fee of anywhere between $20–35 that includes all lectures and food for the day. Larger conventions can last up to four days and often have a similar daily rate in addition to a reduced rate for attending the convention every day. However, larger conventions may have additional fees for each lecture and show, but often contain a bigger selection to choose from.

Another aspect of attending these events is lodging. Larger conventions can be held within convention centers close to hotels that give discounted room rates to those attending the event, so make sure you mention your trip agenda when booking reservations. However, it's also a good idea to look into motels in the surrounding towns to find room rates that are generally a bit lower, though a short distance away.

If you can, attend a Halloween convention with a fellow monster buff who will dive right into the corpse pit with you. You'll also be able to cut costs by sharing a room, cab fair, and even get discounted tickets to Halloween parties if you buy them as a couple — same-sex couples apply!

Tell Me Where! Some Halloween conventions are put on in the same location each year while others move around the country to cover more areas. Some of the best conventions to check out include:

HauntCon
Milwaukee, Wisconsin
Hauntcon.com

Midwest Haunters Convention
Columbus, Ohio
Midwesthauntersconvention.com

National Haunters Convention
Valley Forge, PA
Nationalhauntersconvention.com

New England Haunters Gathering
Salem, Massachusetts
HauntClub.net

Transworld Haunt & Attractions Show
St. Louis, Missouri
Hauntshow.com

Horror Conventions

Ah, the world of horror... what would life be without it? A horror convention is another vacation that takes your passion for the dark and demented and turns it into a party for the masses. They are similar to Halloween conventions in set-up, but tend to focus more on horror fiction writing and film. Writers of the darker genres often come to display their latest short stories and attend lectures to learn from the masters of horror. Beginner film-makers may show the world premier of their first slasher films in addition to selling them on DVD in the showroom.

Like Halloween conventions, horror conventions can last from one day to a long weekend. They can also be held right in the middle of the Halloween season as well as throughout the year. This can make for a great October getaway because you'll have an array of haunted attractions in the area to run to in between those horror seminars and midnight costume balls. Whether you're involved with writing or film making or are a fan of the two, you can look forward to partying, learning and trying out all the horror that these conventions have in store.

Horror fans appreciate a good party just like Halloween buffs... probably because so many of us live in both twisted realms! Go running into the madness for a few days of:

- **The Horrifying Boogie:** Head to a costume ball with fellow horror buffs from near and far and boogie the night away with a psycho ward doctor and an escaped lunatic: the perfect couple. You can also enter a costume contest to show off your scabs and slash wounds.
- **Film Festivals:** Attend a horror film festival and you'll forget what it was ever like to go to the movies alone. You'll also be supporting your fellow enthusiasts by checking the works of up-and-coming filmmakers from around the country.
- **Monster Celebrities:** Remember that guy in that movie about the zombies in that town? No? Well you just may meet him! Horror movie celebrities from classics to new releases prowl around the show rooms, so have your quill pen and book of the dead ready.
- **Horror Signings and Readings:** You may never read your favorite ghost stories the same again... Attend horror signings where both new and renowned authors will personalize their most spine chilling chronicles just for you. Some may also read their work aloud to a captive and spellbound audience and offer Q&A sessions after the readings. It's a Halloween story telling like never before!

When it comes to horror, there's always a lesson to be learned. Whether it's to not go through a door that has blue fog creeping under it or to never approach a smoking crater deep in the woods that suddenly appeared from the sky, it's always best to pay attention.

- **Seminars:** Learn from the masters who could whip together a haunted tour storyline in two shakes of a skull rattle. Attend seminars in subjects such as horror writing in fiction and film, acting and promotion.
- **Art Shows:** In need of some more Halloween art for your indoor décor? Attend horror art shows with every type of dark art imaginable. You may get ideas for creating

your own demented artwork while buying prints to use as Halloween gifts and prizes at next year's Halloween business events.

- **Lectures from the Other Side:** Thinking of doing some ghost hunting? Attend lectures from mediums, paranormal investigators and other experts of the supernatural to improve your ghost-hunting techniques and hear about investigations from around the globe.

No need to keep your paws in your pockets and your nightmares to yourself... Try out a little of everything from the Hannibal Lector masks to the creative writing entries.

- **Merchandise Galore:** And just when you thought your Halloween museum couldn't hold any more... Check out horror merchandise and collectibles that could fill a castle and then some. Try out the different props and memorabilia to use in displays, as gifts, contest prizes and more.
- **Contests:** Got a ghost story to share? Turn the storyline from your home display, walk-through or haunted attraction into a short story and enter it into all kinds of contests in horror fiction. Share your tale of killer pirates or taunting ghosts and read the work of so many others.

Admissions and Fees. Admissions for horror conventions are similar to Halloween conventions and depend mostly on the size of the event. Some will cover any and all lectures and food while others charge separately for each. You may also want to keep an eye out for ticket sales on the convention's website to get a discounted rate rather than paying at the door.

Another expense to expect at these conventions is paying to see your favorite movie stars. Actors and actresses from your favorite monster films all come equipped with photographs to sell and personalize. Keep in mind, however, that the photographs can cost anywhere from $10–20 each, and even asking to take your own picture with the star can cost a separate fee.

Tell Me Where! You don't have to be a horror writer or filmmaker to party hardy at a horror convention. They're the perfect getaways for the ultimate horror enthusiasts to have a great time, meet new people and get ideas for your own horrifying events back home. Some of the best conventions to check out include:

Screamfest Horror Convention
Orlando, Florida
www.spookyempire.com

World Horror Convention
Alternating locations each year
www.worldhorrorconvention.com

Horrorfind Weekend
Baltimore, Maryland
www.horrorfindweekend.com

Rock and Shock
Worcester, Massachusetts
www.rockandshock.com

Warning: After attending a Halloween or horror convention for the first time, you may be changed forever. You may find yourself returning home, only to look around your neighborhood, workplace and long-time friends and think: "But where are all my fellow monsters? Where are those I can talk to about my new tombstone designs, my new haunt storyline and my upcoming trip to Transylvania? ... *My god, I have nothing to say to these people!"*

HORRORFIND WEEKEND CONVENTION
Road Trip, Weekend Summary

Friday, March 27
  The Rocky Horror Show, live performance, midnight

Saturday, March 28
  Tradeshow Room, 9–10
  Art Show, 10–10:30
  Meet the Grim Reaper! 10:30
  Lectures:
    Corpsification for Beginners, 11–12
    Monster Genocide, 1–1:30
    Paranormal Investigating, 2–3
    Cast Developing, 3–4
  Costume Contest, 8 P.M.
  Film Showing: *Dawn of the Dead,* 9 P.M.

Sunday, March 29
  Scares that Care Charity Auction, 10 A.M.

Trip Costs

Hotel and Parking	$130
Convention Tickets	$ 50 (included RHS, trade show, lectures, movies and contest)
Gas	$ 90
Tolls	$ 35
Food	$ 50
Dealer's Room Goodies	$ 15
TOTAL	$370

15

STONE HUNTING

To some, graveyards call.

To those who do not hear it, the concept may elude them. But for many enthusiasts, the spirit of Halloween is seen throughout the layout, artwork, history and overall atmosphere of graveyards. These still and silent grounds are worlds all their own that cry out to be explored, from the smallest group of stones to the most grand and elaborate cities of statue.

When it comes to our favorite places to escape to in the world, we return to them because of the way they make us feel. For many, graveyards provide a peaceful atmosphere, serving as areas of reflection, soul-searching and clarity. Our minds become free to wander in a way not so easily achieved in our everyday lives. This sense of tranquility may be why many of us choose to create

a haunted graveyard as a regular Halloween display, bringing a peaceful atmosphere to our own Insane Asylums... and then load it up with monsters because they're just so *cool*.

Graveyards are just as much places of life as they are of death. They are outdoor museums that reflect changes in culture, language and beliefs throughout the ages, as well as the evolving creativity in stonework. In this chapter, we'll explore all kinds of graveyards for keeping the Halloween spirit alive in many ways. We'll seek out inspiration for future Halloween displays, go on graveyard tours and possibly write our own, meet others who share a passion for the graves, and all the while wander in that awesome scenery that beckons us.

Cemetery Day Trips

Stone hunting: a pastime for the lovers of tombstones. Different people are drawn to graveyards for all sorts of reasons. Some go to learn about the history and culture of their town, its previous inhabitants and the families that have settled there over time. Others may study their family's genealogy, tracing back generations to learn more about their own history.

Other interests in graveyards include searching for stones of famous men and women, or seeking out stones with epitaphs that are philosophical, funny, or just plain weird. And still others go searching in graveyards that have a reputation for being visited by ghosts and housing other inexplicable happenings.

For Halloween buffs, stone hunting can be a fun pastime for another reason, as well. Graveyards can be the perfect source of inspiration for designing your own tombstones, an entire graveyard display or other haunted attraction. The engravings, language and layout of the grounds can be incorporated into your own fun and demented uses while exploring and enjoying the vast surroundings.

Of Graveyards and Cemeteries.

Here's some quick trivia: why are some burial grounds referred to as graveyards and others as cemeteries? Is it just to confuse us and drive us crazy? Maybe. But oftentimes, the difference in the term used lies in the timeframe in which the burial ground was built.

What are commonly referred to as graveyards are burial grounds built before the Victorian era, or approximately before 1837. Graveyards were typically constructed on rocky, hilly land that wasn't suitable for farming, but served just fine for burying the dead who kept quiet with complaints. Cemeteries, on the other hand, are burial grounds built in the late 1830s and onward. The word *cemetery*, which is Greek for *sleeping place*, was introduced during this time to give a more pleasant-sounding name to the areas. Cemeteries began to take on completely new roles than the graveyards before them, serving as grounds for the public to enjoy with wide paths, trees, shrubs and flowers in a quiet, serene atmosphere. Such cemeteries are also referred to as garden cemeteries.

Both ancient graveyards and not-so-ancient cemeteries are equally good places for stone hunting. Graveyards are usually small and contain stones that read much differently

than those of modern day. You can find spellings in the engravings that may look awkward in just the right way for your tombstone designs, such as the long "s," which looks a lot like the letter "f" but is pronounced as "s." You may also come across descriptions of the cause of death on these older stones, a practice which has become lost over time.

In larger garden cemeteries, the engraved images of the stones become much more detailed and decorative, which can also be fun to incorporate into your own displays. You'll find symbolic carvings of cherubs, wings, trees, flowers and other images of the afterlife used in the late nineteenth century. Larger cemeteries very often contain a number of exquisite mausoleums, statues and obelisks that can also give the grounds the look of being an entire city of the dead and make for great Halloween pictures.

Picking Your Stones.

When looking for ideas for your own stones, check out a couple different types of burial grounds. Stone hunting with the eye of a stone carver on a mission makes for a great day trip. You may want to start with local graveyards and cemeteries you've previously visited, as chances are you'll pick up on subtle details of the stones that you never even noticed before.

Discovering new graveyards is another adventure where you never know just what you'll encounter. Road maps can be a helpful resource for this type of stone hunting, as graveyards are oftentimes marked on them with a special symbol (usually a cross), so you can easily locate them. Pick an area that has a couple different graveyards you've never been to before and plan out your route for the day. Take notice, though, if some of them are located on private property and do not allow trespassing.

Another fun way to stone hunt is to throw caution into the wind and just start driving down country roads to discover the graveyards as you come across them. Take the roads you've always wanted to explore and see what turns up. Though, if you use this route and find a graveyard that you really like, write down how you got there so that if you want to go back again you won't be driving around lost trying to find it!

Stone Hunting Essentials.

For the perfect day of stone hunting, make sure you have all the essentials. Pack a backpack that includes the following:

Roadmap
The Grave Hunter's Nosh
Bottles of water
Camera and extra batteries
Notebook
Pens or pencils
Cell phone

Extra winter supplies:
Hat, gloves, tissues

Extra summer supplies:
Sun screen, bug spray

Cemetery Ponderings.

With each new graveyard you explore, you'll no doubt see how each one has its own unique look. Some may have a "peaceful full moon night" atmosphere while others cry out "night of the living dead: keep alert." Both surroundings will probably contain aspects that you want to bring into your own haunted graveyard.

For some good starting points, consider making the following observations with each stone hunting adventure:

- Where are the older sections of the graveyard? Where are the most recent stones? Are you finding random eighteenth- or nineteenth-century stones among the more modern sections?
- How would you describe the layout of the cemetery? Are there wide, paved roads for easy strolls? Are the paths composed of only dirt and rock? Are there any paths at all? Is there an entranceway for vehicles or did you have to park your car along the side of the road?
- Is the cemetery surrounded by a stone wall or fence? If so, how old does the wall or fence appear to be? Does it look like it's been restored over the years or is it in need of repair?
- What are the surroundings like beyond the borders of the cemetery? Is it surrounded by forests? Is it on a main road? Are there houses close by?
- What is the land of the cemetery like? Is it rocky and hilly or smooth and flat?
- Do the majority of the styles of stones look similar or is there a big variety of size and shape? What about the type of stone they are made from, such as granite, sandstone or schist?
- Can you tell which stones were made by the same carvers based on the similarities in shape and engraved images?
- Are there many small stones throughout the graveyard, used both as footstones (usually containing initials only) and headstones? Are some of the stones sunken into the ground so that they are almost completely overgrown?
- How have some of the different types of stones weathered over time?

Seeing the Spook of It All. As you notice all these differences in stones and cemetery layouts, make notes on how some of them can be used in your displays, walk-through or haunted attraction. Draw small sketches and write how you want to work with each one.

For example, you may come up with a completely different look for your display by using a few small, overgrown stones. Make these by using the extra pieces of Styrofoam left over from your bigger tombstones. Shape them with a basic curved top and place them so that they stand only 3–4 inches high. Next to these slowly disappearing stones, bury a skeleton hand so that it is just barely exposed, giving the look that both the stone and the person/skeleton/zombie were overgrown by the earth over time.

You can also make notes on the styles of language used on the stones so that each of your own will be slightly different. For example, some can read "Here lies the body of..." while others read "Here lies interred" or "In memory of...," and so on. Other items to take note of can include items found beside the stones, such as flags, flowers and urns. These sketches and notes can lead to all kinds of new ideas for next year's graveyard display.

The Perfect Shot. In addition to taking notes on the stones and grounds, you can also take pictures during your stone hunting adventures. These can serve as good visuals for reproducing engraved images, as well as serving other Halloween endeavors. Need a few more Halloween pictures to put up for your next Grim Reaper's party? Include some old mausoleums and statues to his wall collection. Or take pictures of old, unusual-looking stones to use as indoor décor for your next haunted graveyard opening.

To get the best visibility of the epitaphs and carvings in your pictures, photograph around high noon, when the sun is shining from straight above and there won't be any shadows from neighboring stones. If you take pictures during other times of the day and you're not getting enough light on the stone, you can also use a full-length mirror to direct the sunlight onto it and remove any shadows.

Most cemeteries close at sundown, but if you find yourself around during that last hour as the sun sets, you're in for a big treat: red, orange and purple skies will create a breath-taking backdrop behind the trees and stones, making for great pictures and a perfect autumn evening!

Hooked on Graves. You may find that even though you started going to graveyards specifically to stone hunt, you've become attached to them simply because they're awesome. If so, embark on stone hunting adventures in graveyards and cemeteries all throughout your state, making regular trips before it's your last. Enjoy the grounds by walking, reading, writing, picnicking and exploring, and just for getting away from the hustle and bustle of all the outside insanity.

If you find that after a few stone hunting adventures you want to learn more about tombstones and graveyards, check out some of the titles in "Recommended Readings" at the end of this book. Also, search your local bookstore or library, online or even the museums in your area to see what they have on the subject.

Graveyard Tours

In addition to visiting cemeteries to stone hunt on your own, another fun way to explore the grounds is to go on a graveyard tour. You'll find that the graveyard tours that take place year-round are much different than the haunted graveyard tours put on around Halloween. Rather than centering on ghosts stories, eerie legends and other unexplained events connected with the graveyard, year-round graveyard tours are much more informative on the non-spooky history of its inhabitants, stone carvers, epitaph and symbol interpretations and how the graveyard has changed over time. There are a couple different ways to enjoy the surroundings with a good graveyard tour. And who knows... you may find that the stroll brings you back to your own tour-writing days at the Insane Asylum!

Following the Leader. The most popular way to take a graveyard tour is to sign up for a scheduled tour with a guide. These guided tours are fun because you get to learn all sorts of tidbits about the grounds that you may never have known just strolling around by yourself. A plain, faded stone that you never even noticed in your favorite cemetery may turn out to be one that has actually been reused and bears another name and inscription upside-down in the ground. Or a nineteenth century, million dollar mausoleum may not even hold anyone inside, whereas the large area of land beside it are resting places for many unknown souls who could not even afford simple markers.

Going on a guided tour also gives the advantage of having someone there to answer any questions you may have about the grounds, such as why some of the stones look the way they do, read the way they do, or if any stones have been restored or destroyed over time. Just dying to ask if anything unusual *has* happened within the graveyard? Odds are that your tour guide has done enough research on the place to know — and tell — all the gory details... if you ask the right questions.

To search for upcoming guided graveyard tours, check with the cemetery organizations and historical societies in your area that hold tours of their own and may have information about others.

Following the Paper. Another type of graveyard tour is a self-guided tour. These involve reading information from a tour pamphlet and following a specific trail throughout the graveyard. Cemetery tour pamphlets can be found at libraries, community centers and even at the cemeteries themselves. Self-guided tours are nice in that you get to set your own pace and choose when you want to take the tour, so you won't be learning about eighteenth-century stone carvers with a 20-degree wind blowing past you in April.

With self-guided tours, you'll also have all the information in a handy pamphlet to take home afterwards, containing pictures and quotes from the various spots on the tour. These pamphlets can serve as great examples for making your own haunted graveyard storyline pamphlets, haunted attraction pamphlets and even writing your *own* graveyard tours.

Follow Me! With so many of your own haunted tours and storylines under your belt, you may decide to take grave matters into your own hands. After a couple stone hunting adventures and graveyard tours, take that leap and pick your favorite burial ground to write your own tour for it.

Putting on a graveyard tour can be as simple as packing a picnic and taking some

friends on a stroll of the grounds to
discuss the different images, epitaphs,
mausoleums and more that have
caught your interest and you want to
share. You can also go a step further
and create a tour pamphlet with
pictures of the areas you discuss,
keeping all those self-guided tour
pamphlets you came across for inspiration and models. Just like you did
with your attraction pamphlets, give
this written tour to friends and family for a keepsake after the tour and
keep one for yourself as an awesome
souvenir.

If you find that you want to put
together a more detailed graveyard tour, such as the ones you've collected, do some reading on the different topics you want to discuss. Pick up a few books at the library, your
town historical society or research online to learn about the people buried in the grounds,
the stone carvers of the area or the symbols on the stones. Choose a cemetery that doesn't
already have a tour written for it and donate yours to the town library for all the other stone
buffs out there to enjoy.

The Victorian Era & Stonington Cemetery:
A Cemetery Walking Tour

*The Stonington Cemetery, also referred to as Evergreen Cemetery, is located at the intersection
of Route 1 and North Main Street in Stonington. It was chosen for a walking tour because of
its variety of historic mausoleums and elaborate gravestones that reflect the life and times of the
Victorian era.*

MAUSOLEUMS

We begin our tour with two Gothic mausoleums of the Victorian era. From the entrance just
past the gate, turn left, heading west down the path and passing a series of obelisks on your
left. Notice how the path is not paved but is simply composed of dirt, rock and grass, originally
fitted for wagons rather than automobiles.

The first and larger of the mausoleums comes up on the right. It was built in 1875 by Cottington Billings who, oddly enough, was never put to rest here but is buried elsewhere in the
cemetery. Notice how the mausoleum bears no writings on the outside: no family name, dates
or even engraved symbols. This is an unusual feature for a mausoleum, as only wealthy families
could afford such a resting place and would usually want their family name to be clearly visible
and remembered. A tomb of this proportion was usually built to rest several family members,
and others of its size and style were built by well-to-do families to serve as chapels within a
cemetery for private prayer. However, there is only one person put to rest in this mausoleum: a
descendant of Cottington who was cremated and had his urn placed inside in 1940, 65 years
after its construction.

The second mausoleum is on the left and was built by Albert Gallaton Palmer, D.D., a
reverend of the town and descendent of one of the founders of Stonington. Although much

smaller, this size mausoleum was often used to rest several family members, as well, and is the resting place of four people: Palmer, his daughter Sarah and two relatives who have not been listed in the cemetery's burial records. Their coffins are stacked in the alcoves on either side of the tomb. Note how the burial plot was chosen right along the main road, allowing for easy viewing for all who pass by.

Mausoleums were a popular resting place for many reasons in the nineteenth century. They served to make an impressive statement of family significance, they kept the family together and secured a burial spot for extended family members, they protected the dead from being vandalized, and they were a good alternative for those who did not like the thought of underground burial.

HOLDING VAULTS

From the Palmer mausoleum, retrace your steps to the main entrance and notice a smaller tomb on the eastern side of the cemetery, which will be to your right. It is made of gray granite and contains a stained glass window above the arched door. This chamber was actually used as a holding vault, constructed by the cemetery in the late 1800's. It was used to store the bodies of those who had died during the winter, when the ground was too frozen to conduct a burial. The inscription on the door denotes the peaceful and uplifting view of death during the Victorian Era:

RESURGAM
THEY LAID THE
PILGRIM
IN A CHAMBER WHICH LOOKED
TOWARD THE SUNRISING
THE NAME OF THE CHAMBER WAS
PEACE
AND WHEN THE MORNING CAME
HE AROSE AND SANG
(Resurgam is Latin for "I will rise again.")

Notice a rope coming out of a tiny opening in the door of the chamber. Although it only serves to pull the heavy stone door shut, it also resembles a type of device of the time period used to protect people against being buried alive.

BURIED ALIVE

In the nineteenth century, not all doctors attended medical school, nor were they required to. Many doctors had only studied under another physician — one who also may not have attended medical school. With so little knowledge in medicine, many patients were being misdiagnosed, and even pronounced dead when they were actually in comas or deep trances. These symptoms could occur to those suffering from cholera and tuberculosis, as well as other diseases of the time. The person would appear dead, and as a result, being buried alive was not uncommon.

Precautions that were sometimes taken to prevent such a tragedy were to wait with burial until a few days after death, when the signs of decay would become evident. In other circumstances, creative devices for the grave were made that would allow a person to call for help if they had been buried before their time. One such device was a string that ran from the person's finger in the coffin to a wooden post on ground level. A bell was attached to the post so that any movement of the person's hand would cause the bell to ring, sounding an alarm. A family member or paid watchman would stand guard in the cemetery in the case of such an event. This post was referred to as the "graveyard shift."

In some mausoleums, the door would be constructed so that it could open from the inside. In other cases, a loaded gun would be placed within the tomb, so that the unfortunate person could end their suffering.

MEMORIALIZED TOGETHER

For the next stop on our tour, round the corner by the stone wall and head north for a few paces towards the rear of the cemetery. The stone of Mary Ann Poe Dieter stands out against others, due to its unique style of carving. This eloquently-lettered stone stands for both Mary Ann and her husband, who died at sea. Erecting stones for those who died at sea was quite common. However, since the price of a stone was costly, the lost person would often be later memorialized on the marker of another, such as their spouse or parent, rather than on a stone specifically for them.

TABLE STONES

Follow the path along the stonewall heading east until it turns left, or northbound. Walk straight about 25 paces until you come to a narrow passage on your right, lined with short stone pillars which once linked a chain fence. By the third pole on the left lies a flat table stone so withered with age that it is now illegible. Although the Stonington burial records are incomplete, it is known that this plot was purchased by Reverend Hart. The carved image of an open bible you see on the stone was also a common symbol for a reverend or minister, and the shape of the stone itself represents an alter for one who was close to God.

Back in Europe during the eighteenth century, it was customary for people to be buried within the town church. Being buried close to the alter was considered being closer to God, and achieving a higher place in heaven. As space within the church filled up, burials took place close by its surrounding walls. Eventually this burial method led to overcrowding of the land, creating stench and the spread of disease. Bodies were being excavated after only a few months in the grave to be replaced with the recently deceased, while the older bodies were moved to graveyards further from town. Those who had the unfortunate job of removal were exposed to the smell of decay, bodily gases and disease. Breathing this foul air caused serious illness and often death within just a few days. Such circumstances are why Victorian Americans abandoned this type of burial. Cemeteries were built away from the church, often outside of town on rocky or hilly land not suitable for farming.

REFERENCES

Boylan, James. *Stonington's Forgotten Heroes of 1861–1865*. Stonington, CT: The Stonington Historical Society, 1999.

Brown, John Gary. *Soul in the Stone: Cemetery Art from America's Heartland*. Lawrence, KS: University Press of Kansas, 1994.

Jackson, Kenneth T., and Camilo Jose Vergara. *Silent Cities: The Evolution of the American Cemetery*. New York: Princeton Architectural, 1989.

Morbid Outlook. morbidoutlook.com.

Stevenson, Louise L. *The Victorian Homefront: American Thought and Culture 1860–1880*. Ithaca, NY: Twayne, 1991.

Wilkins, Robert. *Death: A History of Man's Obsessions and Fears*. New York: Barnes and Noble, 1990.

Special thanks to Michael Nolan,
Superintendent of Stonington Cemetery,
and to the Stonington Historical Society.

Cemetery Organizations

When it comes to cemeteries, the fun never stops... though it takes a true graveyard buff to believe it. You may have noticed through your stone hunting adventures that graveyards aren't exactly jam-packed with people sketching stone symbols and photographing grand mausoleums. And yet there was always a crowd at each guided graveyard tour you signed up for. Where are all the graveyard buffs hiding?

Before getting out your shovel to begin your search, look into if there are any cemetery organizations held in your area.

Cemetery organizations are groups for graveyard buffs who are hooked on graves and have all kinds of ways to prove it. You just may find that your haunted graveyard layout and cemetery tour is just the icing on the Dessert of the Dead when it comes to the selection of stone and bone activities out there. To go all out with your interest in the world of tombstones and cemeteries, become involved with one of these groups that may provide all kinds of activities and involvement.

Getting Into the Grave. Want a fun way to step into the grave? Cemetery organizations primarily focus on preserving and restoring tombstones, providing maintenance to graveyards and educating the public on the teachings of cemeteries. They are often run solely by volunteers, so help is needed in just about every area. By getting involved, you could take part in activities such as:

- **Bringing It Back to Life:** Volunteer for projects in cleaning, repairing and restoring tombstones. As cool as it was to paint all that lichen and residue on your haunted graveyard stones, removing it from the real ones means you get to help bring the stone back for the world to see again.

- **Saving the Grounds:** Help with renovating graveyards that have become dilapidated over time. Some towns just can't afford the maintenance of all its cemeteries, so volunteers come in and save the day. Keep that 18th century graveyard from disappearing beneath a field of six-foot grass so that another spot for stone hunting is back on the map.
- **Grave Courses:** It's not everyday that you can attend lectures on crypts and tombstones, so take advantage while you can. You may find lectures on unique stones and renowned carvers in the area to learn about several cemeteries throughout your state... some of which you may have never known existed!
- **Excavations:** In addition to lectures, attend presentations on tomb excavations that have taken place throughout the country. Watch how historians and archeologists perform excavations step by step, and how the coffins and remains appear decades or even centuries after burial.
- **Turning Your Stone Carving Professional:** You've practiced on Styrofoam, now are you up for the challenge of some *real* stone cutting? Learn carving techniques from ages past, how the stones were constructed from start to finish and try it all out for yourself. Who knows, next year's display may include a *real* stone or two!
- **Rubbings:** Another popular interest that many cemetery organizations go into is stone rubbing. Stone rubbings give you a wonderful piece of history to take home and put in your indoor décor, Halloween museum, or to use in other Halloween displays. Going through a cemetery organization to learn proper stone rubbing methods is the best way to go, since the wrong handling can lead to permanently damaging the stones.

In addition to learning from the pros and getting nice and messy in the dirt, becoming engaged in a cemetery organization allows you to meet others who hear the call of the grave and express their interests in all kinds of ways. You may meet graveyard buffs who spend their free time writing, painting and doing other artwork in graveyards, holding public tours with a unique angle or making jewelry based on the different images on the stones. Share your own interests in graveyards, such as photography, sketching Halloween displays and more. You may pick up a new hobby in graveyard design that you had never thought of before!

Many cemetery organizations also arrange day trips to historical cemeteries, both big and small, near and far. Discover new cemeteries by going with stone hunters with years of experience and who have dozens of stories to tell. Bring your notebook, camera and the Grave Hunter's Nosh on a number of field trips to die for.

16

GHOST HUNTING

Who better to share the spirit of Halloween with than those who dwell on the other side? Most of us are familiar with the concept of ghost hunting: it's covered in many TV shows, there's a Halloween library full of haunting books about it, and if you're a real spookster buff, you may have even gone out to search for your friendly neighborhood ghost yourself.

For some, ghost hunting is a science. It's a means to try to explain, and possibly even prove, life beyond our own mortality, answering any number of questions, doubts and fears about life and death. For others, ghost hunting is a form of adventure and entertainment; a fun way to get out there and seek out the unknown while exploring new areas in sometimes spooky or unusual locations.

Whether you fit into either of these categories, fall somewhere in between or you've never gone out into the spook before, ghost hunting can be great fun. Getting into the spirit of it all, you embark out into a world you think you know, possibly to leave you questioning your certainty as time goes on.

This chapter deals with the adventure of ghost hunting for strictly entertainment purposes only. There is no emphasis put on any particular belief system or religious doctrine, but rather deals with the concept of ghost hunting as a means of good, clean and safe fun: a pastime into an aura of mystery and excitement that coincides so well with the spirit of Halloween.

Into the Spook

Ghost hunting: the exploration of the supernatural. It may be that what makes ghost hunting so interesting is that it can make us question what's real, what could be, and if we should really trust what only our basic senses tell us. With each exploration, we consider if what we are searching for is right there before us, unseen, or even all around us. Our mind is open, our eyes alert and ears perked when suddenly something is glimpsed out of the corner of an eye. Was it a trick of the light? The leaves blowing in the breeze? Or the appearance of a figure moving in and out of view? Memories of ghost stories heard long ago come fleeting back: those of white, floating apparitions emerging from dark cemeteries down quiet country roads... just like this one! And we begin to wonder: *was that what I thought it was?*

There are all sorts of investigations that can be done out in the spook, and in several types of places. After all, you've written so many stories, tours and attractions based on those from the other side, so let us now head out into a realm where there are no props, actors or scripts, but just the world as it is, and all that there may be hidden within it.

Searching for the Spook.
To start off your ghost hunting adventures, look up places in your area that are known for housing paranormal or other unexplained activity. Odds are there will be a lot more than you thought, and in a variety of locations. In the same fashion that you researched many of your Halloween adventures, begin your search for the spook online. Look to sites that list reportedly haunted areas in each state throughout the country, such as:

www.hauntedhouses.com
www.theshadowlands.net
www.americanghosts.com

www.hauntedtraveler.com
www.strangeusa.com

No matter which haunted state you live in (because you know it's haunted *now*), you'll come up with a big list of spookster areas worth investigating. And to add a bit more adventure to your endeavors, pick a few locations with completely different surroundings. For example, choose one indoor location and one outdoor, or one where unusual activity has taken place during the day and the other only at night. You may also want to pick one location that you've been to before and one where you've never gone.

Different types of haunted areas you may come across include:

Graveyards
Restaurants
Inns
Lighthouses
Forests
Caves

Bed and Breakfasts
Museums
Stretches of road
Private homes
(to drive by without
disturbing the owners!)

By choosing a few locations, you can try out a variety of ghost hunting methods for each investigation. You may discover that things look and feel pretty different depending on your specific surroundings, which can affect your research and how you interpret any events that occur.

Planning the Adventures.
Once you've got a couple places picked out, plan your first few ghost hunting adventures. Make a short list so that you have some fun, haunted outings to look forward to, just like you did during the Halloween season. Include the location of each site and directions if you've never been there before.

Ghost Hunting Destinations:

1. White Horse Tavern
   26 Marlborough Street
   Newport, Rhode Island
   Saturday, January 10

2. Shrub Hill Cemetery
   Exeter, Rhode Island
   Off Route 138
   Saturday, February 7

3. Lighthouse Inn
   Six Guthrie Place, off Route 32
   New London, Connecticut
   Sunday, March 15

4. Bara-Hack Cemetery and Woods
   Pomfret, Connecticut
   Route 97
   Saturday, April 25

Spooky Research. When it comes to reading up on the areas you'll be investigating, there are a couple different approaches you can take. Some people choose to do a lot of research on the haunted happenings that have taken place at a site before doing their investigation. The theory is that the information may lead them to specific areas to check out and possibly give hints of what to look for. This way they won't scope out the kitchen of a haunted bed and breakfast for three hours only to learn later that the strange activity has only taken place in the basement.

On the other hand, you may find that you get more out of an investigation if you *don't* know the whole story. Being too informed about what's been experienced in the past may keep you looking with too narrow a view, and actually limiting your concentration. Focusing on listening for a ghostly voice of a 4-year old boy could make you miss the fleeting image of a 35-year old woman who walks right past you. In this respect, the less you know about the site, the more open you may be to exploring it with a broader mind. After the investigation, then go ahead and read about what others have witnessed there, and compare it to your own findings.

Another thing to consider before heading out into the spook is when to go. Some claim that the best time to ghost hunt is at night. However, there are countless occurrences of unexplained activity taking place during the day, as well. When choosing what time of day or night would be best for you, keep things in mind such as when the location will be open to the public, when activity has occurred there in the past and your comfort level of being in the area during certain hours.

Bringing It All, Minus the Proton Pack. Make sure you have all the essentials before going out into the spook:

- Road map
- Camera and extra batteries
- Notebook and pens
- Flash light
- Cell phone
- Extra cash
- Snacks (the Grave Hunter's Nosh works great for ghost hunting, too!)

In addition to the essentials, other items for a good investigation may include equipment for trying to capture moving images, sounds and kinetic energy of spirits. Video cameras and tape recorders can be used for picking up any subtle moving images and voices that may be otherwise undetectable. Other equipment may include an electromagnetic field (EMF) meter for detecting magnetic fields and a Geiger counter to detect radiation, both of which may attribute to paranormal activity in the area.

When going out to do any investigation, try to have at least one other person with you for safety reasons, and always tell someone where you're going. If you're investigating at night, carry a flashlight, extra batteries and a cell phone if you have one. Never put yourself into any dangerous situations, such as trespassing on private property, going into areas that are unsafe, or staying in an area that makes you feel uncomfortable. Remember, you're there to have fun, not remain forever!

Taking It All In. With each site you investigate, from a cave to a lighthouse to a sea vessel, concentrate on all that's around you. Be sensitive to lighting, sound, temperature, and how you feel in the different areas you explore. Take plenty of photos of anything and everything that you find interesting, even if you're not sure why it seems interesting at the time. If you have a digital camera and you find yourself peeking at the photos right after you take them, keep in mind that there will be a lot more to the pictures than what you can see in the small window.

Throughout the investigation, make notes on everything that occurs, including anything unusual you think you see or feel. Did you repeatedly see a quick glimmer of light by a particular tree in the woods? Did an area of the restaurant feel unusually cold? Did a certain space in a motel room make you feel queasy? Writing it all down could mean putting together different pieces of the puzzle later on. If you use a tape recorder or video camera, try to remain as quiet as you can so that you'll be better able to hear any subtle sounds that are picked up.

After the investigation, listen to your recordings and look closely at your photos.

Look for anything out of the ordinary, such as lighting that wasn't there at the time you took the photo and any unusual images captured in the background. It's also a good idea to go back and review your pictures and tapes again a few days later. You may find small subtleties that you didn't notice the first time when you were looking for something more distinctive.

The Lone Spook vs. the Crowded Spook. If you've already ventured on some ghost hunting adventures, you've probably discovered that several circumstances can affect the type of investigating you're able to do at each site. In particular, if the site is in a populated area, under ownership, or if you're free to do as you damn well please. For instance, you're free to take out that EMF meter and tape recorder in the middle of the woods and cover every square inch of the grounds, but it was frowned upon at that four-star restaurant. This is one of the reasons why doing all kinds of investigations is so useful, because you can try out several methods and see which works best for you. At the restaurant, you may want to stick with simply watching for unusual occurrences that happen in the areas you're in, such as the dining room, bar, hallways and bathroom, talking to the owners and taking notes.

However, you can also ask permission from the business owners to investigate areas not commonly open to the public, such as the attic of a reportedly haunted bed and breakfast or the surrounding grounds of an inn. If you want to investigate areas that are typically closed after dark, such as graveyards or a state park, ask permission from the owners or groundskeeper ahead of time and you may get the ok.

Once you've done a couple investigations in areas with haunted histories, you may also want to check out some places without them. Is there a particular stretch of road that has always given you an odd feeling or a graveyard where you swear you've seen something that you just can't explain? Check it out with all your equipment and see if you discover anything unusual. Perhaps there was a reason why you always got that strange feeling... and now you've caught it on film!

The Ghost Hunting Journal

Now that you've got a couple ghost hunting adventures under your belt, are you starting to see ghosts left and right? Are they hiding under your bed at the Insane Asylum and sneaking around the bathrooms at work? Or are those just the skeletons you hid in there last September? Either way, it may be that you're hooked! And who can blame you? There's so much exploring to be done, so many mysteries to unravel, the world becomes limitless with haunting adventures.

And since you'll be embarking on all kinds of ghost hunting investigations in the coming months, you may want to start keeping a record of all your experiences. One fun and useful way to do this is to make a ghost hunting journal. With a ghost hunting journal, you can store all your research and materials to keep track of your progress, compare findings and come up with new locations and techniques for future investigations.

The Supplies. An easy and efficient way to make a ghost hunting journal is to use a 3-ring binder. This way you'll be able to add as much information as you want for each

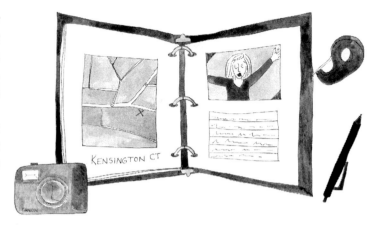

investigation, including any materials you discover after the fact. You'll also be able to easily insert sketch paper, photo sheets, maps and other useful information.

Some good supplies for putting together a ghost hunting journal can include:

- 3-ring binder
- 3-hole punch
- Notebook
- Sketch pad
- Photo sheets
- Single-page map of your state (or each state you'll be investigating)
- Highlighter
- Markers or stickers

Journal Guts. Include in your ghost hunting journal anything and everything that you researched, used and discovered for each investigation. You don't need a picture of a levitating bed with skeletons dancing on it to have an investigation worth remembering (but don't forget to include that one, if you have it). Useful information can include:

State Map: Insert a one-page printed map of your state as the first page of the journal and mark the areas you investigate with a marker or stickers. Use one symbol for sites where you experienced something unusual and a different symbol for those that left no indication of unusual activity. For example, a star sticker can symbolize an investigation you did in the area, and a ghost sticker can refer to a site where something was sensed or seen. You may even notice patterns of activity within certain areas over time.

Pictures of the Site: Use photo sheets to store pictures of each investigation. These can be pictures that show something unusual or something that's just plain cool. Do you think you snapped a photo of an orb, a small ball of light that could actually be a spirit or entity? Or maybe there's an area of the photo that came out blurry for some unknown reason, strange lights that were not visible at the time you took the picture or other bizarre images shown in the shot. Don't think you caught anything unusual? Throw in a picture or two of the general area you investigated so that you'll remember it more clearly later on.

Printed Maps of the Area: A map of the area of each investigation can be a useful tool to keep in your journal, especially if you want to go back a second time and it's in a hard-to-find location or if you want to go back after dark. Use a highlighter to mark the best way to get there and get back. An area map can also come in handy if you want to do investigations in surrounding areas, such as patches of woods alongside each other or intersecting roads. This way you can better keep track of each area as you cover them.

The Date and Description of What Took Place: This is probably the most important information to include for each investigation. When did your investigation take place? What time of day or night were you there? What was your first impression as you entered?

What was the general mood of the place? Was anything seen, heard or felt that seemed out of the ordinary? How did you conduct the investigation? For each entry, you can either insert the notes straight from your notebook, write a summary of what took place based on your notes, or both. In addition to keeping a good record, these descriptions will also be useful when you read up on other people's experiences at the site and make comparisons.

Articles: Include any articles that you find online or in the newspaper relating to the areas you investigate. Tales of the history of the site and reports of strange occurrences that happened there may come in useful when going back over all your materials later on. If you were told the history or legends of the area by word of mouth, write a description of what was said, who said it and the date it was told to you.

Monthly Calendar: If you ghost hunt on a regular basis, you may also want to insert monthly calendars to mark the days of each investigation and plan future adventures. Use printable 8½ × 11" calendar pages for the perfect fit. You'll also be able to look back on specific months and see all your investigations at a quick glance.

Using Your Journal. Keeping a ghost hunting journal is a fun way to record all your research and remember things that occurred later on... even if the memories keep you up at night. Add all your notes, maps, pictures and other research to the journal the day of each investigation while everything is still fresh in your mind. Use your journal to share and compare notes with friends who also participated in the hunt. You may also want to flip back through it each time you add two or three more entries to see if you pick up anything new in the notes or pictures, as well as listen to any tapes or recordings you did at the sites.

Ghost Hunting Log

Date: October 21

Location: Southington Cemetery, Southing Road, Kensington, CT

A few people within our paranormal group found information online about a cemetery in Kensington, CT that is reportedly haunted. Don and I opt not to read about it until after our investigation. The cemetery is owned by the town, so Sally and Mike contact the town police to obtain permission to be on the grounds after sundown.

9 P.M.: It's well after dark as Don and I travel up and down the road looking for the cemetery. We call Mike on his cell and he stands by the entrance, waving his flashlight so that we can see him. The road leading into the cemetery is barely visible in the dark. Mike, Sally and Tim have already arrived.

It's cold, in the low 30s or high 20s. The group separates and everyone takes pictures in all areas of the grounds. I focus mainly on taking pictures beside the trees and the parameter of the cemetery.

After about an hour, I walk with Sally and the others around the oldest section of the cemetery. Sally, who is very sensitive to spirits, says she caught the image of a little boy near one of the stones. The others read the stones of that area to see if any children are buried there while I take photos.

Don and I leave at 10:30 because my feet are so cold I can no longer feel my left foot! Once back home, I look at my photos on the computer and find that the first picture I took after Sally felt the presence of the spirit contains several balls of light, which may be orbs all around where the others stand. No one else was taking pictures at the time and it is my only picture from the investigation which contains something unusual.

Ghost Hunting Log

Date: November 9
Location: Southington Cemetery, Second Visit

12 P.M.: Don and I decide to tour the cemetery during the day to get a better view of the place. It's much easier to find our way there in the light! We head to the right of the cemetery where the oldest stones can be found. As we start to look around and take pictures, a man pulls up in his car and waves us over. He tells us that the stones we are looking at were actually put up for several Native Americans and slaves of the area from the late 1700's and early 1800's.

We come across a few stones erected for children around the same area where I took the picture with orbs last month. We don't experience anything unusual, but get a much better sense of the place and are glad we got to talk with someone who was familiar with its history.

Ghost Hunting Log

Background Information for Southington Cemetery

After doing our first investigation at the cemetery, Don and I went online to read about what others had experienced there and why it was believed to be haunted. The information read:

"A very old and angry ghost seems to be the keeper of this burial ground. On his first trip he makes his presence known to you. On the second trip he can make unusual things happen, such as making electrical devices go haywire. He will also follow you. You may have feelings of great sickness, anxiety, even feelings of complete evilness surrounding you. He haunts the graveyard to your immediate right upon entry."

— Information obtained from The Shadowlands website: www.theshadowlands.net

Notes:

Although we didn't feel any negative activity in the graveyard on either occurrence, it is very interesting that the grounds are reportedly haunted in the same area where Sally felt the presence of a young child and where the visitor told us that Native Americans and slaves were primarily buried.

Could it be that the presence felt by others could have been misinterpreted? Could it be that something resides in that cemetery that did not make itself known to us on either occurrence?

Paranormal Societies

If you discover that ghost hunting is an adventure right up your haunted alley, consider spooking it up with some fellow hunters. Do an online search to see if there are any paranormal societies in your area.

In paranormal societies, people from all different backgrounds and beliefs come together for fun social gatherings to explore, share and teach about investigations and all that lies in the beyond and possibly into the next dimension.

You could meet people, from life-long mediums to those on their first investigation. Some in the group may specialize in technical aspects of investigations, such as using different EMF meters and other recording devices, while others focus more on photography or research. Learn how others go about doing their research and bring in your ghost hunting journal to share your own stories and experiences. You just may be surprised at the tales you hear from others while embarking on group investigations all throughout the state.

An additional bonus of ghost hunting with a paranormal group is that it can often-

times lead to the opening of some creaky doors, especially if someone in the group is a well-known paranormal investigator or psychic. This may involve the group gaining access to performing investigations in areas that are not normally open to the public, possibly staying after hours or even overnight. Many business owners are willing to let paranormal groups investigate on their property because any unusual findings could lead to good publicity, bringing in new customers who want to be in an area that just may be haunted!

Lessons from the Other Side. In addition to ghost hunting, paranormal societies also tend to engage in other activities that deal with paranormal research. You may have the opportunity to get involved with classes and lectures on supernatural studies, group séances and even weekend retreats dedicated to different methods of research. You can learn from world-renowned ghost hunters who give advice on research techniques and share their own experiences in famous hauntings.

In addition to doing a broad search, look for some paranormal societies in your area at either of these great websites:

www.ghostvillage.com   www.paranormal-nyc.com

And remember: if there *aren't* any paranormal societies in your area, you can always go out there and start one yourself! It doesn't have to be a new global alliance... just a few friends exploring and investigating the unknown for a fun hobby to keep the spirit alive with a little help from the other side.

17

FULL MOON NIGHTS

Do people really change during the full moon? Could it be that the gravitational pull of the moon is strong enough to affect our emotional states in the way it does the force of the tides? Could the simple sight of it cause our personalities to become wilder, freer, or even uncontrollable? As of yet, there is no evidence to support that it does. But even if the tales really are just legend, it still makes for a good excuse to act a little crazy.

Each month when the full moon shines down on the werewolves, floating spirits and escaped mental patients in each of us, the spirit of Halloween shines with it. It's a night to engage in the spookiness and chaos of the season that we so desperately need to stay insane in the world.

Full moon nights can also be a time to try out some new kinds of horrifying adventures. We learned a while back that there are countless forces that have shaped Halloween into what it is today, so just imagine how many different ways we can celebrate them all! You can party with creatures from every corner of the grave, study lycan- thropy to prove that the werewolf in the back yard really *is* your Uncle Hubert and you knew it all along, seek out flying saucers, paint a life-size mural of zombie Elvis and explore other activities you've always wanted to experiment with. What better time than now, when the affects of the full moon have made you a little mental, anyway?

Adventures

In this chapter, we'll explore these odd and ill adventures and more for taking part in a little full moon madness each month.

The Night of the Werewolf. It's a full moon party in honor of our favorite furry killer: the werewolf! Celebrate the full moon by throwing an off-season costume party for werewolves only. Deck out the place as a true werewolf's pad with tattered and torn tablecloths and curtains, pictures of the full moon and claw marks on the walls and shredded clothes hanging from the window panes.

Make the silent star of the evening out of a Halloween dummy and werewolf mask to be seated at the dinner table, on the sofa or climbing out the window. Send out invitations that have been clawed through or bitten and see how many different styles of shape shifters arrive once the sun sets. Play your favorite monster tunes and dance the night away before the rising sun changes everyone back to human form.

You can also make it a *Night of the Werewolf* party with a series of movies. Set up the same décor as for a dance party but show films with werewolf culprits (or heroes, depending on your standpoint), such as:

The Wolf Man	*Silver Bullet*
Frankenstein Meets the Wolf Man	*Underworld*
The Howling	*Van Helsing*

But hey, werewolves don't have to take the spotlight for *every* full moon. Work with a variety of party themes with the passing months, such as:

Night of the Ghost	*Night of the Mad Scientist*
Night of the Vampire	*Night of the Mummy*
Night of the Living Dead	*Night of the Killer Klowns*
Night of the Alien	

Alternate your full moon parties between costume dance parties and movie nights, setting up the Insane Asylum as a different monster dwelling each month.

The Game Playing Spookster.

Another type of full moon party is one that involves playing horrifying games... because who would want any other kind? There are many board and card games out there that center on murder, monsters and other horrors for a fun get-together around the lab table.

Choose from games such as:

- **13 Dead End Drive:** Who needs other players around when you could shove them all into the fireplace? In this game of mass murder, you get to kill off as many other characters as you can to be the conqueror of a big inheritance up for grabs.
- **Arkham Horror:** It's the ultimate adventure game based on H.P. Lovecraft's *Cthulhu Mythos*. Fight a band of monsters from another dimension throughout the streets of Arkham or die trying.
- **Betrayal at House on the Hill:** It's never the same game twice: create your own haunted mansion filled with guests and unruly ghosts. But beware, for there's a traitor among your guests... but will you know who?
- **Clue:** It's the who-done-it mystery game that started it all. Case out the joint as Mr. Green, Professor Plum, Mrs. Peacock or one of the other famous, shady characters to discover just who killed Mr. Boddy, in what room and with what weapon.
- **Fury of Dracula:** Live up to your life-long goal by becoming a vampire hunter... or the legendary Dracula himself! Create an army of the undead to gain ultimate power over millions of mortal slaves.

- **Goth: The Game of Horror Trivia:** Show off your true genius for everything in the world of horror. Set up lucky-number 13 tombstones with each defeat and become the champion of the dark side.
- **Hellrail:** In this game based on *Dante's Inferno*, you become an engineer who knows how to get things done. Build a railway that leads straight into the gates of hell. Need a lift?
- **Mall of Horror:** The zombies are loose and invading the mall! And of course it all had to happen the *one day* you go shopping. Players flee from store to store to try and escape the undead.
- *Monster Parties and Games*: This book is actually a collection of 15 games that you can create yourself, each based on a different horror, science fiction or dark comedy film. Throw a murder mystery where anyone could end up dead or make a zombie card game where each hand could be your last — as a human.
- **The Rocky Horror Picture Show Trivia Game:** Kick butt with your knowledge of Rocky Horror and the transvestites from transsexual Transylvania. Now didn't all those midnight stage shows pay off?
- **The Simpsons Treehouse of Horror Monopoly:** This monster edition of Monopoly takes you through the different episodes of The Simpsons Halloween specials. Can you survive the House of Evil, Springfield Cemetery and other disastrous domains?
- **Vampire Hunter:** Embark on a journey through dark graveyards and evil forests to hunt out and destroy the head vampire. But vampire hunting is just never easy as monsters suddenly appear from every corner when day turns to night without warning.
- **Werewolves:** And just when you thought you could trust your neighbors... In this card game, some players are townsfolk, but others are werewolves... and discovering who is who could mean your life!

The Literate Escape Patient.

Sometimes after a night of escaping from the psych ward, you just want to sit back in your favorite chair and enjoy a good book by the light of the moon. You can delve into the spirit of the season each month by adding a new subject to your Halloween library. Choose from topics you've always wanted to explore, such as:

Ancient Egypt: What was life really like during the time of the pharaohs... just before the curse of the mummy destroyed them all! Step into stories that take place in these ancient lands of remarkable landscapes and horrifying traditions that we can only catch glimpses of on the big screen.

Myths and Monsters: Does the Loch Ness monster really exist? What goes on in the Bermuda Triangle? Is Big Foot out there, or has your neighbor just started a new life for himself deep in the woods? Read up on the theories, research and eye-witness accounts of myths and monsters from around the globe.

Astrology: Do the moon and stars really affect the course of our everyday lives? What does your zodiac sign say about you? Read the different teachings and literature of astrology and kick butt at your next Fortune Telling party.

Death in Different Cultures: How is the subject of death dealt with around the world?

Learn about various funeral rites, beliefs in the afterlife, customs honoring past ancestors and how people's lifestyles reflect their views on death. You may never look at your rack and guillotine scene in the same light again.

Studies in Horror: How do vampires, werewolves, lab monsters and other horror characters reflect our own personalities and civilizations? And how do they make it all look so *cool?* Engage in studies of horror in fiction and film that give a deeper meaning to so many classic films and novels.

Monster Guides: Could you take on a zombie if you had to? Are you knowledgeable in the art of vampire slaying? These are important subjects that could save lives... and inspire future interactive haunted attractions. Get all the information out there on how to tackle the creatures that roam the night.

The Making of Horror Films: If you're a big movie buff, consider reading a few titles that give you all the secrets, inspirations and goofs from your favorite monster films. Biographies on Alfred Hitchcock, Vincent Price, Bela Lugosi and other famous directors and actors are fun insights into seeing your favorite flicks like never before.

Parapsychology — The Study of the Paranormal: Have you ever known something was going to happen before it did? Have you ever been able to do something you couldn't explain? Whether you feel you've had an experience with the paranormal or not, learning about the different studies and practices of parapsychology makes for a very interesting read. Learn about abilities that people have reported for hundreds of years, how the subject has grown over time and is practiced around the world.

Other Howling Activities.

Other ways to make each full moon a new adventure include getting out there and taking part in different howling activities. Is there a craft, class or other ungodly endeavor that has been sitting in the back of your mind, just waiting to be unleashed? If so, bust through that window and make a run through the woods to try it out. Such monthly exploits may include:

Howling at the Moon: Interested in astronomy? This subject has planted its roots in the spirit of the season with science fiction in many forms. How can you build a decent alien invasion display if you're not sure which planet the aliens came from? How rude! Astronomy clubs and state universities often hold public observing nights for learning about the moon and stars. Check out the planets for some galactic exploration and become a *real* space traveler... in some sense.

Howling in Class: Monster education is invaluable. If you've been thinking about getting back into the classroom for a fun night class, check out the adult programs and community colleges in your area. You may start off the next full moon night with a course in horror classics, clothes and costume design, scene design and more. It's an endeavor to keep you howling for the next few full moons.

Howling at the Ghosts: Does the full moon affect those on the other side? Find out by grabbing (or kidnapping) some friends to venture out into the night and ghost hunt by the light of the moon... just bring flashlights, too. Spend the night at an inn or bed and breakfast that is known for their regular ghost sightings and ask the owners if these haunting visitations have ever been affected by the phases of the moon. By scheduling different investigations once a month, your ghost hunting journal will fill up faster than you know it.

Howling at the Easel: After painting a few pictures like a true mental patient, there's just no going back. Another howling activity is to get out those art supplies for more artwork of insanity. Head to an open field or other area with a good view of the moon and take photographs for future Night of the Werewolf parties or paint with a sky full of inspiration. Just keep a look-out for other howling creatures running wild while you're out there.

Howling with the Other Howlers: You know that there are other werewolves, spirits and crazies out there, and they just may be throwing a howling bash of their own. Look into local events going on that deal with celebrating the full moon such as full moon dances, dinners and parties. Do a search online and keep alert for special event advertisements in the paper.

Howling with Props: The full moon can also be a good time to continue with your haunts and displays for next Halloween. Add a new set of stocks to the torture chamber or work on a new theme for next year's interactive attraction. Check out Chapter 18, "Expanding the Spook," for all kinds of ways to howl it up with display building.

The Businessman Werewolf. Sometimes there just aren't enough full moon events going on out there, leaving a majority of monsters roaming the streets lost and confused the following morning, wondering why they're wearing a plastic wristband and why they're naked. But you can bring a variety of full moon events to your place of business and to the whole community, just like you did for Halloween. Now that you've drawn in a big crowd of vampires and warlocks from last year's Ball of the Undead, don't leave them alone in the graveyard until next October. Throw a Masquerade of Murder Victims for the full moon and other horrifying events to keep them coming back each month.

Other full moon events to throw at the workplace can include:

- **Psych Ward Shows:** If you run a movie theater or drive-in, hold special full moon night admissions for late-night movie goers who come dressed in costume. Use a different theme each month that revolves around the showing, such as half-price tickets for axe murders and their victims during the full moon slasher film festival and aliens receiving free small popcorns on sci-fi night.
- **Werewolf Sale:** If you own or run a bookstore or library, put on special sales during full moon nights (post the exact dates to avoid confusion). Select books that deal with horror, fantasy, science fiction, hauntings or other titles that go with the theme, and include other merchandise such as posters and DVDs. Alter the selection each month and hold special book signings with local authors.
- **The Howling:** Throw a dance party at your business for the true werewolves among us. Deck out the place as if werewolves had invaded and trashed it all and hire a local band to perform dressed as victims of the beasts. Set up a costume contest for best 80's werewolf, most disturbing werewolf and so on.

For more full moon events, refer to Chapter 5 for some fun and demented themes that can be put together for the full moon, as well as Halloween.

If you have a Halloween website, dedicate one of the links to all your full moon adventures. Post pictures and tell the tales of your monthly monstrous transformations.

18

EXPANDING THE SPOOK: CONTINUING YOUR HAUNTS AND DISPLAYS

After a few months of putting away all the glowing gargoyles, urns of black flowers and mutilated farmers, you may find your thoughts drifting back to the decaying stones of the Halloween graveyard and the silent stares of the scarecrows. The glaze in your eyes may resemble the whirling fog from the torture chamber as you ponder: *A mausoleum would look really good in next year's graveyard* or *Maybe I should expand the haunted tour into the garage.*

If these and other developing thoughts of dementia start to arise, run with them now while they're fresh in your mind. What would you like to improve or expand on from last year's displays, attractions, party themes and tours to take them to a whole new level in the coming season? Did you have a yard display that you would like to turn into more of a walk-through, or are you toying with a new story for next year's ghost story shack?

In the Off-Season

Continuing with your haunts and displays is a great way to keep in the spirit of the season and expand the spook throughout the year. You can either work with your creations

from last year or try something completely different for a whole new nightmare for home or Halloween business events. Building and writing in the off-season also gives you the advantage of being able to work at a slower, easier pace without rushing around like crazy come September.

Oh, the Possibilities...
The possibilities are endless when it comes to making your dark and disturbing creations even more sinister. Take out that Halloween scrapbook and look back at your display photos and storylines to dream up your next big endeavor. You can also reminisce with your other adventures from the season, such as indoor décor, business events, Insane Asylum parties and Halloween story telling and poetry readings for sparking new ideas.

Prop Building: Put that mad scientist's lab coat back on for building props in future window displays, outdoor and indoor décor and Halloween parties. Make a new coffin for a party in the afterlife window display or build graveyard pillars to support skulls and jack-o'-lanterns around the fence. Make new tombstones of all shapes and sizes for your Reaper's party or a hangman scene for next year's haunted tour.

Haunted Attractions: Come up with a completely new theme for next year's haunted attraction. You had the killer klown attraction last year, so how about a Jack the Ripper interactive attraction for next year? Start on all the necessities such as making a new sound effect CDs, borders, backdrops and costumes. Work on floor plans and scripts. Create a new link for the upcoming attraction on your Halloween website and even send out early invitations to friends.

You can also read up on different methods of prop building and constructing commercial haunted attractions in magazines such as Haunted Attraction Magazine and Haunt-World. Check out their websites at:

www.hauntedattraction.com   www.hauntworld.com

Halloween Story Telling and Poetry Readings: Have you been dreaming about your next Halloween story telling and poetry reading since the curtain fell at the last one? Encore! Schedule the next event to be held in the first week of September to kick off the season with a bang. If you'll be having a public event, secure your location well in advance and contact everyone who was involved last year to once again take to the haunting stage.

The Halloween Museum: Build up that Halloween museum with photos and memorabilia from last season, the Halloween and horror conventions you've gone to, ghost hunting adventures you've embarked on and full moon events you've thrown. Can't wait until next Halloween to show your next exhibit? Why wait? Open the museum in the off-season for a special showing and include the new props and projects you've been working on throughout the year.

Party Themes: Was your Grim Reaper's party and Fortune Telling party a big hit last season? Write new grisly crimes and riddles for next year's gathering of murderers and thieves and pick up new fortune telling games and prizes for your next gathering of the mystics. You can also use the same concepts to make up new party themes. Instead of a Reaper party, throw a mad scientist's party where guests have been invited by the mad doctor to come and build their own creations from body bags and coffins filled with bones and body parts.

Or have a party in the mummy's tomb where groups must write a map in Egyptian hieroglyphics (provide symbol charts to avoid mind explosions) for the other groups to decipher and seek out the secret burial chambers of treasure.

Business Events: How can you ever look at your place of business the same again now that it's been the home of a hearse display and 50's science fiction invasion? It's now an official Halloween landmark! In addition to those full moon events you've got going on, get the demonic wheels turning for some fun events for next year's Halloween season. Will there be a dark art show with a specific angle, a Reaper display contest throughout town or a Halloween festival with a vampire rock group performing? Think up new contests, prizes and special advertisement designs that will bring in a new scene of horror.

Year Round Spookster Display.
Stop crying because you took down the Grim Reaper and his throne of skulls back in November... you know he'll be coming for you soon enough. Or if not him, how about some other demented creature?

In addition to working on Halloween displays for next fall, you can also work on one to keep up in the Insane Asylum year round. Make it a special display that's completely different from those you had during the Halloween season, such as a window display of floating ghosts, using sheer draped over hanging skeletons and surrounded by red and orange lanterns. Or set up a special dinner display in the kitchen alcove with skeletons dressed in black suits seated before platters of skulls and bones, black candles and gothic goblets.

19

FRIDAY THE 13TH
AND MURDER MYSTERY

There's one calendar day — other than October 31st — that always catches the eye of the Halloween enthusiast. It's an infamous day that creeps up only once or twice a year, and if we're lucky, we can spot them early and make our plans accordingly... for going all out on Friday the 13th!

Friday the 13th is a day that has come to be regarded as dark, unpredictable, unruly, and a day when teenagers should avoid sketchy summer camps. And you know what a day associated with devious mayhem means... that it just *has* to be celebrated.

But how? Since Friday the 13th's don't come around too often, consider embracing them with an event that's out of the ordinary: something fun, sinister and has unpredictability and death written all over it. One celebration that fits the bill just right is throwing your own murder mystery party.

A murder mystery party isn't your typical Reaper party (no offense, Reaper). It's a game

where treacherous characters come to life and right to your door. Guests arrive as their assigned roles for acting out a series of clues in a fun and challenging real life who-done-it.

Do It Yourself

There are a variety of murder mystery games out there available for purchase, but it can be much more fun to write one yourself. By putting together your own storyline and ensemble of characters, you can create any kind of scenario you want. And with so much practice in writing display storylines, haunted attraction scenarios and tour scripts, making your own murder mystery will be as simple as a Sweeney Todd pie.

A Scandalous Scenario.
To begin writing your murder mystery, come up with a basic scenario: someone somehow got killed somewhere with a certain number of people around who could have done it. Brainstorm with a couple different scenarios under a variety of circumstances.

For example:

Dracula's Castle: A woman was poisoned at a costume ball in a castle in Transylvania. The party-goers at the scene of the crime are on vacation for all different reasons: photographing the landscape, researching a book, exploring the legends, partying, and one believes that he actually *is* a vampire. None of the guests knew each other before the trip, but some had met along the way. The victim was the host of the party, who everyone had met at one point in time.

A Fancy Hotel: A man is found hanged in the stairwell of a high-class hotel in New York. The group of people staying there had come for different reasons: a convention, business, vacation, to have an affair, and to see an exhibit in the city. Some know each other, while others don't. The victim was staying in the penthouse of the hotel. All guests had met him at one point or another.

A Local Tavern: A man is stabbed outside a tavern in a small town. Everyone who was at the tavern that night knew each other, though some not so well as others. Some had been drinking, some had been working there, and others had just arrived. The victim had not gone into the tavern, but had been out back. He was known by everyone in town.

When brainstorming scenarios, make them as down-to-earth or as far-fetched as you like. After you've got a few different ideas, pick the one you like best.

The Rotten Scumbags.
Next, think about how many characters you want in the story based on how many guests you'll invite to the party. Do you want to invite just your four closest friends or all fifteen people from the sci-fi class you took during last month's full moon? With a particular number in mind, you can get into the specifics of each character in the story and what happened that led up to the murder. Since you'll be writing the game and will already know everything that happens, set yourself up as the host of the party rather than one of the characters.

For example:

Murder at Gloss Hotel — 8 Characters (and the dead dude):
- *Niels:* The victim (an un-played role), a rich businessman
- *Jalen and Beth:* convention attendees, neither of them knew each other before they met at the hotel
- *Morris:* a vacationer, seeing the sights
- *Jake and Ruthy:* secret lovers, gave the excuse of going away on business
- *Maxine:* a local who's treating herself to a fancy hotel and art exhibit
- *Harold:* the janitor of the hotel
- *Mary:* the housekeeper of the hotel

The Crime: The housekeeper discovered the victim hanged in the stairwell leading up to the penthouse suite at 11:45pm. No one was seen using the stairwell up to the penthouse all night, as shown on the front desk monitors. The suspects had all been seen with Niels the day of the murder.

Next, think about what *really* happened that your guests will be trying to figure out through the clues.

The Nitty-Gritty: Niels was Jake's former boss. He had fired Jake 3 years ago after he lost a big business deal with some very important clients. As a result, Jake lost his house, car, and his marriage went down the tubes. He has been unable to find a decent job ever since. Two weeks ago, Jake overhead that Niels would be staying at Gloss Hotel all week and made plans with Ruthy to travel there for a secret affair. He specifically got a room with a window view so that he could climb up the fire escape, sneak in Niels' window and strangle him in the night, then make it look like suicide in the stairwell for his final revenge.

Rotten Scumbags Come to Life. Now that you've got the story of what *really* happened, go into more detail about what each character was up to at the hotel, what their motive could have been to murder the victim and what they had access to for completing the job. Remember that for a murder mystery to be suspenseful, each character must look like a possible suspect.

For example:

Victim: Niels Jensen, 50. Successful businessman meeting clients in the city. He always stays in hotels owned by his friends, and always in the penthouse.

Jalen: 39, convention attendee. Met Beth during a seminar. They met Niels in the hotel down in the lobby. Jalen overheard the front desk attendants say that Niels was one of their richest hotel guests. Jalen has been flat broke for years, and is attending a seminar about good business practices. He makes it a point to notice when Niels enters and leaves his hotel room, and has stolen items from his own room such as soaps, towels and coat hangers. He also notices the janitor keeping tabs on him.

Beth: 42, convention attendee. Had seen Jalen at the hotel and introduced herself at a seminar. Ran into Niels in the elevator one morning and made chit chat. He strongly hit on her, which she didn't like. She shared quite a few drinks with Jalen and didn't acknowledge that she had met Niels when they ran into him in the lobby. She keeps a bottle of mace in her purse at all times.

Morris: 30, tells people he's vacationing from New Jersey and came to see the sites. He has actually been hired by Niels' leading business competitor to set him up in a public scandal. He met Niels while waiting for a cab outside the hotel and offered to meet him for a drink later. He keeps a small pistol in his right sock.

Next, give each character an alibi. They all may have reasons as to why they could be the killer, but they will also need an alibi of where they were at the time of the murder. The actual killer also needs a false alibi to mislead the others.

Jalen: in his hotel room alone.
Beth: in the hotel bar.
Morris: in the lobby.
Jake: killing Niels, but claims he was in the hotel room with Ruthy.
Ruthy: taking a bath.
Maxine: receiving pizza delivery in her hotel room.
Harold: on the floor below, changing light bulbs.
Mary: sneaking her way up to the penthouse to steal from Niels.

Clues of the Game: Physical Evidence.
With the story falling into place, make clues that will slowly reveal all the information to the guests throughout the evening. To use all kinds of evidence in the game, create both physical clues and verbal clues.

For the physical evidence, choose everyday objects that will somehow be connected to each character. Each object will be a clue that was found at or around the murder scene. For example: a shoe with blood on it, a biography of the victim owned by one of the suspects, sun glasses, lipstick and so on. Make notes on which item belongs to which character.

For the second piece of physical evidence, draw a rough sketch of the crime scene on a piece of poster board, including the surrounding areas where the suspects claim to have been at the time of the murder. (Don't worry, you don't have to be an artist or architect... remember those Insane Asylum drawings?) For example, draw a rough diagram of Gloss Hotel's penthouse, the floor below it, stairwell in between, the lobby and the bar.

Verbal Clues.
With the physical evidence taken care of, write each character's verbal clues. This will be information revealed over time so that everyone learns secrets about one another. The clues will add suspense and suspicions to each player as more secrets are revealed and it becomes clear that *anyone* could be the killer... but finding out what really happened is what makes the game.

For these clues, make an information sheet for each character. These sheets will list specific facts that they will reveal at certain times throughout the party. Write the clues in the following order:

- A general introduction
- 1–2 pieces of information to reveal to the group
- Which piece of physical evidence to discuss
- 2 clues to reveal during dinner

- Information about another character to reveal after dinner
- An alibi
- Secret clues (that will be revealed by others throughout the evening... those scumbags!)

An information sheet will look something like this:

Jalen

Introduction: You're 39 and attending a seminar in the city with Beth.

Reveal about yourself: The seminar you're attending is about good business practices, but you're basically trying to get rich quick. Cuz come on, isn't that what life's all about? You met Niels one night in the hallway while getting ice and heard from the people at the front desk that he was really rich.

Evidence to pick up: A bottle of pills which belongs to Beth. Give it to her, revealing that she told you she accidentally forgot her *real* medication back home, and hasn't taken it for the past week.

Reveal during dinner: You happened to see Niels' billfold when he accidentally dropped it after tipping a bellhop. It was stacked with hundred dollar bills. If you had that kind of money, you wouldn't go carrying it around. Who knows what people might do to get it... After all, you already saw Mary, the housekeeper, making sure no one was looking when she took the elevator up to the penthouse earlier that morning.

Reveal after dinner: You heard Morris talking to someone on the phone about setting Niels up in some kind of scandal. He claims to be vacationing from New Jersey, but it's obvious he's really here for something he's not admitting. You also saw what looked like a gun sticking out of his sock.

Alibi: You were in your hotel room alone at the time of the murder.

Secret clues: You are flat broke and have done desperate things for money in the past, such as hold people at gun-point, break into homes and steal cars. You've been seen stealing things from your hotel room, such as soaps, towels and coat hangers. You're attending the seminar in hopes to get rich and retire early, no matter what the cost. You notice when Niels enters and leaves his hotel room, as well as noticing the janitor who is often around and would make a good fall-guy.

In addition to each character sheet, write a short summary of the scene of the crime that the host (you!) will reveal at the start of the party. This will give everyone the who, what, when and where that is known before the game begins.

Scene of the Crime: At 11:45 P.M., Niels Jensen, CEO of Big Top, the top ad agency in Chicago, was found dead and hanged in the stairwell outside his penthouse suite of Gloss Hotel. He was discovered by Mary, a housekeeper of the hotel. He had been dead for almost 20 minutes.

Invitation to Murder. With all your characters and clues ready to be brought to life, send out invitations to the party, giving the overall theme of the story. Stress the importance to RSVP, since you'll need one guest for each character being played. (If it turns out there will be more guests than there are characters, don't worry. They may not be able to take on a role, but they can still have fun trying to solve the murder.)

Invitations may read something along the lines of:

Greetings Murder Mystery Fans!

You are invited to take part in a murder mystery dinner at The Cannibal's Diner, 14 Elmwood Road. It is to be held on Friday, February 13th from 7 to 11 P.M.

The murder mystery dinner involves the story of 8 characters who have gathered at Gloss Hotel in New York for business and pleasure when **murder** strikes! Throughout the night, each suspect will reveal information and clues about him- or herself, each seemingly more and more guilty of the crime. At the end of the evening, everyone will make accusations of what they think *really* happened until the actual killer is discovered.

If you would like to be a part of this murder mystery dinner, please RSVP by January 20. The game requires a total of 8 players.

Hope to hear from you soon and watch your back...

Once you receive all the responses of who will be attending, assign the character roles to the guests. Mail guests their individual character sheets at least one week in advance so that they get a chance to know their part and play it well. Encourage everyone to come in character, including dressing in appropriate attire. Instruct all guests to not discuss their character with anyone else who will be attending the party.

The Party Layout. Now you've got everything you need for your murder mystery: the story, the characters, the clues, and the guests. On the night of the party, set up some indoor décor to go with the theme of the story. For example, to create an atmosphere of a hotel lobby, put out some nice linens, a few vases of flowers, tourism pamphlets and a large mirror in the center of the room.

Here's how the party will be played throughout the night:

1. When the guests arrive, make sure they each have their information sheet. (It's always best to have an extra of each in case people forget or lose theirs!)

2. To begin the party, the host (you) reads the summary of what was discovered at the scene of the crime. Name everyone present and tell them that they have all been gathered as possible suspects.

3. Instruct each character to introduce himself using the "introduction" information on their sheet.

4. Once each character has been introduced, the host then brings out the poster of the crime scene, placing it on a table where all can see it. The host points out where the murder was committed.

5. To start the interrogation, the host asks each character to reveal information about why exactly they are staying at Gloss Hotel, and how (and if) they met the victim. Guests answer by revealing the 2 sentences about themselves listed on their information sheet.

6. With all this information revealed, the host then brings out the pieces of physical evidence that is somehow related to each suspect. The evidence is placed on the same table as the crime scene photo. The host states that each piece of evidence belongs to someone in the room, and may be somehow linked to the murder.

7. One by one, each character takes the piece of evidence indicated on their information sheet and gives it to the appropriate owner. They go on to accuse that person of being the murderer (trying to clear their own name), stating the clue they are instructed to give.

8. Once all the physical clues have been given out, everyone breaks for separate dis-

cussion until it is time for dinner. During the course of dinner, each character brings up in conversation the clues listed on their sheet.

9. By the time dinner is over, everyone looks like a killer. Players can once again break up into groups for private discussions. At an appointed time, they retire to the room of evidence for a last attempt to lay the blame on someone else and reveal information they have acquired about others.

10. To try to prove their innocence, players each say where they were at the time of the murder (the killer is allowed to lie, which is stated on their sheet). While everyone takes turns giving his or her alibi, they place their piece of physical evidence on the crime scene photo (which the host lays flat on the table) in the general vicinity of where they were at the time of the murder.

11. Once all the physical evidence is on the photo, everyone is allowed to study it for a few minutes to draw their conclusion of what really happened. In turn, they then make accusations and give their reasoning to support it.

12. The conclusion of what really happened is revealed by the host (refer back to The Nitty Gritty), after which dessert is served.

20

GROWING YOUR OWN PUMPKIN PATCH

Are you in pumpkin withdrawal? Months after the Halloween season has passed by, do you miss seeing those fields of spotted orange beside the farm stands and the giant mounds of pumpkins at the country stores? Do you find yourself on the lookout for them as early as April, when the leaves and flowers return and so maybe the pumpkins have somehow returned as well? If so, growing your own pumpkin patch could be the perfect solution to all those painful months of waiting and yearning.

How many pumpkins did you go through last year with your displays, walk-through, Halloween business events, parties and trick-or-treat station? And how many more would you have *liked* to use? By growing your own patch, you can find yourself with all the pumpkins you could ever want, while also creating a fun and horrifying atmosphere to your summer Insane Asylum.

Planting the Patch

You don't need an extra crop field lying around to plant a pumpkin patch. Any section of your yard that gets plenty of sunlight will do. Just keep in mind that pumpkin vines need a lot of room to spread out, so pick an area that's a bit bigger than the space squeezed between your year-round mausoleum display and ghost story shack in-the-works.

Use the following guidelines for setting up your patch:

1. Pick out any variety of pumpkins seeds at your local store or farm stand, such as seeds for large pumpkins, mini pumpkins, sugar pumpkins or jumbo pumpkins. (Get the seeds in early spring, because they sell out fast!) Beginning in early to mid–June, plant them in small pots filled with fertilizer and keep them in direct sunlight indoors.

2. Choose the area of your yard where you want to grow the patch. Dig up the grass and loosen and turn the dirt. Water the area daily so that it stays moist.

3. Once the pumpkin plants have started to grow so that they are about 6", transplant them into the soil outside. Refer to the seed packages as to the correct length of spacing between the different pumpkin types. Plant each in a thick layer of manure compost and give plenty of water.

4. Water the plants at their stems each morning, keeping the leaves dry.

The Look of the Patch. Since your pumpkin patch is one that's grown in a true Insane Asylum, give it the Halloween atmosphere it deserves. Set up the surroundings in any number of ways that reflect the spirit of the season, while also serving to keep away night critters and other demons who may be tempted to invade the grounds.

Scarecrows: Setting up a scarecrow in the patch will actually serve two purposes: firstly, it will look damn cool. But more importantly, the flapping of its cloth will pose a threat to lurking animals who may be tempted to enter the patch and eat the flowers and pumpkins. These scarecrows don't have to be life-size, but only a few feet tall to make them good guardians of the grounds.

The Shining: In addition to flapping cloth, objects that shine and make noise in the breeze work well for keeping away night critters. Set up 2–3' lawn posts at each corner of the patch and hang metal star and moon lawn ornaments or other decorations for a mystical defense mechanism.

Marigolds: Marigolds produce a scent that animals tend to keep away from, so they're good for planting right alongside the pumpkins or even around the parameter of the patch. These flowers come in a variety of colors, but if you want to keep that autumn atmosphere, go with the orange!

The Stone Wall: Another way to create an awesome look for your patch is to build a stone wall around it, just like you did for your Halloween graveyard. But don't go exploding those rock outcroppings in the forest just yet. To save strain on your back and get the same spooky look of a real stone wall, use the stones you came across while loosening the dirt of your patch, as well as the leftover stones from your graveyard.

If you want to use bigger stones for your wall, check out some places that don't mind giving their discarded rocks and stones away, such as town graveyards and state parks. These areas usually have piles of discarded stones that were unearthed while constructing paths on the property, or, in the case of cemeteries, while digging new graves. Ask permission from the cemetery owner or your state park division and you may be able to pick out as many stones as you like. (A word to the wise: when moving stones, watch for sleeping snakes!)

Pumpkin Evolutions. You can also make your pumpkin patch the first outdoor display of the season, even before the season starts. Set up standing lanterns throughout the patch to light at sundown and pose spotlights to shine up on the scarecrows. You can also use the patch on Halloween night as a stop on your trick-or-treaters' haunted tour, or convert it into a jack-o'-lantern light show after the big harvest.

Have more pumpkins than you need? Is that possible? If so, spread the spoils of the season around: donate some of the pumpkins to local non-profit haunted attractions and other Halloween fundraisers that are asking for donations.

Reflection

Well, it's been a season like no other. One never to be forgotten, and perhaps leaving us never to be the same again.

How does celebrating the spirit of Halloween throughout the year change the way we look at the world? How has it made us change our *own* world? With each haunting event, spookster party, investigation and gathering, we may find ourselves looking forward to the little things more, scheduling more time for fun, and trying out new horrifying hobbies to see what unfolds. And for each of us, the results will be different.

But what may be the same for all Halloween enthusiasts is that the Halloween season is an entire culture that makes us feel at home and be ourselves — whether that home is an Insane Asylum or a haunted mansion, and whether our inner self is an escaped mental patient or the Reaper.

We have discovered that for Halloween buffs, the season can never really leave us. And by celebrating it in so many ways, we continue to learn, explore, change and grow. Embarking on new and exciting endeavors is what makes life ghastly and great — and each adventure can lead to another and another.

It may be that the Halloween season is one big party with short breaks in between. It may be that that's what life is. And if that's the case, then let each of us allow our inner monster to break free once and for all. May this book have served you well for inspiring ways to celebrate your favorite holiday, and sparked a long line of countless adventures.

Recommended Readings

Outdoor Décor

Budge, E.A. Wallis. *The Egyptian Book of the Dead*. Mineola, NY: Dover, 1967.

Choundas, George. *The Pirate Primer: Mastering the Language of Swashbucklers and Rogues*. Cincinnati, OH: Writer's Digest, 2007.

Hawass, Zahi. *Tutankhamun and the Golden Age of the Pharaohs*. Washington, DC: National Geographic, 2005.

Rumbleow, Donald. *The Complete Jack the Ripper*. Boston, MA: New York Graphic Society, 1975.

Silva, Freddy. *Secrets in the Fields: The Science and Mysticism of Crop Circles*. Charlottesville, VA: Hampton Roads, 2002.

Halloween in the Classroom

An Elementary Halloween

Brown, Marc. *Arthur's Halloween*. New York: Little, Brown, 1983.

_____. *Scared Silly! A Halloween Book for the Brave*. New York: Little, Brown, 2000.

Layne, Steven L., *Teacher's Night before Halloween*. Gretna, LA: Pelican, 2008.

Robinson, Barbara. *The Best Halloween Ever*. New York: HarperCollins, 2004.

Speirs, John. *The Best Halloween Hunt Ever*. New York: Scholastic, 2000.

Ziefert, Harriet, and Renee Andriani-Williams. *On Halloween Night*. New York: Puffin, 2001.

A Teen Halloween

Bannatyne, Lesley Pratt. *A Halloween Reader: Poems, Stories and Plays from Halloween Past*. Gretna, LA: Pelican, 2004.

_____. *Halloween: An American History, An American Holiday*. Gretna, LA: Pelican, 1998.

Irving, Washington. *The Legend of Sleepy Hollow & Other Stories*. New York: Lancer, 1968.

Tabori, Lena, and Natasha Tabori Fried. *The Little Big Book of Chills & Thrills*. New York: Welcome, 2001.

A Halloween Story Telling and Poetry Reading

Barker, Clive. *Books of Blood, Volumes I–III*. New York: Berkley, 1998.

Dickinson, Emily. *The Complete Poems of Emily Dickinson*. New York: Little, Brown, 1960.

Grimm, Jacob, and Wilhelm Grimm. *Grimm's Fairy Tales*. Ann Arbor, MI: Borders, 2001.

Lovecraft, H.P. *The Best of H.P. Lovecraft: Blood-curdling Tales of Horror and the Macabre*. New York: Ballantine, 1987.

Poe, Edgar Allan. *Edgar Allan Poe: Complete Tales and Poems*. Edison, NJ: 1985.

Travel

Citro, Joseph A. *Weird New England*. New York: Sterling, 2005.

Jones, Richard. *Haunted Castles of Britain and Ireland*. New York: Barnes and Noble, 2003.

Lankford, Andrea. *Haunted Hikes: Spine-Tingling Tales and Trails from North America's National Parks*. Santa Monica, CA: Santa Monica, 2006.

Party Nights

Parker, Julia, and Derek Parker. *The Complete Book of Dreams*. New York: Dorling Kindersley, 1995.

Pielmeier, Heidemarie, and Marcus Schirner. *Illustrated Tarot Spreads*. New York: Sterling, 1995.

Tenton, Sasha. *Simply Palmistry*. New York: Sterling, 2005.

Collections and Libraries

Anson, Jary. *The Amityville Horror*. London: Prentice-Hall, 1977.

Coleman, Penny. *Corpses, Coffins and Crypts: A History of Burial*, New York: Henry Holt, 1997.

Curran, Dr. Bob. *Lost Lands, Forgotten Realms: Sunken Continents, Vanished Cities and the Kingdoms that History Misplaced*. Franklin Lakes, NJ: New Page, 2007.

Genzmer, Herbert, and Ulrich Hellenbrand. *Mysteries of the World: Unexplained Wonders and Mysterious Phenomena*. New York: Parragon, 2007.

Kronzek, Allan Zola, and Elizabeth Kronzek. *The Sorcerer's Companion: A Guide to the Magical World of Harry Potter*. New York: Broadway, 2001.

Rattle, Alison, and Allison Vale. *Hell House and Other True Hauntings from around the World*. New York: Sterling, 2008.

Skal, David J. *Death Makes a Holiday: A Cultural History of Halloween*. New York: Bloomsbury, 2002.

Stephens, John Richard. *Captured by Pirates*. New York: Barnes and Noble, 2006.

The Trick-or-Treaters' Haunted Tour

Cawthorne, Nigel. *Witches: History of a Persecution*. New York: Barnes and Noble, 2004.

Haining, Peter. *The Mammoth Book of Twentieth-Century Haunted Ghost Stories*. New York: Carroll & Graf, 1998.

Simons, D. Brenton. *Witches, Rakes and Rogues*. Beverly, MA: Commonwealth, 2006.

The Ghost Story Shack

Christensen, Jo-Anna. *Campfire Ghost Stories*. Auburn, WA: Lone Pine, 2002.

Scott, Beth, and Michael Norman. *Haunted Heartland*. New York: Warner, 1985.

Stephens, John Richard. *Into the Mummy's Tomb*. New York: Penguin, 2001.

Stone Hunting

Greene, Janet. *Epitaphs to Remember: Remarkable Inscriptions from New England Gravestones*. Chambersburg, PA: Alan C. Hood, 2005.

Rogak, Lisa. *Stones and Bones of New England*. Guilford, CT: Globe Pequot, 2004.

Shushan, E.R. *Grave Matters: A Curious Collection of 500 Actual Epitaphs, from Which We Learn of Grieving Spouses, Fatal Gluttony, Vengeful Relations and All Manner of Parting Commentary*. New York: Ballantine, 1990.

Ghost Hunting

Kermeen, Frances. *Ghostly Encounters: True Stories of America's Haunted Inns and Hotels*. New York: Warner, 2002.

Southall, Richard. *How to be a Ghost Hunter*. St. Paul, MN: Llewellyn, 2003.

Warren, Joshua P. *How to Hunt Ghosts: A Practical Guide*. New York: Fireside, 2003.

Full Moon Nights

Broughton, Richard S. *Parapsychology: The Controversial Science*. Toronto, Canada: Ballantine, 1991.

Greer, John Michael. *Monsters: An Investigator's Guide to Magical Beings*. St. Paul, MN: Llewellyn, 2002.

Gregory, Constantine. *The Vampire Watcher's Handbook: A Guide for Slayers*. New York: St. Martin's, 2003.

Keel, John A. *The Mothman Prophecies*. New York: Tom Doherty Associates, 2001.

Quasar, Gian J. *Into the Bermuda Triangle: Pursuing the Truth Behind the World's Greatest Mystery*. Columbus, OH: McGraw-Hill, 2005.

Schneider, Kirk J. *Horror and the Holy: Wisdom Teachings of the Monster Tale*. Peru, IL: Open Court, 1993.

Snake, Doktor. *Doktor Snake's Voo Doo Spellbook*. London: Eddison Sadd, 2000.

Steiger, Brad. *The Werewolf Book*. Canton, MI: Visible Ink, 1999.

Van Helsing, Abelard. *The Demon Hunter's Handbook*. New York: Barnes and Noble, 2006.

Wilkins, Robert. *Death: A History of Man's Obsessions and Fears*. New York: Barnes and Noble, 1996.

Index